Customer Service Delivery

THE PROFESSIONAL PRACTICE SERIES

The Professional Practice Series is sponsored by the Society for Industrial and Organizational Psychology (SIOP). The series was launched in 1988 to provide industrial/organizational psychologists, organizational scientists and practitioners, human resource professionals, managers, executives, and those interested in organizational behavior and performance with volumes that are insightful, current, informative, and relevant to organizational practice. The volumes in the Professional Practice Series are guided by five tenets designed to enhance future organizational practice:

1. Focus on practice, but grounded in science
2. Translate organizational science into practice by generating guidelines, principles, and lessons learned that can shape and guide practice
3. Showcase the application of industrial/organizational psychology to solve problems
4. Document and demonstrate best industrial and organizational-based practices
5. Stimulate research needed to guide future organizational practice

The volumes seek to inform those interested in practice with guidance, insights, and advice on how to apply the concepts, findings, methods, and tools derived from industrial/organizational psychology to solve human-related organizational problems.

Previous Professional Practice Series volumes include:

Published by Jossey-Bass

Improving Learning Transfer in Organizations
Elwood F. Holton III, Timothy T. Baldwin, Editors

Resizing the Organization
Kenneth P. De Meuse, Mitchell Lee Marks, Editors

Implementing Organizational Interventions
Jerry W. Hedge, Elaine D. Pulakos, Editors

Organization Development
Janine Waclawski, Allan H. Church, Editors

Creating, Implementing, and Managing Effective Training and Development
Kurt Kraiger, Editor

The 21st Century Executive
Rob Silzer, Editor

Managing Selection in Changing Organizations
Jerard F. Kehoe, Editor

Evolving Practices in Human Resource Management
Allen I. Kraut, Abraham K. Korman, Editors

Individual Psychological Assessment
Richard Jeanneret, Rob Silzer, Editors

Performance Appraisal
James W. Smither, Editor

Organizational Surveys
Allen I. Kraut, Editor

Employees, Careers, and Job Creation
Manuel London, Editor

Employment Discrimination Litigation
Frank J. Landy, Editor

The Brave New World of eHR
Hal G. Gueutal, Dianna L. Stone, Editors

Published by Guilford Press

Diagnosis for Organizational Change
Ann Howard and Associates

Human Dilemmas in Work Organizations
Abraham K. Korman and Associates

Diversity in the Workplace
Susan E. Jackson and Associates

Working with Organizations and Their People
Douglas W. Bray and Associates

Customer Service Delivery

Customer Service Delivery

Research and Best Practices

Lawrence Fogli, Editor

Foreword by Eduardo Salas

JOSSEY-BASS
A Wiley Imprint
www.josseybass.com

Published by Jossey-Bass
A Wiley Imprint
989 Market Street, San Francisco, CA 94103   www.josseybass.com

Jossey-Bass books and products are available through most bookstores. To contact Jossey-Bass directly call our Customer Care Department within the United States at (800) 956-7739, outside the United States at (317) 572-3986, or by fax at (317) 572-4002.

Jossey-Bass also publishes its books in a variety of electronic formats. Some content that appears in print may not be available in electronic books.

Library of Congress Cataloging-in-Publication Data

Customer service delivery : research and best practices / Lawrence Fogli, editor.— 1st ed.
   p. cm. — (The Society for Industrial and Organizational Psychology Professional Practice series)
 Includes bibliographical references and index.
 ISBN-13: 978-0-7879-7620-0 (alk. paper)
 ISBN-10: 0-7879-7620-2 (alk. paper)
 1. Customer services. 2. Customer relations—Management. I. Fogli, Lawrence. II. Professional practice series
 HF5415.5.C839 2006
 658.8'12—dc22

                                                            2005021210

Printed in the United States of America
FIRST EDITION
HB Printing   10 9 8 7 6 5 4 3 2 1

The Professional Practice Series

Contents

Foreword

Good customer service—service that is focused on us, the customers—is all we really want when we buy our groceries, when we fly, when we go to the hospital, when we eat at a restaurant. We expect to be treated as valuable customers by everyone who sells us something—from our accountants to our waste management employees, our veterinarians to our bank tellers. In reality, the service we receive can exceed every expectation or find us feeling disappointed, dissatisfied, or worse. Some companies, agencies, and organizations excel at providing customer service; others do not. Some make it part of their culture, a core corporate value, a norm. Others don't seem to recognize its value. This book seeks to understand customer service on many levels: what it takes to create a corporate culture that nurtures it, how it gives businesses an edge in the marketplace, and how to select and hire individuals who are ready, willing, and able to provide it to customers. *Customer Service Delivery: Research and Best Practices* is a practical walkthrough in the customer service arena. A very welcome book—on a topic not much studied by our profession—but which offers solutions that are based on recent research.

Larry Fogli and associates have tackled a challenging, unique, not-oft-discussed topic in the I-O community, yet one that affects us all every day. These chapters are full of advice, tips, hints, and strategies that can be applied to improve customer service. We hope this information is useful to anyone seeking to learn more about customer service from different perspectives. We know that exemplar customer service matters in organizational performance, so this volume should matter to those who create and manage organizations that rely on customer service to remain competitive. On behalf of the SIOP Professional Practice Series Editorial Board,

I would like to thank Larry and the authors for giving us such a practical and timely gem.

University of Central Florida
October 2005

EDUARDO SALAS
Editor

Preface

Over the past two decades, customer service delivery has become a catchphrase for businesses, as well as an inescapable part of modern life. Not a day goes by without multiple opportunities to engage in service transactions at grocery stores, banks, restaurants, and a host of other businesses. The service sector has become the largest part of the U.S. economy. The explosive growth of the U.S. service sector, coupled with every company's need to compete for market share, has resulted in an increased emphasis on improving customer service delivery as a boon to organizational survival. Business, marketing, and psychological research and practices provide a wealth of knowledge about customer service. Individuals engaged in the application of I/O psychology principles and practices have been involved in assisting organizations to both define the vision and implement the strategies.

The purpose of this book is to integrate our research and practices to provide for common understanding and sharing of our knowledge for best practices in customer service delivery. We will provide a framework for customer service as a process and an outcome. The book is divided into three parts: Part One, "What Is Customer Service?" provides definitions and explains customer service as a process and as an outcome. Topics addressed are customer expectations, loyalty, satisfaction and dissatisfaction, products versus service delivery, tangible versus intangible service, measurement, brand equity, job and industry differences, regional and cultural differences, and organizational impact.

Stephanie Kendall (Chapter One) points out that services differ from products in that services are intangible, occur simultaneously, and involve customer participation. Poor customer service can lead to customer switching, but, she explains, customers do not have to receive the best quality of service to be satisfied because of their "zone of tolerance." Because companies are expanding across the globe, they must be aware that customer satisfaction can be driven by different factors in different countries, as Kendall elucidates. Robert Vance (Chapter Two) reviews how companies are using technology to improve and implement customer service through the Internet and customer relationship management software. He discusses recent workforce and organizational changes that drive the use of technology to service both internal and external customers. Service worker performance is categorized as prescribed, voluntary, and proscribed. Scott Brooks, Jack Wiley, and Emily Hause (Chapter Three) review the service-profit chain, balanced scorecard, and linkage research to provide a better understanding of the relationships of employee satisfaction, customer satisfaction, and organizational performance. They conclude that happy customers are not often loyal customers and that an employee's opinion about the climate for service is a good indicator of organizational performance. Finally, Clifton Lemon (Chapter Four) asserts that customer satisfaction is declining because employee-customer contact is being engineered out, and he describes other negative consequences of technology-driven service systems, like loss of privacy and spam. Lemon reviews how brands and service coevolve and how brand equity and service expectations are related. He notes that service delivery will become more complex as more products are introduced, technology delivery systems develop, and market segments expand worldwide.

Part Two, "Employees and Customer Service," is devoted to HR staffing practices and service delivery. Jerry Kehoe and David Dickter (Chapter Five) discuss task requirements of service jobs, performance expectations, service competencies, specific knowledge skills, abilities, and other characteristics needed to perform service jobs. They provide a selection strategy for hiring service workers, considering job requirements, employee characteristics, and business constraints and priorities. Deborah Whetzel and Michael McDaniel (Chapter Six) review the personality correlates of service performance, including service orientation, sales drive, cognitive ability, and vocational interests. They also provide a comprehensive review of assessment instruments that predict customer service performance.

Part Three, "Organizational Change Management for Service Quality," includes strategies and tactics to improve and manage service delivery and provides case examples of how organizations have successfully improved and managed customer service. Diane Catanzaro and Eduardo Salas (Chapter Seven) describe the aspects of service encounters between employees and customers that lead to customer service improvement. They suggest strategies for improving such encounters, including improving company policies, educating customers about expectations, training employees, and improving the quality of services. Seymour Adler and Miriam Nelson (Chapter Eight) provide a performance management system for improving and managing customer service delivery in a call center. They describe the components of the system, including development and implementation of the service model, measurement, performance evaluation, and reporting. In the concluding chapter (Chapter Nine), I integrate our shared knowledge and describe organizational strategies and tactics to improve customer service delivery in an era of unprecedented organizational change.

Pleasant Hill, California   LAWRENCE FOGLI
October 2005

Acknowledgments

This book would not have been possible without the skill, ability, and diligence of my editorial assistant, Jennifer Ukei. From its inception to final proofs, Jennifer has done the hardest work to meet schedules, make necessary edits, and meet publisher formats and requirements. She was the key contact for all authors and facilitated getting all of us to meet deadlines. We are indebted to her for her unwavering persistence in completing this book.

I want personally to thank all the authors for their commitment and responsiveness to deadlines and editorial changes. The quality of the book chapters is evident.

A special acknowledgment goes to Wayne Cascio of the Professional Practice Series Board and Eduardo Salas, both of whom supported and motivated me to pursue the publication of this book.

To the reader, my goal was to share our knowledge of customer service delivery as a resource for our practice. Our challenge is that customer expectations in service delivery are more demanding than ever before, and my hope is that the readers of this book will use it to meet the challenge.

L.F.

The Authors

Seymour Adler is a graduate of the doctoral program in industrial and organizational psychology at New York University. He is senior vice president for talent solutions consulting at Aon Consulting, where he directs the development and implementation of assessment, performance management, and development programs, with particular emphasis on customer service, sales, and management positions. In addition to a thirty-year career in industry, he has been on the faculties of graduate I/O programs at Tel Aviv University, Purdue University, and the Stevens Institute of Technology, and he is currently an adjunct at New York University. He is a fellow of the Society for Industrial and Organizational Psychology and served as president of the Metropolitan New York Association of Applied Psychology.

Scott M. Brooks is general manager of the West Coast region for Gantz Wiley Research, a consulting firm that helps clients drive business performance through the strategic use of employee and customer input. In addition to survey consulting, he has had special oversight of the firm's projects linking employee surveys to customer satisfaction and business performance measures. Much of Brooks's consulting and research work focuses on leveraging these links in creating human resource metrics, balanced scorecard tools, and other frameworks to help clients make better use of strategic input from employees and customers. Brooks has over fifteen years of experience in survey research in numerous industries, including retail, health care, and service industries. Previously, Brooks worked in organizational development for Mervyn's. He holds a doctorate in industrial and organizational psychology from Ohio State University and is the author of numerous presentations and publications on employee measurement topics.

Diane Catanzaro is an associate professor of psychology at Christopher Newport University in Virginia and teaches undergraduate and graduate courses in industrial and organizational psychology. She has consulted on service quality and service encounter–related issues in a variety of settings, including the health care industry and law enforcement agencies. Her research and practice have included service encounter training and service climate–related interventions in nursing homes, examination of service quality measurement issues, and assessing adoption and implementation of human resource management best practices. Catanzaro has a Ph.D. in industrial and organizational psychology from Old Dominion University and an M.A. in industrial and organizational psychology from Fairleigh Dickinson University.

David N. Dickter is an industrial-organizational psychologist with Psychological Services. He has held personnel selection management roles at AT&T and Aon Human Capital Services, including the development and implementation of selection tools and systems for customer service and sales jobs. He is author or coauthor of several articles, book chapters, and conference presentations. He is a member of the American Psychological Association, the Society for Industrial and Organizational Psychology, the Society for Human Resource Management, and the Personnel Testing Council of Southern California. He earned his Ph.D. in industrial and organizational psychology from Ohio State University.

Lawrence Fogli received his Ph.D. from the University of California, Berkeley, in organizational behavior and business administration. A former corporate executive, vice president of human resource activities, and external consultant, Fogli has had substantial experience in the financial, retail, pharmaceutical, manufacturing, professional sports, entertainment, and insurance industries. His expertise has been applied to several major companies and industries in design and implementation of management and talent staffing systems to improve both individual and company effectiveness. Fogli has expertise in both strategic and specific functional human resource areas such as organizational restructuring, job design and redesign, improving customer service delivery, executive coaching, individual executive assessment, employee hiring and promotion systems, employee and customer surveys, and performance assessment feedback. He is the creator of ServiceFirst, a test designed to hire service-oriented employees, and the developer of the Sales and Service Excellence System. He also coined the term *total service delivery*. Fogli has been published in professional journals and books on a variety of topics and is a member of the American Psychological Association, the Society for Industrial and Organizational Psychology, and the Division of Consumer Psychology. He has taught courses in human resource management and organizational behavior at the University of California, Berkeley; California State University-Hayward, and San Francisco State University.

Emily L. Hause is an assistant professor of psychology at Augsburg College. In addition, she has been appointed to various college posts dealing with service quality, including assessment director, responsible for North Central accreditation activities, and membership on the Quality Improvement Steering Committee. Hause has consulted with a variety of organizations on managerial assessment, performance appraisal design, and synchronous work group effectiveness. Her publications and presentations have focused on decision making and job attitudes. She received her Ph.D. in industrial and organizational psychology from Ohio State University and is a member of the Society for Industrial and Organizational Psychology and the American Psychological Society.

Jerard F. Kehoe received his Ph.D. in quantitative psychology from the University of Southern California. In 1982, he joined AT&T, where he was responsible for various selection programs including manufacturing, customer service, sales, and management jobs. In 1996, he assumed overall leadership and direction of AT&T's selection program. He founded Selection and Assessment Consulting in 2003. Kehoe has written several publications and conference presentations on employment selection topics, including computerized testing, fairness, and test validity. In 2000, he edited the Society for Industrial and Organization Psychology's Professional Practice Series volume *Managing Selection in Changing Organizations: Human Resource Strategies*. He also has served on numerous professional committees, including the SIOP subcommittee that revised the Principles for the Validation and Use of Employment Selection Procedures. He served as an associate editor for the *Journal of Applied Psychology* from 2002 to 2005.

Stephanie D. Kendall is an executive consultant at Gantz Wiley Research, a consulting firm specializing in employee and customer measurement programs with both domestic and international clients. Her area is customer research, and she works across a broad range of clients in the financial service, retail, and business service sectors. Her research programs include loyalty studies, competitive perception studies, win-loss assessments, and internal customer satisfaction programs. Previously she was manager of service quality research for Questar and a research consultant for Control Data Business Advisors. She specializes in designing integrated research programs that link organizational effectiveness measures to customer satisfaction and business performance and has made numerous presentations on survey research to professional associations. She has completed four years of graduate coursework in applied sociology at the University of Minnesota.

Clifton Lemon is the founder and president of BrandSequence, a San Francisco–based brand consulting and management firm. He has extensive experience in brand research, brand development, and marketing communications. He has worked with a wide range of companies and organizations throughout the United States and abroad, from small technology start-ups to multibillion-dollar corporations. Before founding BrandSequence, he founded a full-service marketing communications firm in 1979 in San Francisco that specialized in corporate identity, print collateral, Web development, user interface design, advertising, and interactive media. He was a department director for Hirsch Bedner Associates, overseeing branding, identity, collateral, and environmental graphics for large hotel projects in Australia, Hawaii, and Hong Kong. He is the recipient of awards from organizations including the AIGA, San Francisco Art Director's Club, and the Art Director's Club of Los Angeles. Lemon's work and quotations have been featured in several publications, including *ID Magazine, Communication Arts, Shopping Centers Today,* the *San Francisco Chronicle,* and *USA Today.* He has a B.A. from Notre Dame de Namur University, Belmont,

California, and pursued independent studies in design at California College of Arts in Oakland, California.

Michael A. McDaniel received his Ph.D. in 1986 in industrial and organizational psychology from George Washington University. He is internationally recognized for his research and practice in personnel selection system development and validation. In 1996, he received the Academy of Management best paper award in human resources. In 2000, he was made a fellow of the Society for Industrial and Organizational Psychology, the American Psychological Society, and the American Psychological Association in recognition of his personnel selection research. McDaniel has published in several major journals, including the *Academy of Management Journal,* the *Journal of Applied Psychology,* and *Personnel Psychology.* He is noted for his research in customer service measures, employment interviews, situational judgment measures, cognitive tests, reviews of education and experience, and applicant faking in noncognitive measures. He coauthored a seminal article on the validity of customer service orientation measures in personnel selection and has presented a paper on the construct validity of customer service measures. McDaniel has consulted with many organizations, including international temporary staffing firms, major electric and gas utilities, manufacturing companies, and health care organizations.

Miriam T. Nelson is senior vice president for talent solutions consulting and serves as the practice leader for Aon Consulting's Call Center Performance Services. She has responsibility for managing the delivery of performance monitoring and directing a research team of industrial and organizational psychologists working to improve talent management, employee selection and retention, and leadership development in customer service environments. Nelson holds a Ph.D. from Stevens Institute of Technology in industrial and organizational psychology. She has published several articles on the conduct of call monitoring and performance assessment.

Eduardo Salas is trustee chair and professor of psychology at the University of Central Florida. Previously he served for fifteen years as a senior research psychologist and head of the Training Technology Development Branch of the Naval Air Warfare Center

Training Systems Division. During this period, he was the principal investigator for numerous research and development programs focusing on teamwork, team training, advanced training technology, decision making under stress, and performance assessment. Salas has coauthored over three hundred journal articles and book chapters and has coedited fourteen books. He is on or has been on the editorial boards of *Journal of Applied Psychology, Personnel Psychology, Military Psychology, Group Dynamics,* and the *Journal of Organizational Behavior* and is past editor of *Human Factors.* He currently edits an annual series, *Advances in Human Performance and Cognitive Engineering Research* (Elsevier). He is active with the Society for Industrial and Organizational Psychology. He is the past series editor for the SIOP's *Professional Practice Book* series and has served on numerous committees.

Robert J. Vance is a partner in Vance & Renz LLC of State College, Pennsylvania, a provider of customer-focused solutions to problems in personnel training, human resource management, and organizational development. He holds a Ph.D. in industrial and organizational psychology from Pennsylvania State University. Previously he served on the faculty of Ohio State University and Pennsylvania State University. He has twenty-five years of experience in teaching, research, publishing, consulting, and project management. His research and practice interests are in personnel selection, performance measurement, organization development, online surveys, and workforce development systems. His work has appeared in such publications as the *Journal of Applied Psychology, Personnel Psychology,* and *Human Performance.* In recent years, he has served on a National Research Council committee examining future directions for occupational analysis and classification systems and the American Psychological Association Task Force on Workforce Analysis. He is a member of the Society for Industrial and Organizational Psychology, the American Psychological Association, the Academy of Management, and the American Association for the Advancement of Science.

Deborah L. Whetzel received her Ph.D. in 1991 in industrial and organizational psychology from George Washington University. She has directed or conducted research on projects dealing with training development using the instructional systems design model, competency model development and job analysis, performance appraisal, selection, nationally administered test development, research, and implementation. She is the coeditor of *Applied Measurement Methods in Industrial Psychology,* which uses lay terms to describe methods for conducting job analysis and developing various kinds of instruments used to predict and assess performance. Her work has been presented at professional conferences and published in peer-reviewed journals, including the *Journal of Applied Psychology* and *Education Training, Research, and Development.* Whetzel has consulted with many public and private sector organizations including a midwestern police department, an international hotel franchiser, and a nuclear power utility company.

Jack W. Wiley is president and CEO of Gantz Wiley Research, a consulting firm that helps clients drive business performance through the strategic use of employee and customer input. Wiley's thirty years of experience in survey research spans a variety of industries including health care products and services, retail, and financial services. Based on groundbreaking research of over ten thousand business units, Wiley developed the High Performance Model, which demonstrates the link among employee opinions, customer loyalty, and business performance. Previously, Wiley was director of organizational research at Control Data (now Ceridian) and held a personnel research consulting position at Ford Motor Company. He has written several articles and book chapters on survey research topics and has made numerous presentations to professional associations worldwide. Wiley was appointed to Minnesota Governor Pawlenty's Workforce Development Council in 2004. He is a licensed psychologist and an accredited senior professional in human resources, and he received his Ph.D. in organizational psychology from the University of Tennessee.

Customer Service Delivery

PART 1

What Is Customer Service?

CHAPTER 1

Customer Service from the Customer's Perspective

Stephanie D. Kendall

A customer is anyone who receives products or services; customers can be internal or external to the organization and are the foundation of any business. As Levitt (1983) so simply stated, "The purpose of business is to find and keep customers and to get existing buyers to continue doing business with you rather than your competitors" (p. 101). Customer service is important in an organization's quest to keep customers. The relative role of customer service, however, can vary widely across industries, organizations, and customer segments.

Practitioners and line managers use numerous service-related terms, often interchangeably. We speak of measuring customer satisfaction but may focus primarily on the service experience; we have goals for customer loyalty without having any behavioral measures of it. Although they are all related, there are distinct differences in the concepts of customer service, service quality, customer satisfaction, and customer loyalty. Each concept is discussed in this chapter, as defined in Exhibit 1.1.

The framework outlined in Exhibit 1.1 moves from the discrete service experience (customer service) to a broader evaluation of services (service quality). Customer satisfaction is a broad attitude about the organization, taking into consideration service, but also products and available alternatives. And finally, customer loyalty moves from attitude to behavior toward the organization. Each of

Exhibit 1.1. Definitions of Service-Related Terms.

Customer service	Transactions aimed at meeting the needs and expectations of the customer, as defined by the customer. It is the service encounter or series of encounters.
Service quality	A global judgment or attitude relating to a particular service; the customer's overall impression of the relative inferiority or superiority of the organization and its services. Service quality is a cognitive judgment.
Customer satisfaction	Overall evaluation of an organization's products and services versus the customer's expectations. Customer satisfaction includes but is not limited to evaluations of service quality. Customer satisfaction is an attitude.
Customer loyalty	The preference of an organization or its brands over other acceptable products or services, conveniently available. Customer loyalty includes but is not limited to evaluations of service quality and customer satisfaction. Customer loyalty is behavior.

the subsequent concepts includes, but is not limited to, the previous concept. For example, customer satisfaction includes, but is not limited to, evaluations of service quality; customer loyalty is influenced by customer satisfaction, but a satisfied customer is not always loyal.

The difference is more than semantic. It is important that we understand what we are trying to influence or improve. Is it the customer's experience, her perception of our company, or her behavior that is the focus of our research and our initiatives?

Customer Service

Customer service is the interaction between the customer and a representative of the organization and is not limited to a single function or job type within the organization. The core of its definition is that customer service is defined by the customer who receives it. Along this line, Smith (1998) defines customer service as "meeting the needs and expectations of the customer, *as defined by the customer*" (p. 55). The customer is the judge of quality customer service, based on the expectations he or she has for the service.

Customer service is viewed separately from product quality. The distinction between services and products (Albrecht and Zemke, 1985; Bowen and Schneider, 1988) is a well-researched and frequently discussed concept. Three important dimensions of service distinguish it from products:

- *Intangibility.* Customers must experience the service to really know it. Service itself is intangible, although it can be provided in support of a tangible product, and documentation of service (receipts, account summaries, and reports, for example) can be tangibly provided.
- *Simultaneous delivery.* Service does not exist before it is delivered, and it cannot be stored for future use. Unlike a physical product, service cannot be placed in inventory or recalled if performed improperly.
- *Customer participation.* Customers are present for, and often participate, in their own services. Service delivered to customers varies more from customer to customer than product quality, in part because of the customer's role in the delivery process. Both the customer and the service provider react to verbal and sometimes physical cues provided by the other. As a participant, the customer can facilitate or impede the delivery of service.

Measuring Quality of Service

Bittner and Hubbert (1994) define *service quality* as "the consumer's overall impression of the relative inferiority/superiority of the organization and its services" (p. 77). They contrast this with *service encounter satisfaction,* which is the consumer's satisfaction or dissatisfaction with a single service encounter.

When a customer enters into a customer service relationship with an organization, he brings along certain expectations. Schneider and Bowen (1995) state that "customers are generally aware, or easily become aware of what they expect" (p. 3). Drawing on experiences from similar situations, the customer develops expectations for such things as response time, courtesy, empathy, and reliability. If these expectations are not met during the service encounter, the customer is likely to judge the service as poor and is likely to feel dissatisfied (Klose and Finkle, 1995).

Indeed, a common model in the measurement of customer perceptions of service quality focuses on meeting expectations. In this measurement model, service quality is defined as the difference between customers' expectations of what should happen in a service interaction and their perceptions of what actually happens (Schneider, Holcombe, and White, 1997).

Expectations of service quality are seen as desires or wants of the customer—what they feel the service organization should offer (Lewis and Mitchell, 1990). Expectations are based on many sources, including prior exposure to the service (or similar services), word-of-mouth, and market signals such as advertising and price (Steenkamp and Hoffman, 1994). A customer may have never stayed at a Ritz Carlton hotel, but she has expectations of service levels based on her experiences with other hotels, what others have said, the price of the room, and the brand image of the organization.

The dominant paradigm surrounding service quality is that of disconfirmation. Based on their expectations of what the experience will be like, the customer will confirm or disconfirm his expectations after the exchange occurs. If the organization's performance meets the expectations of the customer, his expectations are confirmed. If expectations are exceeded, the customer is said to be "delighted." Disappointment occurs when performance does not meet an acceptable level of expectation. Dissatisfaction, then, may be due to inherently poor service, or perhaps to the continuation of a once-acceptable level of service that no longer meets the customer standards (Rust and Zahorik, 1993). Customers refine their expectations based on their experience with the organization itself, its competitors, or service providers from other categories.

Service quality dimensions are measured in various ways. Three common models are presented below.

Perhaps the best-known measure of service quality is SERVQUAL (Parasuraman, Zeithaml, and Berry, 1985, 1988). Based on research conducted in a number of service settings, SERVQUAL uses the "met expectations" paradigm to measure service against an ideal service provider. A ninety-seven-item questionnaire yielded ten service quality dimensions: tangibles, reliability, responsiveness, competence, courtesy, credibility, security, access, communication, and understanding. The original ten dimensions were reduced to the five that explained the most variance in overall ratings of service quality: reliability, responsiveness, assurance, empathy, and tangibles. Descriptions of the five dimensions of SERVQUAL can be found in Exhibit 1.2.

Exhibit 1.2. Descriptions of SERVQUAL Dimensions.

Reliability	The ability of the organization to perform the promised service dependably and accurately. Examples include accurately posting a deposit or a credit to an account, or the on-time arrival of a flight. Customers consistently rate reliability as more important than the other dimensions.
Responsiveness	The organization's willingness to help customers and provide prompt service. Examples include waiting time, or the time it takes to complete a transaction.
Assurance	The knowledge and courtesy of the employees and their ability to inspire trust and confidence in the customers of the organizations. Examples include greeting and thanking customers for their business, or the knowledge level of employees in electronics superstores. Although it is rated as less important than reliability, assurance is related to higher levels of customer commitment.
Empathy	The caring and individualized attention the organization provides to its customers. Examples include acknowledging the customer's needs or frustrations when resolving problems. Although it is rated as less important than reliability, empathy is also related to higher levels of customer commitment.
Tangibles	The physical facilities, equipment, and appearance of personnel in the organization. Examples include the condition of the ATM, the appearance of the cashier, or the cleanliness of the parking lot. Customers consistently rate tangibles as less important than the other dimensions.

Source: Parsuamann, Berry, and Zeithaml (1998).

To examine the relationship between service and quality gaps, Klose and Finkle (1995) identified ten key service components. The components focus on attributes of the service providers (such as friendliness, appearance, and communication skills), as well as measures of assurance and trust. Highly similar to the SERVQUAL dimensions, the ten components are:

- Friendly and caring employees
- Employees who listen
- Employees who have the ability to communicate
- Employees who are able to make decisions
- Employees who have the ability to make the customer feel special
- Confidence in employees' abilities to solve problems
- Appearance of personnel
- Employees who are accurate
- Confidence that the customer input helped solve the problems
- Assurance that company policy is followed

While the previous models focus more on directly on dimensions of service delivery, Albrecht and Zemke (1985) identified a set of organizational practices and conditions needed for the delivery of high-quality service. These practices include focusing on customers and understanding their wants, needs, and expectations; developing and communicating a service strategy that defines excellent service and how it will be delivered; designing customer-friendly service systems; and having well-trained, service-oriented people at all levels of the organization.

Researchers have pointed out that the behaviors that constitute service quality in one organization may not be the same in another organization (Schneider, Holcombe, and White, 1997) or across positions within the same organization (Lundby, Dobbins, and Kidder, 1995). Speed and consistency may be the defining service behaviors for fast food restaurants, while creativity and appreciation may define service quality in an upscale restaurant. Speed and accuracy may be the most important service dimensions for tellers, while knowledge and advice may be more important from personal bankers. Each organization must focus on the behaviors its customers regard as most important.

Internal Service

An interesting consideration in the delivery of customer service lies in the difference between internal and external customers. In most discussions of customer service, the customer is perceived to be external to the organization. While external customers are, by definition, persons outside the organization, internal customers are employees who work for the same organization and depend on each other to carry out their work (Johnston, 1999). They are parts of the service delivery chain, often working in different departments and reporting to different managers. As examples, the customer service representative depends on the shipping department to pick and ship products accurately; the bank teller relies on the information technology group for reliable systems that are up and running when needed. Internal service quality can thus be defined as employee satisfaction with the service received from internal service providers (Hallowell, Schlesinger, and Zornitsky, 1996). Internal service quality is often measured in department-specific ways—for example, employee satisfaction with the speed and accuracy of benefit change submissions, responsiveness to hardware or infrastructure failures, or assistance in qualifying supplier organizations.

In considering the differences between internal and external customers, it has been suggested that the two types of customers cannot be treated in exactly the same manner. This is due in part to the fact that external customers typically operate in a free market; they usually have a choice of where to purchase products and services. To some degree, internal customers are captive customers.

While understanding the differences between internal and external customers may be useful in defining how customer service may best be achieved in each of these domains, their interrelationships, or the impact of internal customer service on external customer service, should also be considered. Specifically, the quality of service that internal customers receive strongly influences the quality of service that external customers receive (Berry, Parasuraman, and Zeithaml, 1988). For example, the wait staff may assure a customer that a salad can be substituted for fries, or that he can have the sandwich without the tomato, but if they do not have the cooperation of the kitchen staff, the promise cannot be fulfilled. Similarly, the gate agent may correctly tag a piece of luggage, but if the baggage handler sorts it incorrectly, it will not arrive at its intended destination.

Rarely can the efforts of an individual service provider (or department) totally meet the needs of the customer. The degree to which internal service (or the lack of internal service) is visible to the customer varies by industry and setting. For example, a lawyer may prepare a contract that, due to poor internal service relationships, may need to be reworked several times before it is correct. If the client's deadline is met, she may be unaware of the poor internal service relationships. Organizations striving to deliver excellent customer service to their external customers may begin by addressing and meeting the needs of internal customers.

Heskett and others (1994) state that internal service quality is characterized by the attitudes that people have toward one another and the way people serve each other inside the organization. They put forth the well-known service-profit chain, outlining a series of events where internal service quality drives employee satisfaction, which in turn enables the delivery of high-value service, resulting in customer satisfaction and leading to customer loyalty and, ultimately, profit and growth. In this framework, internal customer service is an important antecedent to both customer satisfaction and employee job satisfaction.

Cost of Poor Service

Service need not be of the highest quality to satisfy customers. Customers trade off various factors in their assessments of quality and satisfaction. For some customers, adequate service at a convenient location or a lower price may be more satisfactory than higher service levels elsewhere. Adequate selection at the bookstore down the block may be preferred to one with twice the inventory across town. Zeithaml, Parasuraman, and Berry (1993) introduced the term *zone of tolerance* to represent a range of service quality outcomes that are deemed neither particularly good nor bad by customers. The gap between desired service and adequate service is known as the zone of tolerance. The zone tends to be narrower for the most important components of satisfaction and wider for less important factors. For example, an airline passenger has a narrow band of tolerance for reliability and a wider tolerance for the food served onboard. Once the service falls below the zone of tolerance, disappointment occurs.

Poor service can result in substantial costs to an organization. These costs can include rework, discounts granted as compensation for poor service, and time spent dealing with dissatisfied customers. The most prevalent direct cost of poor service is in dealing with repeat calls to the organization and calls escalated to supervisors (TARP, 1997). These calls result in the need to employ more people than would be necessary if service was satisfactory or if calls were more effectively resolved on the first contact.

Poor service can also decrease revenue as dissatisfied customers find alternative suppliers. In addition, there is the word-of-mouth cost to the organization each time a customer is not satisfied. TARP has found that for small problems, a customer who is satisfied with the organization's response will tell four to five people. If the experience was bad, the customer will tell nine to ten people. For more serious problems (such as those that cost a customer in excess of a hundred dollars) the customer will tell eight people about a good experience and around sixteen about a bad experience. Negative word-of-mouth can affect the organization's image, future purchases, and, in some industries, regulatory relations.

Call Center News (2000) reports studies indicating that of consumers who had recently closed their bank account, more than 60 percent cited poor customer service as a reason for their decision. Another poll of three hundred consumers responsible for household purchasing found that 36 percent had changed insurance providers, 40 percent had changed telephone companies, 35 percent had changed credit card providers, and 37 percent had changed Internet service providers, all due to poor customer service. From these examples, it is clear that poor service can drive customer defection across a number of industries.

Customer Satisfaction

A distinction can be made between service quality and customer satisfaction. As discussed above, service quality is a global judgment relating to a particular service (Parasuraman, Zeithaml, and Berry, 1985), which takes into account the differences between customer expectations of service and customer perceptions of the actual service provided. Neal (1998) defines customer satisfaction as the attitude resulting from what customers think should happen (expectations) interacting with what customers think did happen (performance perceptions). Clearly the two concepts are related. Customer satisfaction includes, but is not limited to, evaluations of service quality. Satisfaction is superordinate to quality, one of the dimensions factored into the customer's satisfaction judgment. The difference can be illustrated by situations where customers are satisfied with a specific service but at the same time feel that the overall transaction was not satisfactory. A customer can be satisfied with the service encounter with the employee but overall dissatisfied with the price, selection, or quality of merchandise available. Satisfaction may reinforce quality perceptions, but only indirectly (Bittner and Hubbert, 1994).

Jones and Sasser (1995) outline four elements that influence customer satisfaction:

- The *basic elements* of the product or service that customers expect all competitors to deliver. Examples: all cars will have air bags; all banks will do wire transfers.
- *Basic support services* such as customer assistance or order tracking that make the product or service more effective and easier to use. Example: the Web retailer will confirm my order and tell me when the product has shipped.
- A *recovery process* for counteracting bad experiences. Examples: product or service guarantees or no-hassle return policies.
- *Extraordinary services* that excel in meeting customers' personal preferences, appealing to their values or solving their particular problems so they make the product or service seem customized. Example: suggesting products or services based on the customer's need or previous purchase experience.

Factors outside the realm of service influence customer perceptions and customer satisfaction. Such factors include price, convenience, and value (Schneider, White and Paul, 1998). The relative importance of these and other factors in determining customer satisfaction varies by industry. Customer service is often an important driver, although not the most important driver, of satisfaction in many industries. In the credit card industry, for example, customer service generally ranks behind interest rates and fees in determining satisfaction levels. In a business product environment, customer service is subordinate to product quality, selection, and price in determining satisfaction. And in a light manufacturing setting, it was found that delivery turnaround time, conformance to specifications, and price were all more important than customer service.

The business strategy of the organization can also influence the relative importance of service in the satisfaction equation. In a study for a retail grocer focusing on creating a high-quality service environment, service (as measured by being treated as a valued customer) was the top driver of customer satisfaction, followed by price and selection. One would expect that a retailer that builds its strategy on being the low-price provider would see price as a top driver and service of less importance.

Schneider, Holcombe, and White (1997) suggest that it is not enough to simply measure customer perceptions of an organization. In addition to these perceptions, they suggest it is critical to know how customers view the organization's competitors in order to help identify the need for change. When an organization has not only the ratings of how customers see it but also how competitors are seen, it can better determine key marketplace strengths and weaknesses, or the opportunity to differentiate the organization. An organization's own customer survey may show that service is rated high; employees are seen as courteous and friendly, responsive and knowledgeable. Service is not a competitive advantage for this organization, however, unless its service levels are higher than the competition. But if customers across competitors rate delivery systems poorly, the organization may not suffer from its own low ratings, or it may choose to invest in this area and differentiate itself from other providers.

Customer Loyalty

Customer satisfaction has been shown to be related to customer loyalty and organizational profits (Rust, Zahorik, and Keiningham, 1995). Researchers debate whether customer loyalty is an attitude or a behavior, or both. Neal (1998) strongly believes that customer loyalty is the proportion of times a purchaser chooses the same product or service in a specific category, compared to the total number of purchases the customer makes in that category, under the condition that other acceptable products or services are conveniently available. He sees loyalty as a behavior that is best measured as a proportion.

A customer who continues to repurchase from an organization because he sees no convenient alternatives is not loyal. Should a convenient alternative become available, the customer may well try it, especially if he was not "very satisfied" with the original provider. Jones and Sasser (1995) refer to such customers as "hostages," where the absence of market alternatives, and not loyalty, accounts for repurchase behavior.

Classic marketing literature defines loyalty as having both attitudinal and behavioral components (see Jacoby and Kyner, 1973). These definitions go beyond purchase behavior to offer a broader perspective of loyalty. Exhibit 1.3 highlights some attitudes and behaviors commonly attributed to customer loyalty.

Exhibit 1.3. Common Attitudinal and Behavior Indicators of Customer Loyalty.

Attitudes commonly attributed to loyal customers	*Behaviors* commonly associated with customer loyalty
• An intention to buy again or buy additional products or services • A willingness—hopefully, an eagerness—to recommend the company or brand to others • Little motivation to seek or explore alternative providers or brands	• Actual repeat purchases or renewals of contracts • Purchasing more or a broader array of products from the same company • Positive word-of-mouth communications or referral behavior
Attitudinal measures are *leading indicators* of customer loyalty.	Behavioral measures furnish *lagging indicators* of customer loyalty.

Source: Gantz Wiley Research (2005).

Significant work has been conducted that documents a link between customer satisfaction and customers' intent to repurchase (Oliver and Swan, 1989). More recently, however, research shows that the empirical link between satisfaction and actual repurchase is weak (Bemmaor, 1995; Hennig-Thurau and Klee, 1997; Kendall and McGoldrick, 2003). In a study in the automotive industry, Quick and Burton (2000) found that the closer in time to actual repurchase, the weaker the link was between customer satisfaction and actual repurchase of the same brand. Reinartz and Kumar (2002), studying four separate companies, found weak to moderate associations between customer longevity (a measure of loyalty) and profits; correlation coefficients were 0.45 for a grocery retailer, 0.30 for a corporate service provider, 0.29 for a direct brokerage firm, and 0.20 for a mail-order company.

Other conditions bear on repeat purchase, often despite customers' satisfaction. A satisfied customer may choose another brand just to try something new, or may purchase less frequently because of reduced need. Satisfied customers may nevertheless continue to purchase because of convenience (the gas station is on their route to work, the airline offers more direct flights), high switching costs (cancellation penalties, set-up charges), or just inertia (they do not want to take the time to investigate alternatives).

Customer Segmentation

Understanding that the relationship between service quality, customer satisfaction, and purchase behavior varies by customer segments helps an organization set service policies or standards for various segments and helps focus retention efforts on the most profitable segments. The notion of focusing service strategies on specific customer segments has a long tradition in marketing research and practice (Davidow and Uttal, 1989).

Research on market segments suggests that service organizations should not serve all customer segments equally, because different segments have different needs (Zeithaml, Parasuraman, and Berry, 1990). For example, Deitz, Pugh, and Wiley (2000) looked at customer segments based on frequency of face-to-face interactions. They found that the relationship between service climate and customer satisfaction was stronger in bank branches where employees and customers interacted frequently. They concluded that service organizations with frequent-interaction customer segments can benefit from the creation and investment in climates that foster service; service organizations whose businesses do not require frequent face-to-face interactions may consider devoting resources to areas more likely to have an impact on customer attitudes, such as technology to improve the speed and efficiency of the service transaction.

Kendall and Barker-Lemay (1999) investigated the relationship between service and share of wallet in a retail setting. In this study, share of wallet is the proportion of times the customer shops a specific store in the context of all the times she shops that category of store—for example, the number of times a customer shops at Safeway as a proportion of the total number of times she shops at grocery stores. Customers were segmented by purchase volume and frequency: high and low volume and increasing or decreasing from the previous quarter. Heavy purchasers had high volume in the current and previous quarters; upgraders had high volume in the current quarter, with a significant increase from the previous quarter; lapsed customers had light volume in the current quarter but heavy volume in the previous quarter; and light customers had light volume in both the current and previous quarters.

As shown in Exhibit 1.4, customer service elements such as staff knowledge and a "fun place to shop" were related to share of wal-

Exhibit 1.4. Key Drivers of Share of Wallet by Market Segment.

Heavy	Upgrader
• Fun place to shop	• Friendly staff
• Staff knowledge	• Helpful staff
• Store location	

Lapsed	Light
• Policy	• Value for price
• Store location	
• Convenient parking	

let for heavy-volume customers; friendly and helpful staff were also important drivers for customers' increasing their purchase volume. Service elements showed no relationship to share of wallet for declining- or light-volume buyers; cost and convenience were most important to these segments. Investments in developing and nurturing the service climate in the stores would have a positive impact on the buying behavior of higher-volume customers. To get a higher share from the light buyers, however, discounts or coupon strategies would be more effective.

By clearly understanding which customer segments are most desirable and which are most affected by increased service levels, the organization can better predict the return on the investments needed to increase service levels.

International Differences

As more companies do business globally, customer satisfaction measurement is expanded to various countries and regions. Not only do absolute ratings of satisfaction vary by region, but the relative importance of factors such as service, product quality, cost, and value can also differ. Finding that service is rated higher in Latin America than in Europe does not necessarily mean that Latin American service is "better" in an absolute sense. Interpreting levels of satisfaction across regions of the world should be done cautiously, paying attention to trends within regions.

Research conducted at Northwestern's Kellogg Graduate School of Management, as reported by Maruca (2000), focused on four regions: Asia, Latin America, and Northern and Southern Europe. Customers rated a company's products and services. The ratings of the company's product quality were consistently high across customer regions. At other levels, there were significant differences across the regions. Cost was a driver of quality for all markets except Latin America; quality drove repeat business in all markets except Southern Europe. Perceptions of service drove repeat purchases everywhere except in Northern Europe, and value drove repeat purchases only in Latin America. Research such as this helps companies better understand the relative importance of various factors across the globe.

Implications

This chapter sets the stage for the subsequent chapters by defining the terms and laying out the interrelationships among the concepts. From a scientific perspective, it is important to be precise with our terms—to understand the difference between a service experience and service quality, the distinction between service quality and satisfaction, the difference between an attitude and a behavior.

From a practitioner viewpoint, however, it is the interrelationships among the concepts that are most important. For the success of our organizations, it is important to know the role of service in helping to attract and retain customers. Service is important to all organizations. The relative importance of service and, in turn, of satisfaction, however, varies by industry and customer segment. Not all customers desire the highest levels of service, and not all organizations can afford to deliver it. The availability and performance of competitors influence both customer perceptions and the relative importance of service. The organization's strategy for business success also influences the role that service plays.

The question is no longer "Is service important in today's marketplace?" Instead, the question is "What aspects, to what extent, under what circumstances, and to whom is service important?"

References

Albrecht, K., and Zemke, R. *Service America: Doing Business in the New Economy.* Homewood, Ill.: Dow-Jones-Irwin, 1985.

Bemmaor, A. C. "Predicting Behavior from Intention to Buy Measures: The Parametric Case." *Journal of Marketing Research,* 1995, *32,* 176–191.

Berry, L. L., Parasuraman, A., and Zeithaml, V. A. "The Service Quality Puzzle." *Business Horizons,* Sept.-Oct. 1988, pp. 35–43.

Bittner, M. J., and Hubbert, A. R. "Encounter Satisfaction Versus Overall Satisfaction Versus Quality: The Customer's Voice." In R. Rust and R. L. Oliver (eds.), *Service Quality: New Directions in Theory and Practice.* Thousand Oaks, Calif.: Sage, 1994.

Bowen, D. E., and Schneider, B. "Services Marketing and Management: Implications for Organizational Behavior." In B. M. Shaw and L. L. Cummings (eds.), *Research in Organizational Behavior.* Greenwich, Conn.: JAI Press, 1988.

Call Center News. "Frustrated Consumers Have Little Tolerance for Poor Customer Service." *CC News,* Oct. 2000.

Davidow, W., and Uttal, B. *Total Customer Service: The Ultimate Weapon.* New York: HarperCollins, 1989.

Deitz, J., Pugh, S. D., and Wiley, J. W. "When Climate Matters: Customer Segments and the Importance/Unimportance of Service Climates." Paper presented at the Sixteenth Annual Conference of the Society for Industrial and Organizational Psychology, New Orleans, La., 2000.

Hallowell, R., Schlesinger, L. A., and Zornitsky, J. "Internal Service Quality, Customer and Job Satisfaction: Linkages and Implications for Management." *Human Resource Planning,* 1996, *19*(2), 21.

Hennig-Thurau, T., and Klee, A. "The Impact of Customer Satisfaction and Relationship Quality on Customer Retention." *Journal of Psychology and Marketing,* 1997, *14*(8), 737–764.

Heskett, J. L., and others. "Putting the Service-Profit Chain to Work." *Harvard Business Review,* Mar.-Apr. 1994, pp. 164–174.

Jacoby, J., and Kyner, D. B. "Brand Loyalty Versus Repeat Purchasing Behavior." *Journal of Marketing Research,* Feb. 1973, pp. 1–9.

Johnston, C. G. " 'Knock Your Socks Off' Service: Can Health Care Learn from Industry?" *Nursing Management,* 1999, *30,* 16–19.

Jones, T. O., and Sasser, W. E. "Why Satisfied Customers Defect." *Harvard Business Review,* Nov.-Dec. 1995, pp. 88–99.

Kendall, S., and Barker-Lemay, C. "When Does Service Matter: Linking Service Emphasis to Customer Satisfaction Within Heavy, Lapsed and Light Customer Segments." Paper presented at the Fourteenth Annual Conference of the Society for Industrial and Organizational Psychology, Atlanta, 1999.

Kendall, S., and McGoldrick, T. "What Drives Customer Behavior: Focusing on the Links That Matter Most." Paper presented at the Seventeenth Annual Conference of the Society for Industrial and Organizational Psychology, Orlando, Fla., 2003.

Klose, A., and Finkle, T. "Service Quality and the Congruency of Employee Perceptions and Customer Expectations: The Case of an Electric Utility." *Psychology and Marketing,* 1995, *12,* 637–646.

Levitt, T. "The Globalization of Markets." *Harvard Business Review,* May-June 1983, pp. 92–102.

Lewis, B. R., and Mitchell, V. W. "Defining and Measuring the Quality of Customer Service." *Marketing Intelligence and Planning,* 1990, *8*(6), 11–17.

Lundby, K. M., Dobbins, G. H., and Kidder, P. "Climate for Service and Productivity in High and Low Volume Jobs: Further Evidence for a Redefinition of Service." Paper presented at the Tenth Annual

Conference of the Society for Industrial and Organizational Psychology, Orlando, Fla., 1995.

Maruca, R. F. *Mapping the World of Customer Satisfaction.* Boston: Harvard Business Review Press, 2000.

Neal, W. D. "Satisfaction Be Damned, Value Drives Loyalty." Paper presented at the ARF Week of Workshops, New York, 1998.

Oliver, R. L., and Swan, J. E. "Consumer Perceptions of Interpersonal Quality and Satisfaction in Transactions: A Field Survey Approach." *Journal of Marketing,* 1989, *53,* 21–25.

Parasuraman, A., Zeithaml, V. A., and Berry, L. "A Conceptual Model of Service Quality and Its Implications for Future Research." *Journal of Marketing,* Fall 1985, pp. 41–50.

Parasuraman, A., Zeithaml, V. A., and Berry, L. "SERVQUAL: A Multiple-Item Scale for Measuring Customer Perceptions of Service Quality." *Journal of Retailing,* Spring 1988, pp. 12–40.

Quick, M. J., and Burton, S. "An Investigation of Repurchase in a High Involvement Category." Paper presented at the Australia and New Zealand Marketing Academy Conference, Gold Coast, Queensland, 2000.

Reinartz, W., and Kumar, V. "The Mismanagement of Customer Loyalty." *Harvard Business Review,* July 2002, pp. 86–94.

Rust, R. T., and Zahorik, A. J. "Customer Satisfaction, Customer Retention, and Market Share." *Journal of Retailing,* 1993, *69*(2), 193–215.

Rust, R. T., Zahorik, A. J., and Keiningham, T. L. "Return on Quality (ROQ): Making Service Quality Financially Accountable." *Journal of Marketing,* Apr. 1995, pp. 58–70.

Schneider, B., and Bowen, D. E. *Winning the Service Game.* Boston: Harvard Business School Press, 1995.

Schneider, B., Holcombe, K. M., and White, S. S. "Lessons Learned About Service Quality: What It Is, How to Manage It, and How to Become a Service Quality Organization." *Consulting Psychology Journal: Practice and Research,* 1997, *49,* 35–40.

Schneider, B., White, S. S., and Paul, M. C. "Linking Service Climate and Customer Perceptions of Service Quality: Test of a Causal Model." *Journal of Applied Psychology,* 1998, *83,* 150–163.

Smith, S. "How to Create a Plan to Deliver Great Customer Service." In R. Zemke and J. A. Woods (eds.), *Best Practices in Customer Service.* New York: AMACOM, 1998.

Steenkamp, J., and Hoffman, D. "Price and Advertising as Market Signals for Service Quality." In R. Rust and R. L. Oliver (eds.), *Service Quality: New Directions in Theory and Practice.* Thousand Oaks, Calif.: Sage, 1994.

TARP. *How Good Is Your Service—and in a Monopolistic Environment, Does It Matter?* Arlington, Va.: TARP, 1997.

Zeithaml, V. A., Parasuraman, A., and Berry, L. L. *Delivering Quality Service: Balancing Customer Perceptions and Expectations.* New York: Free Press, 1990.

Zeithaml, V. A., Parasuraman, A., and Berry, L. L. "The Nature and Determinants of Customer Expectations of Service." *Journal of the Academy of Marketing Science*, 1993, *21*, 1–12.

Chapter 2

Organizing for Customer Service

Robert J. Vance

Profit and nonprofit organizations, privately held and publicly traded companies, government agencies, educational institutions, and volunteer community groups, businesses with hundreds of thousands of employees and home-based part-time entrepreneurs have at least one thing in common: they exist to serve needs outside their boundaries. Needs imply customers, and boundaries imply a distinction between customers and the producers and servers who fulfill those needs. This distinction is at the heart of every enterprise: external customers pay those inside to provide goods and services that they either cannot or will not produce for themselves.

Organizational boundaries are as fundamental to work and commerce as are division of labor and specialization. The latter two hallmarks of modern labor, characteristic of work since at least the first industrial revolution, increase productive efficiency by allowing individual workers to become highly skilled at a narrow range of tasks. This allows standardization, so that work skills can be easily taught and learned, and quality control, so that products and services reliably meet customers' expectations. In traditional organizations, the efforts of individual workers are organized and coordinated by their employers to yield marketable products.

The boundaries of the organization make this possible: they shield those inside from the vagaries and turmoil of the marketplace. By providing islands of relative calm in a tumultuous stream of commerce, organizational boundaries enable work to be orderly, predictable, and efficient (relatively speaking, at least). There is a downside, however, and it is the flip side of this great advantage. The boundaries that make efficient work possible, that foster a sense of belonging and commitment among members, also foster an us-versus-them mentality that creates a kind of disconnect between the organization and its customers. This is the inherent dilemma that modern organizations continually face. How do you simultaneously shield yourself from marketplace dynamics while keeping abreast of, and preferably ahead of, the curve of changing customer needs and wants? How do you distinguish between the signals of a changing environment to which you must adapt and the noise of momentary fluctuations in the marketplace that are best ignored? Getting this right can make a successful world-class enterprise; getting it wrong can mean extinction.

Getting it right depends on a continual series of decisions and actions by business owners and executives. Foremost among these is the definition of the organization and its mission. Who are its customers? Which of their needs does it endeavor to meet? What does it take to meet customer needs? Cappelli and others (1997) noted that the collection of functions and tasks that are brought inside the company reflect management's choices in this regard. Why does a company produce goods that could be purchased from the market (outsourced)? Why does it have its own legal and accounting departments when these services could be subcontracted? As Cappelli and others put it, "In short, why are there companies at all?" (p. 21). The collection of entities within the company (that is, whose company is kept—for example, production lines, legal, finance, accounting, human resource departments) constitute its response to its environment. Implications of choices organizations make in defining themselves in relation to their customers and environments are examined in this chapter.

Organizations and Their Environments: A Brief History

Executives and managers strive to attain company goals by managing what to them is manageable—the internal workings of the organization. Of course, success is never guaranteed, so minimizing risk of failure is a constant concern. The design and structure of an organization reflect its approach to managing risk and exerting control over its internal environment in order to achieve success in its external environment.

The forms that organizations take span a broad range, from traditional tall bureaucracies with rigid hierarchies, many layers of authority, narrowly defined jobs, and highly formalized rules, to more modern flat and nimble organizations with few levels, broadly defined jobs, and permeable internal and external boundaries. Traditional forms remain common, but in the past twenty-five years, many companies that once dominated their industries have disappeared (for example, Pan American Airlines, Bethlehem Steel) or been acquired (for example, Chrysler Motors became Daimler-Chrysler). Companies that dominate their industries today did not exist thirty years ago (for example, Microsoft); in some cases, the industries they dominate did not even exist (for example, America Online and the Internet). Companies using nontraditional business models have driven traditional competitors into oblivion. For example, Wal-Mart leveraged supplier relationships to achieve cost advantages over rivals in the discount retail industry, from large national and regional chains to a host of small local businesses. Southwest Airlines and other no-frills carriers appear to be challenging and dominating rivals in the U.S. airline industry in much the same way.

To understand how and why things began to change in the last two decades of the twentieth century, it is helpful to consider the forces that created the traditional organization earlier in the century. A brief examination of the history of organizational forms over the past one hundred years yields insights into the external forces that shaped them and drove their evolution.

The Traditional Model

Cappelli and others (1997) provided a cogent analysis of the pressures that produced both traditional and modern organizations. What we think of as traditional industrial employment—paternalistic organizations that promised job security in return for unwavering commitment—was in fact a product of many years of efforts to rationalize and standardize employment relations. At the outset of the twentieth century, industrial concerns had little control over staffing, relying instead on foremen and their workers. Companies hired foremen, and their workers came with them. Foremen had control over hiring, training, paying, and firing. There could be considerable variability in these practices across foremen in the same plant, and a foreman could change the rules as needed to manage his workers. From the company's perspective, control was externalized to the foremen, who could leave at any time and take their work crews with them.

These practices changed as companies began to adhere to the principles of scientific management (Taylor, 1980). Taylor prescribed the techniques of time and motion studies to simplify and standardize work, such that unskilled and inexpensive workers could quickly learn to perform their assigned tasks with a minimum of training. Control of workers was through a combination of incentive pay (usually piece work) and disciplinary procedures. Planning and organization were left to managers, who were assumed to have a greater stake in the company's success and therefore could be entrusted with greater responsibility.

For these practices to be effective, the psychological employment contract, together with the worker's allegiance, had to shift from the foreman to the company. Employers began to internalize the labor market by standardizing hiring practices, rates of pay, training, and job progression (from unskilled entry-level jobs to higher-skilled, better-paying jobs). By thus internalizing the labor market, they gained control over it and diminished the uncertainty inherent in the previous system. Of course, internal labor markets are more costly because they are less flexible; to maintain an internal labor market, you have to keep employees on the payroll even in slack times. World War I spurred this trend along through pressure for more productivity and better quality control of wartime industrial output. Paper-and-pencil selection tests developed during this period by the U.S. Army (in an effort led by Robert Yerkes, then president of the American Psychological Association) added a systematic and scientifically grounded aspect to personnel selection.

In the postwar years, military officers returning to civilian jobs brought with them new ideas about standardization of everything from work tools and processes to worker selection and training.

These practices found wide acceptance in businesses throughout the 1920s, in part because they complemented investments by companies in the technologies of the day (for example, machine tools and assembly lines) that fostered efficiency through mass production. Standardization also made the jobs of managers easier because work within the boundaries of the company became more routine and predictable, shielded from the vagaries of the external environment. Mass-produced goods appeal to consumers because they are affordable; they are not custom-tailored to individual needs and preferences, however. As Henry Ford was famously quoted as saying of the Model T and consumer preferences, "The customer can have any color he wants so long as it's black."

Additional pressures to rationalize employment practices during this period came from trade unions, which sought to counter arbitrary and capricious management practices (Cappelli and others, 1997). To resist union inroads, employer associations adopted standard employment practices that addressed worker complaints (such as "the American Plan"). As unions gained a greater foothold, they bargained for and won agreements governing wages, work rules, and work hours that were applied across entire industries. The effects of this shift can be seen today in industries such as the automotive industry.

Social pressures on the employment system were institutionalized through federal legislation beginning in the 1930s and continuing to the present. The Fair Labor Standards Act of 1938 requires overtime pay for employees who are paid by the hour when they work more than forty hours per week and makes a distinction between nonexempt employees (hourly wage employees to whom the law applies) and exempt employees (salaried, temporary, and contingent employees to whom the law does not apply). The National Labor Relations Act (amended in 1947) distinguishes between workers and managers and addresses issues of union representation of workers. The Civil Rights Act of 1964 addressed equal opportunity in employment, the Age Discrimination in Employment Act of 1967 prohibited discrimination against those forty years of age or older, the Occupational Safety and Health Act of 1970 addressed workplace conditions, the Employee Retirement and Income Security Act of 1975 addressed employee pensions, and the Americans with Disabilities Act of 1990 and the

Family and Medical Leave Act of 1993 addressed employment access issues.

These statutes, plus many other laws (federal, state, and local), executive orders, court decisions, and labor agreements, placed significant constraints on employers. As Cappelli and others (1997) noted, the employment model that most of these laws and regulations assumed was the traditional industrial model of the 1930s and 1940s. Although organizations ultimately exist to serve their environments and are therefore controlled by them (Pfeffer and Salancik, 1978), business owners nevertheless had considerable incentives to restructure employment relationships to increase internal and decrease external control. How and why this happened will be examined next.

Forces for Organizational Change

Cappelli and others (1997) made a distinction among owners, managers, and workers. Owners (stockholders in the case of most publicly traded companies) are assumed to take all the risk for the success or failure of a business, whereas executives, managers, and workers, as hired help, are paid regardless of whether the business makes a profit or loss in a given year. Through boards of directors, stockholders exert pressures on executives and managers to run a profitable business and thereby justify their investments, often by tying executive compensation to company performance. In the middle part of the twentieth century, the trend among companies was to grow larger through acquisitions. Conglomerates were formed from a diverse array of companies as a way to even out revenues and profits in the course of the economic business cycle. General Electric is an example. In a given period, companies within the conglomerate that did well (for example, aircraft engines) could offset the performance of other companies that did poorly (for example, light bulbs).

Conglomerates, however, are often difficult to manage. They are slow to adapt to changing external environments (the same can be said for most traditional bureaucracies), and as the century progressed, their environments began to change with increasing rapidity. As a National Research Council study (1999) pointed out, these changes included changing technology (particularly information technology), a changing geopolitical climate (the breakup of the Soviet Union, the end of the cold war, and the rise of international terrorism to name a few), changing population demographics (an aging population in Europe and Japan, an increasingly multicultural population in the United States), and changing markets and global competition.

Increasing Competition

Among the forces driving these changes was increasing global competition. Companies in the traditional system tended to enjoy stable product markets and readily available resources. Many industries, such as transportation, steel, and agriculture, were protected from competition by government regulations and trade restrictions such as import tariffs. For example, in March 2002, the Bush administration sought to protect the domestic steel industry, long in decline, by imposing 30 percent tariffs on imported steel. Although these were met with howls of protests from foreign producers as well as domestic industries hurt by higher steel prices, as politically expedient actions they were not rescinded until December 2003.

The world began to change in the 1970s with a series of economic shocks imposed on the global economy by the Organization of Petroleum Exporting Countries (OPEC), an international cartel that began increasing the price of oil, in part in response to political turmoil in the Middle East. Rising prices for oil and gasoline led to increasing demand for fuel-efficient and clean-burning automobiles. The Japanese automotive industry produced such vehicles and began taking market share from U.S. automakers, which were slow to respond to these changing conditions. Inroads into American markets by Japanese automakers also heightened the salience to consumers of factors such as quality, reliability, and customer relations. Competition became increasingly global, forcing companies to rethink their business models. In one survey conducted in 1993, 75 percent of 736 large companies indicated that economic pressure from competition caused them to restructure (*Wyatt's*, 1993).

This trend continues, such that today, most large companies are multinational, with production operations in multiple countries serving a global marketplace. Deregulation of some industries (for example, airlines, trucking, railroads, and electric utilities in the United States), relaxation of regulations of other industries (for example, banking and financial services), and the breakup of monopolies (for example, telecommunications) have hastened the spread of competition. International treaties that break down protectionist barriers (for example, the North American Free Trade Agreement of 1994) have contributed immeasurably to this trend. One aspect of globalization that was a major focus of the 2004 presidential campaign was the outsourcing of jobs from the United States to lower-wage countries. The first years of the twenty-first century have seen the export of upwards of 3 million manufacturing jobs from the United States to such countries as China, Malaysia, and India. Increasingly, high-paying nonmanufacturing jobs (for example, computer programming, accounting) are being exported to countries where typical wages for college-educated workers are one-fifth or less those of their U.S. counterparts. Although these developments are painful for displaced American workers, they are inevitable consequences of efficient use of capital in a global free market system.

Changing Markets

Another factor driving changes in organizational forms was changing markets. Spurred by Japanese automakers, which began introducing many new models each year throughout the 1980s, the life cycles of products became shorter. Globalization of markets made it harder to transfer sales of products falling out of fashion domestically to developing markets overseas, a common practice in earlier decades that effectively extended production runs. Rapid changes in products required expensive investments in flexible production systems. Workers were also affected, as skills required by flexible production systems, emphasizing teamwork, digital technology, and quality control, were frequently different from the skills required by older production methods. It was more cost effective for many employers to close old plants and open new ones elsewhere, with new technology and new employees, than to retool older operations and retrain their workers. Today this trend is receiving daily attention in the media as companies close plants in the United States and transfer their production facilities overseas. A related trend is to outsource production to smaller, newer shops that employ the latest technology and younger workers with current skills (who are also less likely to be unionized).

Investor Pressures

The 1980s and 1990s saw yet another force for organizational change, this time from the financial sector. As Cappelli and others (1997) described, new ways of financing corporate debt let to a dramatic upsurge in attempts at hostile takeovers of public companies by groups of investors who offered attractive premiums over current stock prices to shareholders. Once acquired, corporate raiders would often sell off corporate assets and lay off employees in order to cut costs and raise cash to pay off "junk bonds" that financed the takeover. Companies whose book value (the estimated market value of all tangible assets) exceeded their stock value were particularly vulnerable, as successful raiders could then sell off the assets piecemeal, pay off the junk bonds used to finance the deal, and reap a profit over the acquisition cost. To thwart such unwanted acquisitions, corporate boards adopted a variety of strategies, including poison pill defenses (shareholder rights agreements designed to thwart hostile takeovers, for example, preferred stock purchase rights), friendly mergers (agreeing to be acquired in what was hoped would be a mutually beneficial partnership), and leveraged buyouts (a company's managers lead a group of investors who pool their assets to acquire the outstanding shares of a company and take it private). Cappelli and others reported that in the 1980s, one-third of the Fortune 500 companies in the United States received a takeover bid, and one-third ceased to exist as independent businesses.

Corporate hostilities caused many companies to redefine themselves as dedicated solely to their core business competencies—the parts of the business that turned the greatest profits—divesting less profitable parts of the enterprise. Corporate executives also faced growing pressures from investors during this period, particularly large institutional investors such as pension fund managers who often controlled large blocks of stock in major corporations. Stock prices are driven fundamentally by corporate earnings and dividends (even now, according to Morgenson, 2004), and higher stock prices increase the value and long-term solvency of pension funds. Corporate boards responded to these pressures by hiring executives with reputations for cutting costs and focusing on the bottom line, and they tied their compensation ever more closely to company performance by granting stock option packages that could be worth many millions of dollars if stock prices rose in value.

Perhaps at its most extreme, this trend culminated in the accounting scandals that broke in the 2001–2003 period but had been brewing for at least ten years. With the complicity of major accounting firms, until then regarded by the investment community as models of propriety and integrity, executives of many firms began to fabricate crucial elements of corporate balance sheets, such as revenues and expenditures, to mislead investors about the value of their companies and thus drive up stock prices and, with them, their personal income and net worth. Revelations of these practices by government prosecutors produced the spectacle of the "perp walk," whereby corporate executives accused of fraud were led into court in handcuffs in full view of the assembled media and the world. *CFO* magazine abandoned its annual "excellence awards" after two winners for 1998 and 1999, high-profile chief financial officers of major companies, pleaded guilty to financial fraud charges (O'Donnell, 2004). A third award winner for 2000 was found guilty in June 2005 on twenty-two of twenty-three counts of grand larceny and conspiracy, falsifying business records, and violating general business law. Collectively, these executives assisted in looting their companies of many billions of dollars, representing only a small portion of the accounting fraud in U.S. companies during that period.

These scandals led to the downfall of several formerly respected companies, including one of the "big five" accounting firms. They contributed to the stock market slump of 2001–2002 as investors questioned the financial disclosures of many companies tainted by questionable accounting practices. They led to still more government intrusion into the inner workings of companies when Congress passed the Sarbanes-Oxley Act of 2002 that required CEOs to annually sign off on corporate financial statements, personally attesting to their accuracy.

Organizations in Today's Economy

Many forces led to a continual churning in corporate America throughout the 1980s, 1990s, and into the twenty-first century as companies merged, were acquired, divested, outsourced, reengineered, restructured, and downsized. Companies that could not compete successfully disappeared, usually through acquisition by other companies. Those that remained found themselves to be flatter, with fewer hierarchical levels and broader spans of control. These reinvented companies rely on highly skilled workers with expanded scope of responsibilities at each level, often organized as empowered teams (without traditional foremen or supervisors). They are likely to embrace a customer focus that links producers within the organization more closely to customers and end users (National Research Council, 1997, 1999).

Employees with "outdated" skills are displaced while others are simultaneously hired. The stock market bubble of the late 1990s that burst early in 2001 was due in part to "irrational exuberance" (Greenspan, 1996) surrounding stocks, especially stocks of information technology companies driven to stratospheric levels by the digital revolution and the advent of the Internet with its promise as a virtual superhighway of commerce. The recession of 2001 wrung out much of this excess—both excess information technology capacity and investor enthusiasm about its profit-making potential.

This was followed in the United States by a "jobless" recovery from 2002 through the first quarter of 2004, with a gradual increase in business activity but little concomitant increase in job growth. Labor remains the most expensive resource of most businesses. Digital technology can dramatically increase the productivity of individual workers, and companies have made enormous investments in this technology in the past twenty years. They have learned to use it well; hence, job growth was flat, but productivity increases were at historic highs in this period. Fewer workers produce more output now than ever before. Outsourcing is preferred to hiring new workers because costs are lower, particularly ancillary costs such as health and pension benefits. The latter factors, along with wages and work hours, are the hallmarks of labor agreements with American unions, so outsourcing also tends to diminish the strength of unions. Manufacturing jobs are being created elsewhere to supply United States companies with cheap labor and products. Stock prices rose dramatically in 2003 from their lows of 2001–2002, and with them the value of executive compensation packages.

These changes in organizations have increased the risks borne by the typical worker in the U.S. economy. Gone are the days when getting a good job in a good company meant lifelong employment and a nice pension on retirement. Workers are now responsible for their own skill acquisition and career development (formerly assumed by paternalistic corporations). They are displaced as a matter of course and left to fend for themselves in a turbulent economy (Cappelli, 1999). Consequently, young workers today are likely to look at each new job and employer as a stepping-stone to the next. The irony is that the highly skilled, high-value-added workforce that modern companies require assumes a dedicated and committed workforce concerned with quality and customer service. The optimal strategy of the worker, however, is to have no particular commitment to an employer that considers her to be a completely expendable resource. In the next sections, we examine the challenges faced by modern organizations that adopt a customer focus strategy and a workforce without a vested interest in their employers' success.

Customer Focus Organizations and Customer Service Jobs

In recent years, companies have adopted customer focus as a strategy to link themselves more closely to their changing environments. Companies in the retail, service, and travel sectors of the economy have always had a customer focus, of course, but new technologies such as client tracking (customer relationship management) software and the Internet have revolutionized marketing and customer service. Traditional companies in manufacturing, utilities, and defense, where most employees do not interact with external customers, have expanded on the service philosophy by recognizing that there is a customer for every job (or the job would not exist) and distinguishing between external customers (those outside the organization who purchase the products) and internal customers (employees at successive points in the production chain whose work depends on the output of those at earlier points). Even bureaucracies that formerly regarded themselves as having missions but no customers (for example, government agencies and educational institutions) have seen the light, often in response to pressures from those (taxpayers, parents) who have learned the customer service philosophy in their own jobs and expect to be treated as valued customers wherever they are paying for a product or service.

Much of the burden of customer focus falls on the shoulders of workers who interact with customers and provide the services expected. Customer service work can be classified into three categories: (1) personal services such as child care, housekeeping, and hairstyling, (2) clerical and administrative support, and (3) sales (National Research Council, 1999). The hallmark of service work is interaction with the customer. According to Leidner (1993), in some service jobs, this interaction is the essence of what the customer is paying for (for example, child care, elder care, and tour guide), whereas in others, the quality of the interaction can be an important component of the purchase (for example, waitstaff, flight attendants, and hairstylists) but is not a part of what is being sold. According to the National Research Council (1999), service workers increased as a proportion of the workforce from 30 percent in 1950 to 41 percent in 1996.

Consideration of customer service raises different although complementary issues when taken from an organizational perspective versus an individual service worker's perspective. Some of these issues are considered in this section.

Customer Focus as Competitive Edge

To succeed, companies must identify potential customers, determine their needs and wants, develop products and services to meet these needs, produce products and services efficiently enough to sell them at a profit, and reach out to the customer to make the sale. Each of the links in this chain of events requires information that must be gathered and processed. Because external customers reside outside the organization's boundaries, the organization must have ways to reach beyond its boundaries to survey the marketplace for opportunities and obtain feedback from customers. The same can be said of internal customers, who are often separated from producers by internal boundaries (for example, between departments or business units).

Market research, advertising, consumer behavior research, and information technology have played increasingly large roles in these processes. As with other trends in the evolution of organizations, the digitization of these processes has increased, and, with it, the roles of workers have altered (Barley, 1996; Stewart, 1997). This trend toward digitization is relentless because it reduces the cost of doing business, and it often expands the scope of business that can be done. Techniques for spanning internal and external boundaries to acquire information have become increasingly sophisticated, both procedurally and technologically. We explore some of these in this section.

Inventory Control

Universal product codes (UPCs, commonly referred to as bar codes), first established in 1973 by the grocery industry, were widely used by the 1980s. This technology enables manufacturers, suppliers, distributors, shippers, and retailers to track products from point of production through point of sale. Coupled with optical scanning, database, and communications technology to keep track of goods, this technology has greatly expanded the efficiency of inventory management and control. This enables companies to realize savings through just-in-time production, linking sales demand to production schedules and supplier orders to minimize slack and excess inventories. A recent innovation in the supermarket industry, self-scan checkouts, extends this technology further by removing the cashier from the sales transaction by having customers serve as their own sales clerks, replacing labor with cheaper technology.

Customer Tracking

For many years, the supermarket industry encouraged customer loyalty by awarding "green stamps" for purchases that could be redeemed for common household goods, small appliances, and the like. Food producers attracted customers with discount coupons distributed through newspapers, magazines, and direct marketing. In the 1980s, the travel industry followed suit with frequent flyer and frequent stayer programs. Taking advantage of advances in information technology that allowed customers' purchasing patterns to be recorded and tracked, in exchange for personal information (for example, age, gender, marital status, address, family income), customers could accumulate points based on mileage flown on an airline and cost of accommodations for stays with a hotel chain.

Points could then be exchanged for free travel and travel service upgrades (for example, from economy to business class, from a basic room to a suite). These programs have proven to be popular with travelers, particularly business travelers who reap the program rewards while their employers pay the costs. They are popular with travel and tourism companies because, by securing customer loyalty, they provide a more reliable and predictable revenue stream. They track customers' habits and preferences, allowing segmentation of the market, targeted advertising and promotions, and inventory control (for example, how many seats to offer on each flight in each class of service and at what price). According to Fonti (2003), the airline industry regards frequent flyer program membership as the third-ranking factor, after schedule and price, in travelers' purchase decisions, accounting for 18 to 20 percent of sales.

The supermarket industry has followed suit in recent years with shopper card programs. Customers in possession of these cards, which are scanned at checkout along with the items purchased, typically receive special discounts on selected items along with periodic bonus discounts. In return, supermarkets track buying habits and preferences of individual shoppers based on basic demographic information obtained when the customer signs up. With this information, they can individualize marketing and plan everything from inventory through displays to staffing levels in order to attract and retain the most desirable customers.

Online retailers have taken this trend a step further. The Internet equivalent of frequent flyer and frequent stayer cards, from a company's perspective, are "cookies." These are electronic tags stored on one's personal computer in the course of Web surfing. Cookies enable a company to determine such things as whether a Web surfer has previously visited a Web site, the identity of the Web surfer (if the individual has previously registered with the Web site), and particular preferences for the product or service offered. Amazon.com, the online retailer that has grown from originally selling books to music, movies, clothing, and appliances, is perhaps the best-known example. In addition to purchases, Amazon.com tracks customers' searches on its Web site and uses probabilistic modeling to suggest items that might be of interest to the customer based on similarity of browsing and buying habits to other apparently like-minded customers.

Technology and Self-Service

Industrialization in the eighteenth and nineteenth centuries transformed the production of goods from local artisans and tradesmen, who crafted items for individual customers, to mass-produced goods that were stamped out and mass-marketed. The shift was from small-scale, labor-intensive operations to large-scale, technology-intensive operations. Makers of goods in the preindustrial era were also often responsible for selling them, to either local customers or to local or regional middlemen (for example, shopkeepers, peddlers). Along with industrial production systems came new occupations such as sales and marketing. Companies created entire departments devoted to finding out what customers wanted, convincing potential customers that what they wanted were the company's products, and making the sale.

Whereas the trend throughout most of the twentieth century was to replace expensive production labor with cheaper, more controllable, and more reliable production technology, a parallel trend became evident in the last twenty years of the century in the areas of marketing and sales. Advances in information technology and telecommunications made this possible. Sales and service, which once depended almost exclusively on face-to-face interaction between a salesperson or service person and a customer, increasingly happen from afar. Many brick-and-mortar retailers (a term that differentiates the old way of doing business from the new) now have an online presence, and an ever-increasing portion of their business is done online by shoppers who never interact with a salesperson. For them, the Internet is the equivalent of the mail order catalogue, which continues to play a large part in retailing. Some companies have abandoned the brick-and-mortar model altogether, maintaining an online or call center presence but no actual establishments that one can visit to shop for purchases. Examples include Amazon.com, which has adopted the online model as its sole way of doing business, and Dell Computer, which conducts its sales and service online and by telephone. A number of airlines and hotel companies offer incentives in the form of frequent flyer bonuses to customers who use their Web sites rather than calling a reservations agent to purchase tickets, reserve seats, and obtain boarding passes.

Technology is cheaper than labor, so customers are being trained to use it. The trend is to assign the customer another role, that of sales or reservations clerk. Through Web sites, telemarketing, self-scan registers, ATM machines, and various types of self-service kiosks, companies achieve enormous savings by reducing and even eliminating the expenses of local retail stores and the clerks who staff them. They use these savings to compete more effectively on price, particularly against old-style competitors slow to adopt the new model. They can offer a wider assortment of goods and provide sales and service twenty-four hours a day, seven days a week. A recent and controversial trend has been to outsource call centers overseas, particularly to India where English is commonly spoken and wages are a fraction of their counterparts in the United States. The success of the application of information and telecommunications technology in the domain of customer service continues to put pressure on traditional companies, which face a rising tide of expectations from customers who demand around-the-clock access to their services.

Customer Service and Sales Jobs

Performance of customer service work requires interaction with a customer. This interaction can be an end in itself (what is being sold, as in child care or counseling), or it can be a means to an end, as when a persuasive salesperson sells you more than you intended to buy. In some service jobs, the worker exercises considerable autonomy in assessing the customer and determining the optimal sales or service strategy, whereas in others, the worker follows a completely scripted protocol in interacting with the customer, with any deviation passed along to another representative specifically trained to deal with the issue. Employers make choices concerning these options in designing customer service jobs.

A useful model of job performance is Campbell, Dunnette, Lawler, and Weick's person-process-product model (1970). As adapted by Vance and Brooks (1990), this model (see Exhibit 2.1) proposes that performance involves attributes of the worker performing a set of tasks and duties in order to produce an outcome or result. Performance occurs in a context that either facilitates or constrains accomplishment of objectives. Worker attributes may be

Exhibit 2.1. A Model of Work Performance.

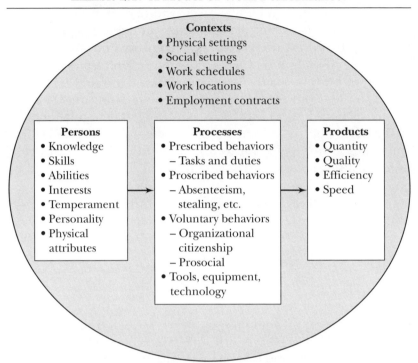

enduring, such as knowledge or skill, or relatively short term, such as attitude or mood. Similarly, situational context factors may be enduring, such as one's group of coworkers, or short term, such as a rush of customers just prior to closing time.

Work processes are usually accomplished through a combination of worker behaviors and technology. Worker behaviors can be conceptualized as prescribed, proscribed, and voluntary. *Prescribed behaviors* are those required by the employer and deemed necessary to accomplish assigned tasks and duties; these are often listed on job descriptions. *Proscribed behaviors* are those prohibited by the employer, for example, use of illegal drugs, stealing, and unexcused absence. *Voluntary behaviors* (encompassing prosocial behaviors, organizational citizenship behaviors, and contextual performance) are activities needed to keep a workplace running smoothly but are not formally prescribed to individual workers. Examples are offering assistance to a coworker struggling to meet a deadline and organizing an office holiday party. Customer service jobs vary in the mix of work behaviors that the employer defines as prescribed, proscribed, and voluntary. Of course, context factors vary substantially across employers, across jobs, and even from one worker to another performing the same job.

Examples from the airline industry help to illustrate some of these concepts. In the early 1980s, government deregulation initiated a period of fierce competition among domestic carriers that continues to this day. Prior to that time, the government determined routes that each airline could fly and fares that could be charged. After deregulation, airlines competed on routes, fares, and amenities. A series of start-up airlines began service, generally offering cheaper no-frills service. The result was that many more people began flying, and passenger miles flown increased nearly three-fold between 1981 and 2000.

The airline business was greatly affected by the attacks of September 11, 2001. Already suffering from an economic recession that began earlier in the year, passenger volume dropped off dramatically in subsequent months as travelers avoided airlines due to safety concerns. Post–9/11, air travel is seen by many as an ordeal brought on by strict and intrusive passenger security screening, discomfort as airlines abolish amenities such as food and beverage services, crowding as they seek to fill all available seats, and uncertainty as flights are cancelled at the last minute in order to consolidate passengers to ensure that other flights are filled to capacity.

The result is a stressful environment for both passengers and airline employees. This was illustrated by reports in the *New York Times* in a feature section titled, "A Paycheck Weekly, Insults Daily" (Estabrook, 2004). As reported, a survey of transportation workers conducted late in 2003 by Public Agenda stated that 54 percent felt that passenger rudeness was a primary cause of job stress. Almost half of the respondents said that they had witnessed an incident where disrespectful behavior had verged on physical confrontation, and nearly one in five had observed violent acts by passengers (Estabrook, 2004).

An example is cited of a passenger who ran through a terminal shouting expletives, overturning a trash receptacle, and finally assaulting a gate agent before being restrained and arrested by security personnel. In another case, at the urging of her mother, a fourteen-year-old slapped an airline worker. Stating that throwing staplers at ticket counters has become "a particularly common way for unruly passengers to vent," one airline employee went on to observe that "rudeness can definitely ruin your day" (Estabrook, 2004). These were cited as typical incidents that occur daily.

The other side of the coin is also presented. Travelers are frustrated by deteriorating customer service and the uncivil behavior of fellow passengers. One passenger reported that when an airline canceled his flight and he asked to be booked on another airline, a ticket agent responded, "Those days are over. We're going bankrupt. That's your problem." A mother who asked a flight attendant for milk for her two-year-old son was told that she should have brought her own (when she finally got the milk, it was delivered with "a dirty look"; Mansnerus, 2004).

The confluence of misfortune and mismanagement afflicting the airline industry in recent years provides stark illustration of the challenges facing today's customer-focused organizations. The goal of providing safe, efficient, and low-cost travel requires employees who perform their duties in a friendly, professional manner. The examples cited above suggest that the most difficult part of the job for many airline employees is maintaining a positive demeanor in the face of unpleasant and even hostile customers. Aside from the military and law enforcement, in what other occupations are workers regularly threatened with physical violence, for which they are not trained or provided means of self-defense?

These jobs place a premium on emotional labor (Glomb, Kammeyer-Mueller, and Rotundo, 2004; Hochschild, 1983), the conscious manipulation of one's self-presentation to achieve a work objective or standard. In selecting workers for customer service jobs, employers often screen candidates on such personal variables as extraversion, self-control, self-awareness, and social perceptiveness. Service workers are then expected to use these attributes in performing their job duties, many of which can be classified as emotional labor (such as reassuring nervous passengers and calming irate ones). Goals of these activities include safe, efficient, and enjoyable travel that will encourage repeat business from customers. The challenge is maintaining effective performance in the context of a hectic, unpredictable, and sometimes menacing work environment.

The examples cited illustrate how this process can break down. Airline workers, most of whom undoubtedly have the personal attributes as well as the training necessary to provide good customer service, nevertheless are sometimes overwhelmed by the difficult situations they face. It is perhaps not surprising that workers in any industry sometimes ask themselves why they should go out of their way to be helpful to customers when neither their employers nor their customers appreciate it. Why not stick to prescribed job duties, skip the voluntary behaviors, and slip in the occasional proscribed one too?

The challenge for employers is to organize the workplace so that its products and services make customers happy and motivate them to return. They strive to achieve this by managing what to them is manageable: their employees and work processes. In the next section, we examine some of the mechanisms that companies employ to manage customer service.

Organizing and Managing for Customer Service

Gathering, processing, and responding to customer feedback requires reaching beyond the boundaries of the organization to interact with customers to solicit their input. It also requires that their feedback is accessible to those inside the organization who put it to effective use. The latter, in turn, implies that the feedback message should be understandable to those who are expected to make use of it. In this final section, we examine some of the ways that organizations use customer feedback for both performance management and organizational development purposes.

Performance Management

In a sales transaction, there are two roles: the salesperson and the customer. The behaviors that the salesperson must enact to make a sale are situationally dependent; they can vary quite a bit from one customer to the next. Good salespersons use their knowledge, judgment, and social perceptiveness to determine the best way to interact with each customer to make a sale. Inexperienced salespersons or those who are not motivated to do well will rely on a scripted pattern of behaviors that varies little from one customer to the next, whereas bad salespersons might make inappropriate comments or treat customers rudely.

In managing service workers, distinctions among performance of prescribed, voluntary, and proscribed behaviors are important. Prescribed behaviors can usually be placed on continua of quality and quantity such as effective-ineffective, good-poor, always-never, and so on. For prescribed behaviors, more is generally better. Voluntary and proscribed behaviors are usually dichotomies: what matters is whether they occur, not how well they are performed. A salesperson who suggests a competitor to help a customer who is seeking an item that the store does not carry is creating a positive impression on a customer who may return at another time, even though the behavior does not produce a sale (and is not required by the employer).

From a motivational standpoint, the issue for prescribed behaviors is decisional: how to motivate employees to decide to give it their all. For voluntary and proscribed behaviors, it is a question of choice: how to motivate employees to choose to help and refrain from proscribed actions. In many service jobs, such as sales, successful performance requires a combination of prescribed and voluntary behaviors. A salesperson must adapt a basic sales protocol to the needs of each customer, and this often includes an emotional labor component (for example, maintaining a friendly and upbeat demeanor in the face of unpleasant and demanding customers). Because of the difficulties of prescribing every aspect of a salesperson's job behaviors, employers often reward results in the form of sales incentives and commissions, thereby leaving it to each employee to figure out the optimal mix of behaviors to land a sale.

In other service jobs, such as telemarketing and call centers, employers attempt to control quantity and quality of service by prescribing (scripting) every aspect of the worker-customer interaction. Employers of telemarketers and call center workers exert control over the quantity and quality of performance with digital technology that routes calls to available representatives after the customer answers a series of automated questions about the nature of service requested. The customer service agent follows a closely scripted protocol in interacting with the customer. The result is highly routinized and standardized work, mediated by digital technology, easily learned, and easily outsourced to regions of cheap labor. Through technology, many service jobs that once required personal encounters at the local level have become the modern equivalent of mass production jobs of a century ago, with service delivered from a (sometimes great) distance.

Customer service jobs in which there is greater individual variability in performance and employees have more discretion in deciding how to accomplish work objectives generally require more skilled workers. Greater discretion, particularly in jobs where worker-customer interaction is integral to the service, places a premium on the worker's willingness to engage in voluntary behaviors as needed and to avoid proscribed behaviors. Experience in such jobs generally counts for more than in rigidly scripted jobs, because through experience, an employee develops situational awareness and, eventually, expertise. Commitment to one's job and employer is likely to instill a strong motivation to find ways to ensure success. Doing the right thing when it is not technically required is more likely when an employee values his job and believes his employer values him. When employers communicate the opposite—that employees are expendable and their jobs may be eliminated or outsourced at any time—employees are likely to question whether any additional effort than absolutely necessary is wise, and may indeed look for ways to slack off and even sabotage their employer's efforts.

An example of this comes from the airline industry. A story in the news as this is being written tells of a cross-country flight that was diverted to an emergency landing in Tennessee when a flight attendant reported finding a note in a restroom warning of a bomb on board. All passengers were rescreened and questioned, and their journey was delayed by a full day. A subsequent story reported a few hours later that an arrest was made in the case. The note was written and planted by the flight attendant who reported it. This individual pleaded guilty to a charge of unlawful interference with an airline and was sentenced to five years in federal prison ("Flight Attendant," 2005).

Although the motivation of the perpetrator is not known to me, this may be an extreme example of a proscribed job behavior. It illustrates the effects that job stress can have on a worker, particularly when an employer fails to provide the support needed to cope with difficult working conditions. As companies struggle for survival, they pressure their workers and unions for pay cuts, reductions in benefits, and longer work hours. These pressures may well cause workers to act out their frustrations in behaviors intended as retributions against their employers for perceived mistreatment.

Getting customer service right from an employer's perspective requires alignment of the design of the job with its contribution to the bottom line. What is the value-added of the job, and what must the worker do to maximize this contribution? What must the employer do to set the stage for effective individual and group performance and to direct and manage it? Can the job be completely scripted, such that more prescribed behaviors properly performed produce better results? If so, employee selection is fairly straightforward, generally based on cognitive ability (ability to learn the job), interpersonal skills, willingness to work, and resilience in the face of customer rejection. Large employers are likely to invest in technology to manage the activities of workers in highly prescribed service jobs.

If the job cannot be completely scripted and results are a product of both prescribed and voluntary behaviors, particularly if there is a substantial emotional labor component, then selecting the right person for the job becomes critical, because training and technology are necessary to performance but not sufficient to ensure success. Results increase with experience, so employers often require previous experience as a basic employment prerequisite. Compensation may be based on results. Support to help employers cope with the stress of emotional labor is essential, from informal day-to-day social support from supervisors and coworkers to formal stress management training and counseling. Such support systems convey that an employer understands and appreciates what its employees endure for the sake of results. They engender a "we're all in this together" sense of belongingness and support that fosters loyalty and commitment and minimizes the likelihood of proscribed behaviors and unhappy customers.

To revisit the theme of organizational boundaries and changing environments, we note again that systems (for example, employee selection, compensation, performance management, customer feedback) are established to standardize practices and make them efficient. Organizational systems, however, by their very nature have built-in inertia that resists change. To avoid becoming dinosaurs, companies must continually monitor their environments and periodically review and update their systems.

Examples of environmental changes that force companies to reevaluate their management practices include changes in markets (including customer needs and expectations), competition, laws and regulations, technologies, economic conditions, and company mergers, acquisitions, and restructuring. If a new technology is introduced that automates work (for example, customer order tracking software), jobs may need to be redesigned to accommodate the new technology, workers may require training to use it, and the relative mix of prescribed and voluntary activities might change in their contributions to results. For example, the new technology may allow closer monitoring of employee productivity and quality control. Whether the company should prescribe aspects of customer interaction that previously were discretionary (for example, time spent per customer order status query) depends on the potential value-added of discretionary actions.

If good customer service requires that a service representative take the time to ask the right questions to understand a customer's problem, then using technology to completely prescribe work behaviors could be counterproductive. How much time to spend with a customer, what questions to ask, how to respond to a customer's frustration level, and so on may be decisions that are best left to the discretion of the service representative. The organization must understand the means by which a service worker achieves the desired result if, in the change management process, it is to avoid damaging this process. Customer order tracking technology may help a service representative to provide better and faster service, but if the employer also uses it to regulate all aspects of the transaction (because it can), then the risk is that the result will be unhappy customers, and the fundamental value-added of the job will diminish.

Alignment of job design and organizational mission should be assessed periodically and adjusted as needed. If changing technologies supplant activities formerly done by workers, have the remaining jobs been rethought in terms of person and process variables? Do employee selection, training, performance measurement, and compensation systems need to be reconfigured accordingly? If some jobs have been outsourced, are the remaining workers expected to assume more responsibilities and perform a broader array of tasks? If so, are they fairly compensated? If new products and markets are developed, do some jobs become obsolete while new jobs are created? If the organization has changed due to merger, acquisition, restructuring, or downsizing, have jobs in the new organization been reanalyzed with respect to new missions and objectives?

Customer Satisfaction Surveys

In designing surveys of any type it is important to consider survey contents, administration process, and population to be sampled. All of these factors are critical to a successful survey that addresses a company's needs. Some highlights of good survey design and administration include these:

- Identify the purpose of the survey, and consider who will find the information it produces to be useful.
- Design a survey that asks questions that respondents can and will answer while addressing the company's information needs.
- Summarize survey results in ways that are understandable to those who will put them to use.

Internet technology makes it possible for surveys to be continuously available to customers and for managers to create reports of current results at will. Survey feedback can then be used to assess performance relative to other units, stores, sales districts, and over time (versus last quarter, same quarter last year). Exhibit 2.2 illustrates a page from an online feedback report for the customer service dimension of an employee opinion survey. Results are shown for Store 2–1, an outlet in a large retail company, with survey dimension comparisons to other sales districts and the company overall, and detailed item results for that location. Survey feedback can inform a store manager about strengths and weaknesses relative to other areas of the company, and highlight needed improvements.

Research reported in the past twenty-five years has established relationships among customer satisfaction, employee satisfaction, and other indicators of organizational performance and effectiveness (for example, Schneider, Parkington, and Buxton, 1980; Wiley, 1996). Usually conducted at the establishment unit of analysis (retail outlets, bank branches), reliable and consistent correlations

Exhibit 2.2. Sample Page from a Survey Feedback Report.

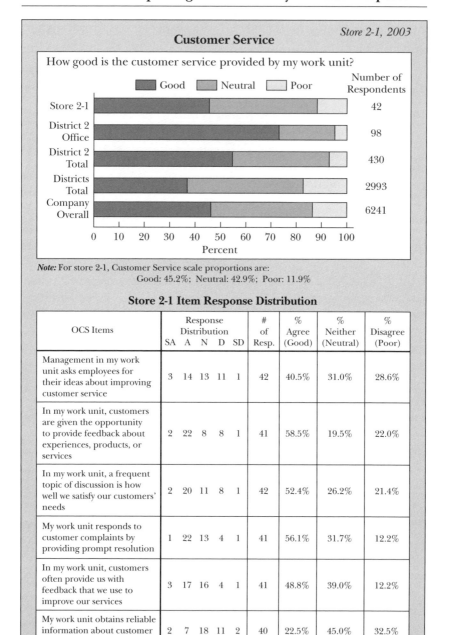

Customer Service *Store 2-1, 2003*

How good is the customer service provided by my work unit?

Good   Neutral   Poor   Number of Respondents

Store 2-1	42
District 2 Office	98
District 2 Total	430
Districts Total	2993
Company Overall	6241

0 10 20 30 40 50 60 70 80 90 100
Percent

Note: For store 2-1, Customer Service scale proportions are:
Good: 45.2%; Neutral: 42.9%; Poor: 11.9%

Store 2-1 Item Response Distribution

OCS Items	Response Distribution SA A N D SD	# of Resp.	% Agree (Good)	% Neither (Neutral)	% Disagree (Poor)
Management in my work unit asks employees for their ideas about improving customer service	3 14 13 11 1	42	40.5%	31.0%	28.6%
In my work unit, customers are given the opportunity to provide feedback about experiences, products, or services	2 22 8 8 1	41	58.5%	19.5%	22.0%
In my work unit, a frequent topic of discussion is how well we satisfy our customers' needs	2 20 11 8 1	42	52.4%	26.2%	21.4%
My work unit responds to customer complaints by providing prompt resolution	1 22 13 4 1	41	56.1%	31.7%	12.2%
In my work unit, customers often provide us with feedback that we use to improve our services	3 17 16 4 1	41	48.8%	39.0%	12.2%
My work unit obtains reliable information about customer satisfaction	2 7 18 11 2	40	22.5%	45.0%	32.5%

Note: The 5-point response scale for OCS items is: SA = Strongly Agree, A = Agree,
N = Neither Agree nor Disagree, D = Disagree, SD = Strongly Disagree

Source: Vance and Renz, LLC (2004).

between workplace practices and customer satisfaction have been demonstrated. These relationships can be used to diagnose reasons for customer dissatisfaction and identify avenues for improvement. An organization that makes internal changes based on feedback from its external environment is likely to remain attuned to customers' wants and expectations, thus contributing to its long-term effectiveness and survival.

Six Sigma

The 1980s saw a dramatic increase in attention to quality by U.S. companies, spurred by competition from Japanese companies. Japanese competitors were producing high-quality, low-cost goods and winning market share from their American counterparts, particularly in the automotive and consumer electronics industries. U.S. producers responded with a series of quality-focused initiatives, including quality circles, Continuous Quality Improvement, team-based manufacturing, employee involvement and empowerment, statistical process control, process reengineering, and others. Most of these initiatives were internally focused, seeking to minimize errors and defects in products by reducing variability in production processes and increasing worker involvement in decision making and responsibility for quality.

A quality improvement process pioneered by Motorola in the 1980s (and subsequently adopted by other U.S. corporations such as GE and Starwood Hotels and Resorts) extended the concept of quality improvement outside the organization's boundaries by beginning with assessment of customers' needs. Called Six Sigma, for the expected magnitude of reduction in variability in processes (to 3.4 defects per million opportunities for defects in the production process, or six standard deviations from the mean number of defects prior to process improvement), the process begins with an analysis of customer requirements. A defect is defined as anything outside customer specifications. To satisfy customer requirements, Six Sigma uses process analysis and statistical process control to identify steps in production where defects can occur. An iterative improvement process is initiated until occurrence of defects is reduced to an acceptable level. Employee involvement in quality improvement, emphasizing understanding of customer requirements, is integral to successful Six Sigma projects.

These projects, which can either address problems in ongoing production systems or aid in the development of new processes or products, are purported to save companies hundreds of thousands and even millions of dollars per year. Higher quality products also yield satisfied customers.

Conclusion

An organization's external boundary serves to shield it from the turbulent forces of its environment, but it also presents a barrier between the organization and its customers. To remain competitive, a company must broach its boundaries to solicit feedback from customers. It must use that feedback to evaluate its products, production processes, the skills and training of its workforce, and its systems for organizing their labors. It must rectify problems and effect improvements when needed, and it must surmount the challenges posed by a complex and constantly changing environment. Techniques such as customer satisfaction surveys and Six Sigma contribute to efficiency and effectiveness, but there is more to it than that. Customer focus also requires an organization to rethink the roles of its employees in relation to its customers, the mix of human labor and technology encompassed in its jobs, and their interplay in meeting customer needs and wants. The range of options is broad and in all likelihood will get broader in the years to come, driven by rapidly evolving technology, rising customer expectations, and increasing globalization and competition. Successful organizations will be aware of their options and make informed choices.

References

Barley, S. *The New World of Work.* London: British-North American Research Committee, 1996.

Campbell, J. P., Dunnette, M.D., Lawler, E. E., III, and Weick, K. E., Jr. *Managerial Behavior, Performance, and Effectiveness.* New York: McGraw-Hill, 1970.

Cappelli, P. *The New Deal at Work: Managing the Market-Driven Workforce.* Boston: Harvard Business School Press, 1999.

Cappelli, P., Bassi, L., Katz, H., Knoke, D., Osterman, P., and Useem, M. *Change at Work.* New York: Oxford University Press, 1997.

Estabrook, B. "A Paycheck Weekly, Insults Daily." *New York Times,* Feb. 15, 2004, pp. 10, 12.

"Flight Attendant Sentenced in Bomb Threat Case," *USA Today,* June 24, 2005 [http://www.usatoday.com/travel/flights/2005-06-24-bomb-threat_x.htm?POE=TRVISVA].

Fonti, N. "Does Loyalty Still Pay?" *Sky Guide.* Feb. 2003 [http://www.skyguide.net/articles/200302/200302_loyalty.html].

Glomb, T. M., Kammeyer-Mueller, J. D., and Rotundo, M. "Emotional Labor Demands and Compensating Wage Differentials." *Journal of Applied Psychology,* 2004, *89,* 700–714.

Greenspan, A. "The Challenge of Central Banking in a Democratic Society." Paper presented at the Annual Dinner and Francis Boyer Lecture of the American Enterprise Institute for Public Policy Research, Washington, D.C., Dec. 1996.

Hochschild, A. R. *The Managed Heart: Commercialization of Human Feeling.* Berkeley: University of California Press, 1983.

Leidner, R. *Fast Food, Fast Talk: Service Work and the Routinization of Everyday Life.* Berkeley: University of California Press, 1993.

Mansnerus, L. "Turbulent Manners Unsettle Fliers." *New York Times,* Feb. 15, 2004, pp. 11–12.

Morgenson, G. "New Math Aside, Earnings Still Reign." *New York Times,* Feb. 1, 2004.

National Research Council. *Enhancing Organizational Performance.* Washington, D.C.: National Academy Press, 1997.

National Research Council. *The Changing Nature of Work: Implications for Occupational Analysis.* Washington, D.C.: National Academy Press, 1999.

O'Donnell, J. "A Couple of Bad Apples Spoiled 'CFO' Award." *USA Today,* May 6, 2004, p. 5B.

Pfeffer, J., and Salancik, G. R. *The External Control of Organizations: A Resource Dependence Perspective.* New York: HarperCollins, 1978.

Schneider, B., Parkington, J. J., and Buxton, V. M. "Employee and Customer Perceptions of Service in Banks." *Administrative Science Quarterly,* 1980, *25,* 252–267.

Stewart, T. A. *Intellectual Capital: The New Wealth of Nations.* New York: Doubleday, 1997.

Taylor, F. W. "Principles of Scientific Management." In D. Mankin, R. E. Ames Jr., and M. A. Grodsky (eds.), *Classics of Industrial and Organizational Psychology.* Oak Park, Ill.: Moore Publishing, 1980. (Originally published in 1916)

Vance, R. J., and Brooks, S. M. "Performance Management and Appraisal." Unpublished manuscript, 1990.

Wiley, J. W. "Linking Survey Results to Customer Satisfaction and Business Performance." In A. I. Kraut (ed.), *Organizational Surveys: Tools for Assessment and Change.* San Francisco: Jossey-Bass, 1996.

Wyatt's 1993 Survey of Corporate Restructuring: Best Practices in Corporate Restructuring. New York: Wyatt, 1993.

CHAPTER 3

Using Employee and Customer Perspectives to Improve Organizational Performance

Scott M. Brooks
Jack W. Wiley
Emily L. Hause

Many organizations focus on employee relations and customer service in order to achieve their business goals. The theory is that treating employees and customers better will lead to stronger financial performance. This may seem like common sense: happy employees create happy customers, who in turn deliver revenues and profit. But research over the past twenty years has shown a much more complex relationship between employee and customer opinions and financial results. Today, the challenge for businesses is to marry sophisticated measurement and strategic analysis of employee and customer data to practical organizational development efforts. This combination of scientific research and applied management tools offers a potent model for predicting and influencing financial performance.

This chapter distills recent research linking employee and customer opinions to an organization's financial performance. Anchored by a case study, we embellish with a thorough review of the literature and conclude by highlighting the most fruitful avenues of pursuit, for both science and practice.

Models of Business Management

Management theories such as the service-profit chain (Heskett and others, 1994) and the Balanced Scorecard (Lundby and Rasinowich, 2003; Kaplan and Norton, 1996) are performance models that link leadership, employees, customers, and financial results.

The service-profit chain is a holistic model of organizational performance. It starts by focusing on the organization's end goals—that is, revenue growth and profitability—and then traces the chain backward. The underlying concept is that profit and revenue growth are stimulated primarily by customer loyalty, which is a reflection of customer satisfaction. Customer satisfaction in turn is largely influenced by the customer's perception of value, which we argue is created by satisfied, loyal, and productive employees. A culture of employee satisfaction results primarily from proper management practices, such as support services and policies that empower employees to deliver high-quality customer service. Thus, the service-profit chain is defined by a special kind of leadership that acknowledges that financial success is achieved through emphasis on exemplary service.

The Balanced Scorecard is another holistic model of organizational performance that starts with the end in mind. The typical scorecard incorporates four perspectives, each of which has to be successfully managed: (1) financial, (2) customer, (3) internal business process, and (4) learning and growth. Kaplan and Norton (1996) explain that the Balanced Scorecard is fundamentally a method for translating management strategy into action. Like the service-profit chain, the scorecard links management practices and beliefs with the interrelated variables that work together to produce financial success. Within a given scorecard, managers distinguish between leading indicators that predict success and lagging indicators that reflect the actual performance achieved. The integrating concept is that every measure selected for the scorecard is part of a system of cause-and-effect relationships, including work environment, business processes, and customer value, that culminate in the achievement of financial goals (Lundby and Rasinowich, 2003).

Linkage Research

Prior to the development of these highly popular management theories, a significant and growing body of literature had already begun to demonstrate the links between employee perceptions of their work environment, customer satisfaction and loyalty, and various measures of business performance and financial success. This body of research, which we describe below, illustrates the power of combining strategic scientific studies with applied management principles, such as the management theories described. Indeed, linkage research offers a road map for creating a high-performance work climate that fosters an enhanced customer experience, which subsequently leads to better business performance.

Wiley (1996) defined linkage research and its purpose as follows: "Linkage research involves integrating and correlating data from employees with data in other key organizational databases. The purpose of linkage research is to identify those elements of the work environment—as described by employees—that correlate or link to critically important organizational outcomes such as customer satisfaction and business performance" (p. 330).

Research linking employee descriptions of their work environment and customer satisfaction was introduced by Benjamin Schneider and his colleagues (Schneider, Parkington, and Buxton, 1980) over two decades ago. Jack Wiley and his colleague Walt Tornow (Wiley, 1991; Tornow and Wiley, 1991) extended the research design to incorporate measures of business performance. Since these original publications, other researchers have contributed dozens of studies that reflect the basic linkage research approach.

The basic design of linkage research involves gathering and correlating employee and customer survey data with other measures of business performance. Typically, employee data are gathered as part of a human resource initiative, and customer data are gathered through marketing research. Business performance data are typically supplied by an organization's financial reporting function. The key requirement of this research is that the measures within these databases be aggregated to a common business unit level, for example, at the store level of a retail chain or the branch level within a banking system. As a result, sample size will equal the number of units for which common data are available.

Wiley (1996) provided the first review of existing linkage research and introduced what he would subsequently call the High Performance Model. This model (see Exhibit 3.1) incorporated all published linkage research studies and tied together the findings of various researchers in a way more comprehensive than any single study. As Wiley explained, the model suggests that where certain organizational and leadership practices are observed in a given work environment, the workforce becomes more energized and productive. In turn, the energized workforce builds greater satisfaction and loyalty among customers, which over time translates to stronger business performance of the organization.

In the second major review of linkage research literature, Wiley and Brooks (2000a) summarized newly published studies that further supported the original conclusions. They derived from the entire body of research a taxonomy of the high-performance organizational climate. This taxonomy (see Exhibit 3.2) describes

Exhibit 3.1. The High Performance Model.

Leadership Practices
- Customer orientation
- Quality emphasis
- Employee training
- Involvement/empowerment

Business Performance
- Sales growth
- Market share
- Productivity
- Long-term profitability

Employee Results
- Information/knowledge
- Teamwork/cooperation
- Overall satisfaction
- Employee retention

Elapsed Time

Customer Results
- Responsive service
- Product quality
- Overall satisfaction
- Customer retention

Work Characteristics

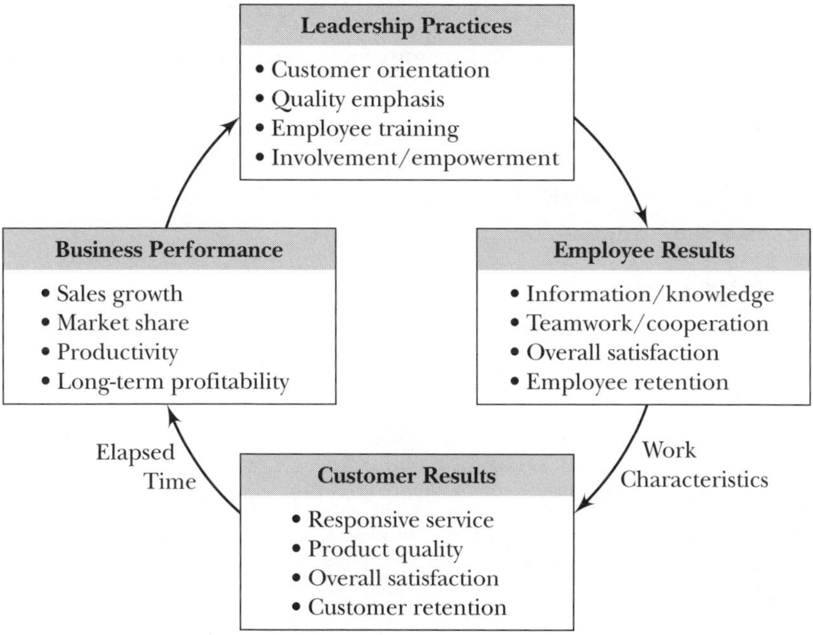

Source: Copyright © Gantz Wiley Research. Reprinted by permission.

Exhibit 3.2. Characteristics of High-Performance Organizations: The Employee Perspective.

LEADERSHIP PRACTICES

Customer orientation

Employees see a strong emphasis on customer service, and in fact believe their organization does a good job of satisfying customers.

Customer needs are attended to quickly, whether in initial delivery of products and services or in the resolution of problems.

Quality emphasis

Senior management is committed to quality and demonstrates this priority in day-to-day decisions. These values are effectively translated and implemented by lower-level managers.

Employees can see that quality is a priority versus cost containment, and especially versus meeting deadlines.

Employees believe their work groups do quality work, as judged by clear quality standards, and are able to improve continuously.

Involvement/empowerment

Employees have the authority and support they need to serve their customers.

Employees are encouraged to participate in decisions affecting their work and, perhaps more important, to innovate.

Management solicits and uses opinions of employees in such a way that employees can see the connection.

Employee training

Employees have written development plans to take advantage of the formal and informal skill-improvement opportunities that exist within the company.

Whether on-the-job or formal, employees see they have the training to perform their current jobs well. This can include specific training on products and services or explicitly on customer service.

New employees are oriented and able to come up to speed quickly, without undue burden on existing staff.

Exhibit 3.2. Characteristics of
High-Performance Organizations:
The Employee Perspective, Cont'd.

EMPLOYEE RESULTS

Information/knowledge

Management creates and communicates a compelling vision and direction for the company.

Employees understand their role in the organization—how their goals fit into overall company objectives.

Employees report having enough information to do their jobs, including company information, advance warning of changes, and information from other departments.

Teamwork/cooperation

Employees both within and across departments cooperate to serve customers and to get the work done.

This teamwork is actively supported by management.

Workload is managed effectively within a given work group—the load is divided fairly, and short staffing is not a significant barrier.

Overall satisfaction

Employees derive intrinsic satisfaction from their work, see a good match among their jobs, their interests, and their skills and abilities.

Employees are satisfied with and proud of their organization.

There is confidence in the company's ability to succeed, leading to long-term stability for the employee.

Employee retention

Employees value their relationship with the organization and have no short-term interest in leaving.

Longer-tenured employees are more efficient and create more value for the organization and its customers.

Source: Copyright © Gantz Wiley Research. Reprinted by permission.

with greater clarity how higher-performing units differ from lower-performing units within their respective organizations.

Despite growing consensus among researchers and management theorists regarding the employee-customer-performance linkage, however, two problems remain when applying these concepts to organizational development.

First, many human resource professionals continue to use survey models that primarily measure employee satisfaction, even though such models are less effective in predicting customer satisfaction and business performance. For example, as we discuss later in this chapter, direct tests show that employee observations of an organization's leadership practices and customer orientation predict customer satisfaction much better than more general measures of employee satisfaction, commitment, and engagement. Human resource practitioners and researchers too often focus on predictors of employee attitudes rather than on the service and financial outcomes that organizations are trying to achieve.

An overreliance on models that emphasize employee satisfaction thwarts organizations from achieving optimal returns on their survey investments. This is not to argue, of course, that employee satisfaction, commitment, and engagement are irrelevant. But using these concepts as the starting point in maximizing the employee-customer-performance linkage is misguided. Schneider and his colleagues (for example, Schneider, Gunnarson, and Niles-Jolly, 1994) define climate for services as employees' shared perceptions of the policies, practices, and procedures that are rewarded, supported, and expected concerning customer service. In understanding how to maximize the employee-customer-performance linkage, the proper starting point is with climate for service.

Second, organizations continue to show weak understanding, and therefore weak implementation, of Balanced Scorecards, dashboard metrics, and other similar integrated measurement systems. Ittner and Larcker (2003) argue that only a few companies realize the benefits of measuring customer loyalty, employee opinions, and similar nonfinancial performance areas. Their research shows that "most companies have made little attempt to identify areas of non-financial performance that might advance their chosen strategy. Nor have they demonstrated a cause and effect link between improvement in those non-financial areas and in cash flow, profit, and stock price" (pp. 88–89). These authors deride the common practice of adopting boilerplate versions of nonfinancial measurement frameworks and insist that companies need to dig deeper to discover and track the activities that genuinely influence financial performance.

Moving Forward

Ideally, frameworks such as Balanced Scorecards and other integrated holistic measurement systems are derived from a careful strategy that lays out how employees work through business processes to deliver customer value and achieve the organization's financial goals. Scorecards achieve their promise when they include the necessary balance of short-term, financial, lagging indicators, as well as long-term, nonfinancial, leading indicators of performance. Indeed, nonfinancial predictive measures are inherently vital in any such tool. Despite Ittner and Larcker's lament that most organizations have failed to assemble scorecards that effectively incorporate nonfinancial measures, that does not mean it is impossible to do it well.

Matching employee and customer data to strategic interests is where organizational science, through the growing body of linkage research, provides information of great value. Properly designed linkage research tells us how the variables in the employee-customer-performance chain interrelate, as well as the strength and direction of those interrelationships. As a result, it can guide the use of stakeholder input by suggesting specific tracking measures that help scorecards fulfill their promise.

In the remainder of this chapter, we focus on aspects of the customer experience that relate to actual financial performance and, in turn, aspects of the work environment that contribute to the customer value proposition. As we will illustrate, and as Schneider's work has emphasized, this approach casts the employee in the role of observer and reporter of organizational effectiveness. Thus, we are less concerned with employee satisfaction or happiness and more concerned with what employees report is working, or not working, within the organization.

Case Study

A case study will help to illustrate the major points. The setting is a specialty products retailer, in which employee opinions, customer opinions, and various business results were available at several points over a three-year period for each of 373 stores.

Employee Survey

The organization had been conducting regular employee opinion surveys using relatively stable content for over a dozen years. The survey's design integrated the topics of the High Performance Model. Sixty-six items measured sixteen theme areas, including Customer Orientation, Quality, Training and Development, and Overall Satisfaction. Over the three years covered by this study, three paper-and-pencil surveys were administered to all employees.

Customer Survey

The organization also regularly asked customers for their opinions about service. The customer survey had fourteen items. The two customer survey measures used in these illustrations include a single-item measure of Overall Customer Satisfaction and a two-item measure of Sales Associate Ability, which rates the sales associate's ability to (1) serve and (2) communicate. The satisfaction measure is included as a representative indicator of typical customer satisfaction constructs. The Sales Associate Ability measure is included because of the clear sense within the organization that the sales associates were critical to creating a successful customer experience.

Over the three years covered by this research, all customers making a purchase were given an opportunity to complete this survey by telephone. Thus, customer data collection was an ongoing process.

Business Results

After considerable discussion with internal subject matter experts, we chose three primary financial measures to reflect store-level organizational performance: sales (a measure of volume), profit (a measure of success), and profit as a percentage of sales (a measure of financial efficiency—how much profit success per dollar of volume).

Key Observations

Three key observations emerged from the integration and analysis of these measures. We start with the issues closest to the financial results and work our way back upstream to the employee issues:

* *A time lag is critical to understand how customer opinions relate to financial performance.* As referenced by the High Performance Model and described in more detail in previous work (Wiley, 1996; Wiley and Brooks, 2000a), a time lag mediates the correlation between Customer Results and Business Results. We accounted for the time lag by using two features of the organization. First, the repurchase cycle of customers for this retail organization was approximately every two years. Given that customer retention and repeat purchasing were expected to play a significant role in financial growth, we knew we had to cover at least two years in time. Second, the organization's passion with regard to both customer satisfaction and sales was improvement. Thus, we chose to focus on change scores (improvements or declines). Although there are alternative statistical techniques for dealing with longitudinal trends, we determined that staying close to the organizational development needs of this project (that is, improvement scores) held priority over other considerations.

To illustrate the importance of a time lag, we documented the relationships between the three financial measures and a customer survey measure of Sales Associate Ability. Exhibit 3.3 lists partial correlations among these measures, which were chosen as a robust measure of relationships, with the ability to take into account store size, age, and type—unit characteristics known to be related to both customer opinions and business results. Concurrent analyses are based on both customer and financial results aggregated within one year. Longitudinal analyses are based upon change scores between year 1 and year 4.

We see a striking contrast in Exhibit 3.3 between concurrent and longitudinal analyses. The concurrent analyses are not simply weaker than the longitudinal analyses in the correlation between

Exhibit 3.3. Customer Opinions Relate to Financial Performance Positively with Longitudinal Analyses and Negatively with Concurrent Analyses.

Partial Correlations: Sales Associate Ability

	Concurrent	Longitudinal
Sales	−.18*	.16*
Profit	−.15*	.13*
Profit as percentage of sales	−.13*	.12*

Note: N = 373 retail stores. Partial correlations control for size (employees per store), age (months open), and type (mall rating, location type).

Sales Associate Ability and unit performance; they are negative. However, both types of analyses are correct, and each supports a piece of the story. The concurrent results illustrate how higher-volume, busier stores (those that are most successful right now) tend to have busier sales associates, who in turn are less able to attend to customers. The longitudinal results illustrate how successful efforts to improve the customer experience (depicted here in terms of customer perceptions of sales associate ability) coincide with improved financial performance.

Given the differences between the concurrent and longitudinal analyses, a sense of time lag is essential to understand very important dynamics in this retail environment.

• *The most potent customer opinion is not always Overall Customer Satisfaction.* While it may seem intuitive that Overall Customer Satisfaction would track most closely with business results, this is not always the case, for reasons we discuss in more detail later in this chapter. In this case study, we found evidence to justify the organization's belief that its sales force played a critical role in creating a successful customer experience.

We contrast here a two-item measure of Sales Associate Ability against the more common customer measure of Overall Customer Satisfaction. Exhibit 3.4 presents the partial correlation results for both Overall Customer Satisfaction and Sales Associate Ability with

**Exhibit 3.4. Customer Satisfaction Not as Potent
as Perceptions of Sales Associate Ability.**

Longitudinal Partial Correlations

	Increases in Overall Customer Satisfaction	Increases in Sales Associate Ability
Sales growth	.09*	.16*
Profit growth	.11*	.13*
Profit as percentage of sales growth	.10*	.12*

Note: $N = 373$ retail stores. Partial correlations control for size (employees per store), age (months open), and type (mall rating, location type).

* indicates $p \leq .05$.

measures of financial performance. These results show that Sales Associate Ability outperforms the general duty Overall Customer Satisfaction measure.

• *The most potent employee opinion is Climate for Service, not Employee Satisfaction.* Common measures of employee satisfaction can provide useful organizational data for research. However, if the goal is to seek measures that can be used in predicting business outcomes, it is more productive to measure how employees describe (as observers) the organization's climate for service. Exhibit 3.5 documents clearly that the employee perception of Climate for Service in our case study outperforms Employee Satisfaction in predicting Customer Satisfaction.

Role of Customer Service

Ultimately the goal of an organization is not simply to provide high levels of customer service. Service is a means to an end, which is usually sustained or improved financial performance. In addition, increased revenues and profit depend not on customer satisfaction but rather on customer behavior: repurchases, larger or more frequent purchases, marketing to friends and colleagues, and so forth (see Chapter One).

**Exhibit 3.5. Employee Perceptions of Climate for
Service Outperforms Employee Satisfaction
in Predicting Customer Reactions.**

	Longitudinal Partial Correlations	
	Increases in Employee Satisfaction	Increases in Climate for Service
Increases in Overall Customer Satisfaction	.18*	.37*
Increases in Sales Associate Ability	.17*	.32*

Note: $N = 373$ retail stores. Partial correlations control for size (employees per store), age (months open), and type (mall rating, location type).

* indicates $p \leq .05$.

Customer Satisfaction Versus Customer Behavior

While less emphasized in the psychology literature, business and marketing research tend to focus on customer loyalty rather than customer satisfaction as more directly related to financial performance (Lundby and Christianson DeMay, 2003). Customer loyalty is defined not as an attitude (like satisfaction) but as behavior, or behavioral intent—for example, intentions to repurchase, purchase more than one product or service, or refer an organization's products or services (for example, Chapter One, this volume; Loveman, 1998). Thus, customer loyalty (and its associated behaviors) is a required intermediate step in the relationship between customer satisfaction and financial performance (Heskett and others, 1994; Chapter One, this volume; Loveman, 1998; Rust and Zahorik, 1993). Customer loyalty, rather than customer satisfaction, embodies the belief that the organization's goal is behavior, not attitude.

These points reinforce advice to focus customer surveys on behavioral intentions. Reichheld (2003) goes so far as to say that the likelihood customers will recommend an organization's products or services to a friend is the one number that organizations need to increase. While perhaps extreme, the logic is consistent. The behavioral intention to provide enthusiastic referrals for the company can be correlated with actually doing so. Customers acting in an unpaid marketing role contribute to financial growth. Reichheld found that this measure of intent predicted far better than the more diffuse item, "How strongly do you agree that [company X] deserves your loyalty?"

Of course, behavioral intentions represent one angle on better prediction of customer behavior, but not the only one. An understanding of a customer's choices can also be highly informative in predicting how that customer spends money. There is evidence, for example, that customer satisfaction measures relative to the alternatives are more potent predictors than absolute satisfaction measures (Colihan, 2001; Neal, 1998). This is illustrated by the extreme case that dissatisfied customers may still be "loyal" if they have no other choices. Conversely, a satisfied customer in a crowded marketplace might experiment with the competition.

Time Lag and Causality

The case study presented earlier in this chapter illustrated how longitudinal analyses can be required to fully understand the relationships between customer opinions and financial performance. Other research echoes this assertion. Bernhardt, Donthu, and Kennett (2000) found that while there was no significant relationship between customer satisfaction and organizational performance using cross-sectional analyses, time-series designs did uncover a positive relationship. Rogelberg and Creamer (1994) concluded that "customer satisfaction in the present can only be related to profitability in the future" (p. 9).

There are four primary points to elaborate on the dynamics of how customer opinions and financial performance interrelate.

First, there can often be a delay between a positive customer experience, the resulting behavior, and improved financial results. While a terrific shopping experience can result in a larger purchase that day, the larger financial payoff often comes from customer repurchases or word-of-mouth referrals over the following years. The length of the time lag depends on the repurchase or service decision cycles of the customer, which vary dramatically according to the nature of the business. The frequency of repurchasing a pair of shoes is much different than, for example, a customer's decision to add new services from her primary financial institution.

Second, when the business performance measure is a raw measure of size (such as gross sales), customer satisfaction and current financial performance can be negatively related (Brooks and Graham, 2000; Lundby, Dobbins, and Kidder, 1995; Wiley and Brooks, 2000b). In the case study, retail stores with higher revenues and profit were more crowded, resulting in a less intimate setting for customers, who therefore sensed a less attentive sales associate staff. Lundby and Fenlason (2003), for example, found that higher-volume bank branches had less satisfied customers than their lower-volume counterparts.

Third, financial and customer measures of growth and improvement can be positively related to one another over time. In fact, in the case study, the negative relationships of the concurrent analyses were not reflected in the longitudinal analyses. Although bigger revenue and profit stores had worse customer opinions, improvements in employee opinions were positively related to improvements in financial measures (see also Wiley and Brooks, 2000b). In a way, this reflects that success is measured not by the hand one is dealt (for example, a large, less intimate store), but in how one plays it (for example, improving or declining customer opinions).

Fourth, there is a methodological side benefit to working with longitudinal data. For example, change scores in the criteria (for example, sales growth rather than sales) will result in stronger observed relationships (Wiley and Brooks, 2000b). These are frequently measures the organization already uses and values. Change scores may also be better suited to organizational development efforts, particularly where the goals are to grow, not just to achieve a certain level of sales. Finally, the self-referential nature of change scores does a better job than raw measures of controlling for unmeasured variables.

These findings emphasize the notion that providing high levels of customer service is an investment. It costs money in the short run to devote time and energy to enhancing the customer's experience and may detract from other development efforts. Maximizing the return on this investment requires time and attention to measurement.

Not All Customers Are Equal

Not all customers behave the same. As a result, some have a larger impact on an organization's financial performance than others. Customer segmentation is an understudied corner of linkage research, but it makes intuitive sense that the opinions of customers who generate more revenues or profit will be more closely linked to business performance (see Wayland and Cole, 1997).

A corollary is that the loyalties (and subsequent behaviors) of these different customer segments may be driven by different factors. For example, one linkage research study found that for high-volume customers, opinions about service were more related to purchasing behavior, whereas for lower-volume customers, purchasing decisions were more related to perceptions of value (Kendall and Barker Lemay, 1999). Thus it follows that a comprehensive model of organizational effectiveness should identify the most potent customers and determine the drivers of their loyalty and purchasing and recommending behavior.

Role of Employee Opinions

Just as customer opinions can help companies understand how customer relationships drive business performance, employee opinions can help diagnose how organizational climate fosters (or inhibits) strong customer relationships. What is critical, however, is that not all employee opinion constructs are equal in their ability to predict customer satisfaction and, more important, customer behavior.

Employee as Participant Versus Employee as Observer

Since the early and largely unsuccessful efforts to document the impact of individual job satisfaction on performance (see Iaffaldano and Muchinsky, 1985), researchers and practitioners alike have never quite let go of the belief that happy employees should lead to higher performance (Lundby, Fenlason, and Magnan, 2001). However, since Ben Schneider's original work in the early 1980s (for example, Schneider, Parkington, and Buxton, 1980), many linkage research studies have emerged that document more clearly how employee opinions (including both attitudes and observations) are related to organizational outcomes (for reviews, see Lundby and Fenlason, 2004; Wiley, 1996; Wiley and Brooks, 2000a).

Two broad classes of theories underlie these findings. First, emerging from satisfaction research is the theory that satisfied, committed, or "engaged" employees drive organizational success. In other words, when the work environment promotes an enriching experience, employees are more likely to devote the time and effort to promote effectiveness (for example, Fulmer, Gerhart, and Scott, 2003; Harter, Schmidt, and Hayes, 2002; Koys, 2001; Rucci, Kirn, and Quinn, 1998).

The second theory views employees as informants, observers, and reporters of organizational effectiveness. The concept here is that employees have well-informed perspectives on an organization's efforts to create value, particularly for customers. That insider view can help organizations predict, understand, and improve performance (Pugh, Dietz, Wiley, and Brooks, 2002; Schneider, White and Paul, 1998).

Employee opinions included in linkage research often use constructs and survey items that measure both climate for service (where the employee is an observer) and individual attitudes of satisfaction, commitment, and engagement (where the employee is a participant). This section covers how these employee opinions relate to customer opinions. While there are certainly cases where employee opinions have a direct impact on financial performance, they are not nearly as potent or consistent as models that include customer satisfaction and behavior.

Employee Satisfaction Versus Climate for Service

There are compelling logical arguments for expecting both employee satisfaction and the organization's climate for service to be related to how the customer views the customer experience. But they offer different uses for organizational development. If one wishes to understand the employee experience and the implications of poor working conditions, employee satisfaction is a fair and valid topic of study. Conversely, if one wishes to understand the customer experience and use the "upstream" input of employees to analyze drivers, then employee perceptions of the climate for service are a potent and promising avenue of inquiry.

There is evidence that both employee satisfaction and climate for service are related to customer satisfaction. Regarding employee satisfaction, Harter, Schmidt, and Hayes (2002) claim that "employee satisfaction and engagement are related to meaningful business outcomes" (p. 276).[1] Climate for service has also been consistently related to customer satisfaction (for example, Dietz, Pugh, and Wiley, 2004; Johnson, 1996; Ryan, Schmit, and Johnson, 1996; Wiley and Brooks, 2000a). As referenced earlier, the climate reflects employees' shared perceptions of the policies and practices that enable employees to deliver results to customers (Schneider, Gunnarson, and Niles-Jolly, 1994).

Discussions of employee satisfaction and climate for service models have tended to favor climate for service as a predictor of customer satisfaction, for both the theoretical reasons implied above and empirical reasons (Schneider, White, and Paul, 1998; Wiley and Brooks, 2000a, 2000b). Direct comparisons of both models have also begun to emerge. While some cases suggest a strong role for employee satisfaction (Colihan, 2003), the clear growing weight of evidence suggests not only that climate for service is a more potent predictor of customer satisfaction (Lezotte and McLinden, 2003; Pugh, Dietz, Brooks, and Wiley, 2003; Thompson, 1996), but that employee satisfaction makes no statistical contribution when climate for service is already taken into consideration (Lundby and Fenlason, 2003).

Beyond their individual impacts on customer satisfaction, there is also evidence that employee satisfaction and climate for service can interact, such that employee satisfaction is related to customer satisfaction only when a climate for service already exists (Dietz and Wiley, 1999).

Time Lag and Causality

Which comes first: the happy employee or the happy customer? This chicken-or-egg question merits exploration. Within human resource circles, it is intuitive that employee attitudes directly influence the customer experience. (This belief may also be associated with an underlying pressure to create a "business case" that documents the financial return of investments made into the human capital of an organization.) But existing research leads to opposite conclusions, depending on whether the employee attitudes in question reflect perceptions of the organization's climate for service or employee satisfaction.

Climate for Service

Generally it appears that changes in employee opinions about service climate precede changes in customer opinions (Dietz, 2000; Schneider, Ashworth, Higgs, and Carr, 1996). In other words, employees see improvements or declines in service delivery before customers do. However, Schneider, White, and Paul (1998) suggested that tighter feedback loops between employees and customers may also be a sign of more effective work groups. Tight feedback loops would tend to blur the differentiation between cause and effect, promoting a circle where enhanced climate for service would improve the customer experience, and effective service teams would learn from customer feedback at the same time and continue to calibrate their service climate.

It is important to note that while there is additional, important research work to do to fully understand these causal dynamics, the organizational development implication is clear. In both cases above, the research indicates that efforts to improve an organization's climate for service are likely to result in an improved customer experience.

Employee Satisfaction

Research dealing with employee satisfaction suggests that improving employee satisfaction sometimes can improve customer satisfaction. There is emerging evidence, though, that a more appropriate view is that employee satisfaction is a side effect of things going well.

On the one hand, satisfied employees are more likely to be good organizational citizens, engaging in citizenship behaviors— the extra things employees do, perhaps outside their formal job duties, to help the organization succeed (for example, Koys, 2001; Organ and Ryan, 1995). This kind of citizenship behavior may promote customer satisfaction (Adcock, 2000); however, Koys (2001) did not replicate this finding.

On the other hand, the reverse relationship—that customer satisfaction actually leads to employee satisfaction—can also occur and may often be more potent. Specifically, customer opinions will lead to employee opinions when satisfied customers enrich an employee's experience (or perhaps more powerfully, when dissatisfied customers create more work or frustrations for employees). This is a plausible interpretation of Ryan, Schmit, and Johnson

(1996), who constructed a longitudinal, covariance structure model that suggested customer satisfaction at time 1 led to morale at time 2. This reverse causality is rarely considered in the literature, yet can be keenly felt by any employee whose customer's opinions can make or break his or her day faster than that employee can influence the customer's own satisfaction.

Not All Employees Are Equal

When considering employees as observers and reporters of service climate and organizational effectiveness, it is plausible to conclude that not all employees are equal in diagnostic ability. In fact, there is ample and growing evidence for this idea.

Employees who are close to the customers and know more about them appear to have workplace perceptions more calibrated to the service delivery process and therefore more correlated with customer satisfaction. For example, opinions of employees with higher tenure (a proxy for more experience; Kendall and Barker Lemay, 1999) or more direct customer contact (for example, Brooks and Kam, 1999; Dietz, Pugh, and Wiley, 2004; Lundby and Fenlason, 2001; Vance, Brooks, Tesluk, and Howard, 1999) are more significantly related to customer satisfaction.

In addition, employees in different jobs can have different perspectives on the same overall value chain. For example, Pugh, Dietz, Brooks, and Wiley (2002) found differences in how opinions of back office production employees and front office service employees related to customer satisfaction. While climate for service perceptions of both groups related to customer satisfaction, the product-related opinions of the production employees were also significantly related to customer perceptions.

It is also important to consider cases where no employees are close to the customer. Self-service environments, for example, have weaker employee-customer linkages. It is logical that with less direct employee-customer contact, employee and customer opinions will be less correlated. Suggestive findings emerge from research within a retail organization, where mall stores had stronger linkages than stand-alone stores (recognized within this organization as more transactional and less service oriented than mall environments; Brooks and Guth, 1999).

Closing the Loop

Most discussion of linkage research describes a flow starting with employee opinions, moving through customer satisfaction, and ending with business performance. But such discussions are incomplete. Anyone working for organizations engaging in layoffs knows all too well that employee opinions are often intimately tied to the financial fate of an organization. This is referenced by the High Performance Model, which highlights how Business Results "complete the circle" and change the way an organization is led.

Employee Satisfaction Caused by Business Performance

The dynamics of the relationship between employee satisfaction and financial performance may parallel that of employee satisfaction and customer satisfaction. Research highlights two broad ways that business performance will influence employee opinions, each acting in opposition. Despite their contrasting natures, each casts employee satisfaction in the role of a result of or side effect of performance, not a driver.

Successful Firms More Easily Satisfy Employees

Recent work by Schneider, Hanges, Smith, and Salvaggio (2003) found that overall job satisfaction (in addition to satisfaction with pay and security) was related to organization-level measures of return on assets and earnings per share. The strongest directional flow was from financial performance to employee satisfaction. Schneider, Hanges, Smith, and Salvaggio found "good support for the causal priority of organizational financial and market performance appearing to cause employee attitudes (Overall Job Satisfaction and Satisfaction with Security)" (p. 846).

In other words, working for a company that is succeeding is more fun (and generally more rewarding) than working for one on the decline. Thus, morale or overall satisfaction will be greater with greater financial performance.

Some of the dynamics underlying this finding may include:

- Organizational rewards (for example, pay, career opportunities, recognition) are often a direct result of reaping the benefits of success.

- Discretionary budgets are more available for "optional" activities, such as training, when profits are up.
- Senior managers have more difficult, controversial, and painful messages to convey in tough times (which can reduce credibility and instill doubt among employees regarding leadership).
- Employees may derive their opinions in part from business performance results. That is, they have more confidence in leadership and the business overall when things are going well.
- Leadership can act in a less rigid and more supportive or empowering way when not preoccupied with financial strain.

The point here is not that employee satisfaction is always caused by an organization's financial fate, but rather that we must consider that the strongest causal flow might be *from* success *to* satisfaction.

High Productivity Levels Are Stressful

While company success would seem to foster employee satisfaction, the cost of success may at times undermine this relationship. Wiley (1998) cited an example of a finding that productivity levels (in this case, open client accounts per employee) were negatively associated with employee morale. Thus, when success depends on a greater load per employee, there can be a cost in terms of lower employee satisfaction and higher stress.

Employee Opinions Leading to Business Performance

Even if the most potent flow is from business performance to employee opinions, it is not inconceivable for employee opinions to have a direct, causal impact on financial results that is *not* mediated and explained by customer opinions and behavior.

There are two conditions under which this could happen, associated with increasing revenue or decreasing costs. First, employees can have a direct impact on increasing revenue (that is, not mediated by customer service) when creating value that existing customers are not aware of (for example, developing new products, attracting new customers). Logically, this is a way to improve revenue without changing the opinions or behavior of existing customers. Second, employees can have dramatic roles in reducing costs. Employee opinions regarding adherence to standards or protocols can reflect increasing efficiencies. For example, in a retail setting, keeping a cleaner store can help reduce theft or damage to merchandise (Brooks and Guth, 1999). Accidents, union relations, employee turnover, and other important outcomes with demonstrated relationships to employee opinions often have significant cost implications.

Outside these two forces, however, most efforts of employees can be expected to flow through customer perceptions and behavior before influencing financial performance.

Not All Employees Experience Success in the Same Way

Success can alternately promote a more satisfied workforce or, depending on the strain it takes to get there, come with a cost of dissatisfaction. If strain and productivity demands are not evenly distributed through organizations, then it is reasonable to find different reactions to success based on an individual's job.

In fact, this appears to be true. Volume or processing job types (for example, tellers, retail associates) have been found to have opinions negatively related to overall financial performance or productivity (Brooks and Guth, 1999; Lundby, Dobbins, and Kidder, 1995; Wiley, 1998; Wiley and Brooks, 2000b). However, even within the same organization where employees in processing jobs have opinions negatively related to success, jobs that focus on quality or relationships (for example, loan officers) can have opinions positively related to performance (Lundby, Dobbins, and Kidder, 1995).

Similarly, employees who are more invested in the business (for example, managers or those with compensation packages tied to financial success) will likely have opinions more strongly related to business performance. There is also a tentative yet intriguing suggestion in one organization that retail managers associate a busier pace with success (and thus have stronger, positive relationships between opinions and sales), and lower-level employees associate a busier pace with chaos (thus, showing weaker or even negative relationships; Brooks, 1999).

Conclusion

The research paints a picture of a value chain where employee opinions, particularly their observations with regard to an organization's climate for service, are a potent predictor of how customers react to the delivery of products and services. In turn, customer loyalty and behaviors are leading indicators of financial performance over time. Exhibit 3.6 summarizes the core findings reviewed above, with special attention to the survey topics for employees and customers that reveal the most about the value chain, as well as those employee and customer segments whose opinions have the strongest impact.

A resonant finding is that satisfaction—both employee satisfaction and customer satisfaction—is not as central to holistic models of organizational effectiveness as popularly thought. Employee satisfaction is best viewed as a side effect of success. Customer satisfaction is best viewed as subordinate to customer behavior. This is definitely not to say that satisfaction constructs are unimportant. Employee satisfaction can be important in working with employee relations issues such as voluntary turnover. Customer satisfaction is often a useful and predictive construct in understanding the

**Exhibit 3.6. Summary of Customer and Employee
Opinions and Segments That Most Affect
Financial Performance.**

	Topics	Segments
Customers	• Behaviors that affect performance	• High volume
		• High profit
	• Evaluations versus alternatives	• Frequent
	• Features core to value	
Employees	• Customer Orientation	• Experienced
	• Quality	• Customer contact
	• Training	• Those who affect costs
	• Involvement	

value chain. It is, however, not a goal unto itself, and service efforts should ultimately be judged by the behaviors they produce.

Implications

Linkage research deals with organizational effectiveness models anchored in a practical measurement reality. As such, it can be counted among the most scientifically interesting and practical avenues of research. Both the science and practice are also growing increasingly sophisticated. We no longer depend on the simple intuition that happy employees create happy customers, who in turn create a happy financial state of affairs. We no longer need to start with employee satisfaction and cross our fingers that it is related to positive outcomes.

Instead, researchers are increasingly building models starting with the end in mind: financial performance or other measures of business results. To predict performance, we enlist employees and customers as allies in diagnosing the value chain. We ask employees to tell us about the effectiveness of customer-directed efforts and then study how those efforts promote customer loyalty, purchasing, and recommendations.

To fulfill its potential, however, linkage research needs to be more than a measurement exercise and must be integrated with organizational development (OD) efforts. Statistical validity and a sound scientific foundation are required for both measurement and OD objectives, yet OD efforts also need greater executive buy-in and clearer, more compelling stories told from the data. Clearly, the data that convince a researcher are not what convince leadership. Too often, linkage research has stopped at the analytical phase, without crafting a compelling story that can influence an organization's leadership to alter or refine its strategy.

This may arise from differing standards of cause and effect. Causality implies a different question to scientists than it does to leadership. Outside a laboratory, causality is notoriously hard to defend to scientific standards. But without a defined assertion of cause and effect, management teams may be more inclined to disregard the potential of linkage research to shape core OD plans and instead file it alongside the soft data of employee satisfaction surveys. Scientific causality aspires to truth—demanding general-

Exhibit 3.7. Criteria for Linkage Research Success: Measurement Versus Organizational Development Intervention.

Linkage Research as Traditional Measurement Science	Linkage Research as Strategic Organizational Development Intervention
Valid methods, sound analyses	Valid methods, sound analyses
80 percent of time spent on analyses	30 percent of time spent on analyses—more on discovery, storytelling, implementation
Ultimate is complete covariance structure model	Ultimate is a steady drip of linkage illustrations
Statistical control	"Control" through better variables
Satisfaction is central, driving force	Employee satisfaction is side effect/supporting construct
	Customer satisfaction subordinate to customer behavior
All employees, customers made equal	Diagnosing value chain not a democracy
Accuracy is required	Usefulness is required
Causality important	Confidence in return on effort is critical, guided by local findings, judgment
Sophisticated statistical models are convincing	Compelling stories with clear examples are convincing
Success is a valid model	Success is leadership influence and insight (validity necessary, but not sufficient)
Models tend toward the complex	Models need to be easy to communicate

Source: Gantz Wiley Research (2005).

izable and replicable findings. The leadership causality question is different. It asks whether money and effort expended in one area (such as climate for service) will result in greater organization success than money and effort spent elsewhere.

Exhibit 3.7 highlights some of the differences between traditional measurement approaches to linkage research and the view proposed here to consider linkage research as an OD activity, not strictly a model-building exercise.

Linkage research is a rare intersection of scientific measurement and practical management concerns. It is this partnership of scientists and practitioners that makes this topic both fruitful and exciting. Science will continue to drill into the dynamics of the relationships among employee opinions, customer opinions, and business performance. But we now believe that the science has matured to the point where the biggest questions and challenges are related not to data but to the application of this management tool to the climate of service, delivery of customer value, and bottom-line performance of organizations everywhere.

Note

1. Note that although this research invokes the concept of engagement, Harter and others' definition of this term is essentially employee satisfaction: "The term employee engagement refers to the individual's involvement and satisfaction with as well as enthusiasm for work" (p. 269). In fact, results of different operationalizations were virtually identical. A measure of employee satisfaction had a meta-analytic validity coefficient of .28 with customer satisfaction, whereas employee engagement had a coefficient of .29.

References

Adcock, B. P. "Organizational Citizenship Behavior in the Employee and Customer Satisfaction Relationship." Poster presented at the Fifteenth Annual Conference of the Society for Industrial and Organizational Psychology, New Orleans, La., 2000.

Bernhardt, K. L., Donthu, N., and Kennett, P. A. "A Longitudinal Analysis of Satisfaction and Profitability." *Journal of Business Research*, 2000, *47*, 161–171.

Brooks, S. M. *Linkage Research in a Retail Setting.* Minneapolis, Minn.: Gantz Wiley Research, 1999.

Brooks, S. M., and Graham, K. E. "Payless Linkage Research: Using Line Management Momentum to Drive the Business." Paper presented at the Fifteenth Annual Conference of the Society for Industrial and Organizational Psychology, New Orleans, La., 2000.

Brooks, S. M., and Guth, T. "When Service Means More: Its Impact on Customer Opinions Across Work Environments." Paper presented at the Fourteenth Annual Conference of the Society for Industrial and Organizational Psychology, Atlanta, Ga., 1999.

Brooks, S. M., and Kam, S. M. "Linking Employee Opinions with Customer Satisfaction and Organizational Outcomes." Paper presented at the Thirteenth Annual Conference of the Society for Industrial and Organizational Psychology, Dallas, 1999.

Colihan, J. "Customer Satisfaction Relative to Competition: Superior Criterion in Linkage Research?" Paper presented at the Sixteenth Annual Conference of the Society for Industrial and Organizational Psychology, San Diego, Calif., 2001.

Colihan, J. "Well-Being, Effectiveness, and Job Type: Differential Effects in Linkage Research." Paper presented at the Eighteenth Annual Conference of the Society for Industrial and Organizational Psychology, Orlando, Fla., 2003.

Dietz, J. "Linking Employee Attitudes and Customer Satisfaction over Time: The Roles of Climate for Service and Customers' Service Experiences." Paper presented at the Fifteenth Annual Conference of the Society for Industrial and Organizational Psychology, New Orleans, La., 2000.

Dietz, J., Pugh, S. D., and Wiley, J. W. "Service Climate Effects on Customer Attitudes: An Examination of Boundary Conditions." *Academy of Management Journal,* 2004, *47,* 81–92.

Dietz, J., and Wiley, J. W. "Serving Employees in Service Organizations: Effects of an Organizational Climate for Employee Well-Being on Customer Satisfaction." Paper presented at the Fourteenth Annual Conference of the Society for Industrial and Organizational Psychology, Atlanta, Ga., 1999.

Fulmer, I. S., Gerhart, B., and Scott, K. S. "Are the 100 Best Better? An Empirical Investigation of the Relationship Between Being a 'Great Place to Work' and Firm Performance." *Personnel Psychology,* 2003, *56,* 965–993.

Harter, J. K., Schmidt, F. L., and Hayes, T. L. "Business-Unit Level Relationship Between Employee Satisfaction, Employee Engagement, and Business Outcomes: A Meta-Analysis." *Journal of Applied Psychology,* 2002, *87,* 268–279.

Heskett, J. L., and others. "Putting the Service-Profit Chain to Work." *Harvard Business Review,* 1994, *72*(2), 164–174.

Iaffaldano, M. T., and Muchinsky, P. M. "Job Satisfaction and Job Performance: A Meta-Analysis." *Psychological Bulletin,* 1985, *97,* 251–273.

Ittner, C. D., and Larcker, D. F. "Coming Up Short on Non-Financial Performance Measurement." *Harvard Business Review,* 2003, *81,* 88–95.

Johnson, J. W. "Linking Employee Perceptions of Service Climate to Customer Satisfaction." *Personnel Psychology,* 1996, *49,* 831–851.

Kaplan, R. S., and Norton, D. P. *Translating Strategy into Action: The Balanced Scorecard.* Boston: Harvard Business School Press, 1996.

Kendall, S. D., and Barker Lemay, C. "When Does Service Matter? Linking Employee Service Emphasis to Customer Satisfaction Within Heavy, Lapsed, and Light Customer Segments." Paper presented at the Fourteenth Annual Conference of the Society for Industrial and Organizational Psychology, Atlanta, Ga., 1999.

Koys, D. J. "The Effects of Employee Satisfaction, Organizational Citizenship Behavior, and Turnover on Organizational Effectiveness: A Unit-Level, Longitudinal Study." *Personnel Psychology,* 2001, *54,* 101–114.

Lezotte, D. V., and McLinden, P. D. "A Test of a Path Model to Determine Climate-Related Antecedents of Customer Satisfaction and Loyalty." Paper presented at the Eighteenth Annual Conference of the Society for Industrial and Organizational Psychology, Orlando, Fla., 2003.

Loveman, G. W. "Employee Satisfaction, Customer Loyalty, and Financial Performance: An Empirical Examination of the Service Profit Chain in Retail Banking." *Journal of Service Research,* 1998, *1*(1), 18–31.

Lundby, K. M., and Christianson DeMay, C. "Leveraging Employee-Customer Linkages to Build Customer Loyalty." *Quirk's Marketing Research Review,* 2003, *17*(9), 46–52.

Lundby, K. M., Dobbins, G. H., and Kidder, P. J. "Climate for Service and Productivity in High and Low Volume Jobs: Further Evidence for a Redefinition of Service." Poster presented at the Tenth Annual Conference of the Society for Industrial and Organizational Psychology, Orlando, Fla., 1995.

Lundby, K. M., and Fenlason, K. J. "Front-Line and Back-Office Employees: Service Climate Ties Them Together." Paper presented at the Sixteenth Annual Conference of the Society for Industrial and Organizational Psychology, San Diego, Calif., 2001.

Lundby, K. M., and Fenlason, K. J. "Service Climate Versus Employee Satisfaction: Which Matters? When? Why?" Paper presented at the Eighteenth Annual Conference of the Society for Industrial and Organizational Psychology, Orlando, Fla., 2003.

Lundby, K. M., and Fenlason, K. J. "Service Climate and Employee Satisfaction in Linkage Research: Which Matters? When and Why?" In A. Buono (ed.), *Creative Consulting: Innovative Perspectives on Management Consulting.* Greenwich, Conn.: Information Age Publishing, 2004.

Lundby, K. M., Fenlason, K. J., and Magnan, S. "New Directions for Linkage Research: Employee Satisfaction as an Outcome or Predictor?"

Research in Management Consulting: Current Trends in Management Consulting, 2001, *1,* 127–142.

Lundby, K. M., and Rasinowich, C. "Using Linkage Research to Make Your Scorecard More Actionable." *Marketing Research,* Winter 2003, pp. 14–19.

Neal, W. F. "Satisfaction Drives Loyalty." Paper presented at the Advertising Research Foundation Week of Workshops, New York, 1998.

Organ, D. W., and Ryan, K. "A Meta-Analytic Review of Attitudinal and Dispositional Predictors of Organizational Citizenship Behavior." *Personnel Psychology,* 1995, *48,* 775–802.

Pugh, S. D. "Service with a Smile: Emotional Contagion in the Service Encounter." *Academy of Management Journal,* 2001, *44,* 1018–1027.

Pugh, S. D., Dietz, J., Brooks, S. M., and Wiley, J. W. "Employees Are the Experts: Improving Linkage Research Through Differentiation Between Employee Functional Groups." Paper presented at the Seventeenth Annual Conference of the Society for Industrial and Organizational Psychology, Toronto, Ontario, 2002.

Pugh, S. D., Dietz, J., Brooks, S. M., and Wiley, J. W. "Employee and Customer-Focused Measures in Linkage Research." Paper presented at the Eighteenth Annual Conference of the Society for Industrial and Organizational Psychology, Orlando, Fla., 2003.

Pugh, S. D., Dietz, J., Wiley, J. W., and Brooks, S. M. "Driving Service Effectiveness Through Employee-Customer Linkages." *Academy of Management Executive,* 2002, *16,* 73–84.

Reichheld, F. F. "The One Number You Need to Grow." *Harvard Business Review,* 2003, *81,* 46–54.

Rogelberg, S. G., and Creamer, V. L. "Customer Satisfaction, Purchase Intentions and Profitability: Introducing a Time Lag." Paper presented at the Ninth Annual Conference of the Society for Industrial and Organizational Psychology, Nashville, Tenn., 1994.

Rucci, A. J., Kirn, S. P., and Quinn, R. T. "The Employee-Customer-Profit Chain at Sears." *Harvard Business Review,* 1998, pp. 83–97.

Rust, R. T., and Zahorik, A. J. "Customer Satisfaction, Customer Retention, and Market Share." *Journal of Retailing,* 1993, *69,* 193–215.

Ryan, A. M., Schmit, M. J., and Johnson, R. "Attitudes and Effectiveness: Examining Relations at an Organizational Level." *Personnel Psychology,* 1996, *49,* 854–883.

Schneider, B., Ashworth, S. D., Higgs, A. C., and Carr, L. "Design, Validity, and Use of Strategically Focused Employee Attitude Surveys." *Personnel Psychology,* 1996, *49,* 695–705.

Schneider, B., Gunnarson, S. K., and Niles-Jolly, K. "Creating the Climate and Culture of Success." *Organizational Dynamics,* 1994, *23,* 17–29.

Schneider, B., Hanges, P. J., Smith, B., and Salvaggio, A. N. "Which Comes

First: Employee Attitudes or Organizational Financial and Market Performance?" *Journal of Applied Psychology*, 2003, *88*, 836–851.

Schneider, B., Parkington, J. J., and Buxton, V. M. "Employee and Customer Perceptions of Service in Banks." *Administrative Science Quarterly*, 1980, *25*, 252–267.

Schneider, B., White, S. S., and Paul, M. C. "Linking Service Climate and Customer Perceptions of Service Quality: Test of a Causal Model." *Journal of Applied Psychology*, 1998, *83*, 150–163.

Thompson, J. W. "Employee Attitudes, Organizational Performance, and Qualitative Factors Underlying Success." *Journal of Business and Psychology*, 1996, *11*, 171–191.

Tornow, W. W., and Wiley, J. W. "Service Quality and Management Practices: A Look at Employee Attitudes, Customer Satisfaction, and Bottom-Line Consequences." *Human Resource Planning*, 1991, *14*(2), 105–116.

Vance, R. J., Brooks, S. M., Tesluk, P. E., and Howard, M. J. "Effects of Work Unit Climates on Customer Service in a Public Sector Organization." Paper presented at the Fourteenth Annual Conference of the Society for Industrial and Organizational Psychology, Atlanta, Ga., 1999.

Wayland, R. E., and Cole, P. M. *Customer Connections: New Strategies for Growth*. Boston: Harvard Business School Press, 1997.

Wiley, J. W. "Customer Satisfaction: A Supportive Work Environment and Its Financial Cost." *Human Resource Planning*, 1991, *14*(2), 117–127.

Wiley, J. W. "Linking Survey Results to Customer Satisfaction and Business Performance." In A. Kraut (ed.), *Organizational Surveys: Tools for Assessment and Change*. San Francisco: Jossey-Bass, 1996.

Wiley, J. W. "Using Culture Survey Results to Predict Dealership Satisfaction and Operational Performance." Paper presented at the Thirteenth Annual Conference of the Society for Industrial and Organizational Psychology, Dallas, 1998.

Wiley, J. W., and Brooks, S. M. "The High Performance Organizational Climate: How Workers Describe Top Performing Units." In N. S. Ashkanasy, C. Wilderom, and M. F. Peterson (eds.), *The Handbook of Organizational Culture and Climate*. Thousand Oaks, Calif.: Sage, 2000a.

Wiley, J. W., and Brooks, S. M. "Longitudinal Versus Concurrent Linkage Research: A Tale of Two Methods." Paper presented at the Fifteenth Annual Conference of the Society for Industrial and Organizational Psychology, New Orleans, La., 2000b.

Chapter 4

Brands, Expectations, and Experience

Clifton Lemon

The rapid global evolution of information technology has created a fundamental shift in the relationship between companies and customers; forced new definitions of customer service, employee roles, and requirements; and made it possible (and necessary) for companies to understand their customers in completely new ways. New knowledge of customer behavior is being created by the combination and evolution of traditional disciplines and the emergence of new ones, such as neuromarketing, customer relationship management (CRM), and behavioral market research. More sophisticated and relevant inquiries into customers' minds (and into the very nature of thought itself) are becoming possible with methodologies engendered by the drive to improve marketing and service delivery.

Companies traditionally have had separate divisions for marketing and customer service; marketing is concerned with acquiring customers and customer service with keeping them. But companies today can take advantage of more and different types of communication with potential customers before, during, and after their transformation into loyal customers. This dictates the need for marketing and service functions to interact more closely. According to Charles Born, vice president of global marketing at Amdocs, a CRM solution provider, "Businesses are still too siloed. They don't have a full view of the customer, [and as a result] the customer experience isn't the same across channels. It has to be, regardless of how the customer interacts with you" (Weinberger, 2004).

Customer service is an integral part of the brand equity of a product or company, especially in service-intensive businesses. Companies communicate with customers through marketing and customer service, reinforcing positive or negative brand associations and expectations of service delivery and product quality before and after service experiences. In order to optimize positive reinforcement and allow service and marketing to co-evolve most productively, companies today need to integrate into their core business processes systems that continually assess the interdependent perceptions and behaviors of customers and employees from many different viewpoints, within the context of competing brands.

Rather than performing a complex equation or calculation in their minds every time they make a buying decision, customers, I suggest, operate in a simple, basic way, and this overall model may be more useful to managers than models with more "moving parts." I refer to this as a cycle of causality—the Brand-Expectations-Experience cycle. Traditionally, a customer service focus deals with internal issues, and a marketing or brand focus deals with external images and communications. What is needed is a way to view the relationship between these functions in terms of causality. How do brands drive expectations and experience?

Much as service delivery has been postulated to have different dimensions or components, so do brands. A best-practices approach to brand analysis indicates that there are five interrelated dimensions that add up to brand positioning, but not in the form of a mathematical equation. Studying each dimension of a brand is valuable, but coming to a deep understanding about how they all contribute to a single competitive differentiation is essential in using customer research to achieve business results.

Customers today are becoming more demanding, better informed, less loyal, and increasingly diverse. Companies must find new ways to partner with customers, listen to their feedback more carefully, ask better questions, interpret the answers more effectively, and send the results back to manufacturing more frequently. New models of service delivery are necessary to develop in companies in order to make this partnership work.

New Externalities Redefine the Relationship

Many factors today are combining to redefine the basic relationship between companies and customers. Classical economic theory defines the unintended effects on society of actions by private corporations as externalities. In the context of service delivery today, many externalities flow from the evolution and adoption of information technologies that increase efficiency and reduce costs for corporations. Some of these externalities are positive for customers—for example, lower prices, more efficient delivery of products, increased selection, increased access to product information, and global-scale self-regulating buyer and seller rating systems such as those that have emerged on eBay. But there are also widespread negative externalities: loss of customer privacy, identity theft, spam overload, loss of customer trust, and the depersonalization (or total elimination) of service encounters. What are some of the unintended effects of information technology on customer behavior, perceptions, and attitudes?

Lower Prices

In general, more efficient information systems and the hyperefficient global supply chains that they have enabled mean lower prices for customers. Customers know this and now expect low prices as a result. Perhaps the most dramatic example of this is the explosive growth of Wal-Mart, the world's largest company. If it were a country in 2003, and its net sales of $244 billion were equated to gross domestic product, its economy would have been larger than Turkey's ($238 billion) but smaller than Austria's ($251 billion) (World Bank, 2004). Wal-Mart has turned low prices into more than a tactic: it is the main component of its brand positioning. Although other mass retailers also compete aggressively on price, none have integrated it into a brand strategy as Wal-Mart has done.

But customers are not just opting for low-quality goods at low prices; they are demanding high-quality goods and premium brands at lower prices across the board. This works out well for companies that can succeed in reducing their costs by keeping customers loyal; they can still turn a profit. But companies whose products are more price sensitive have increasing difficulty keeping customers loyal in the first place as product quality continues to improve and global competition, fueled by information technology and other factors, drives prices down.

Increased Selection

Customers today have more selection than ever before. Some product categories, like consumer electronics and sporting goods, offer a bewildering kaleidoscope of new product choices. For a mass global retailer like eBay, selection is a key component of brand positioning. eBay customers tend to believe, with good reason, that "if you can't get it on eBay, you can't get it anywhere" (Lemon 2004).

Seemingly unlimited product selection (or the perception of it) may be impressive to customers who are browsing. But overloading product categories can actually be detrimental to the buying process. With too many products to choose from or lack of simplified product information or informed, capable sales staff to guide them with their choices, customers may simply decide not to buy rather than invest time in comparing, say, thirty-five or forty different models of cell phones, fifteen different plasma TVs, or sixty-eight flavors of multiterrain Gore-Tex-enhanced, Kevlar-embedded outdoor foot gear systems (formerly known as hiking boots). Retailers call this phenomenon "assortment creep"—the steady growth of the number of product items or categories that customers have to choose from (Hurlbut, 2004).

Rapid growth in the overall number of products that are available is not limited to high-tech products either. According to James Surowiecki (2004a), "Since 1991, the number of brands on U.S. grocery store shelves has tripled." Increased product selection everywhere means many things: customers expect more from the products they do choose to buy, companies have to try even harder to differentiate products and inform customers about them, companies must develop much more agile and decentralized production and distribution systems that rely on a constant stream of quality customer feedback to inform product development decisions, and companies must learn to weed out poorly performing products from their product lines more quickly and with lower associated costs.

Efficient Delivery Systems

Information technology has made delivery of most products and services easier and more convenient. FedEx is said to be the world's largest information processing company, and it faces intense competition from DHL, UPS, and the U.S. Postal Service, as well as a host of upstart delivery companies. The increasing importance of package delivery services is, of course, a result of the rapid growth of e-commerce. U.S. online sales for the 2004 holiday season increased 24 percent over 2003, for instance (LeClaire, 2004). Purchasing nonphysical goods, such as music, movies, and software, online is even more efficient, making for an almost frictionless customer buying experience.

Increased Access to Product Information

Customers today have unprecedented access to information about products and services. Not only do companies themselves provide product information in often exhausting detail, thousands of blogs, online discussion groups, and buyer-seller rating systems exist on the Internet on sites such as epinions.com and eBay. In electronics, buying an item like a digital camera can involve sifting through thousands of ratings of hundreds of models in dozens of categories. This information overload can be daunting to customers, and besides totally paralyzing them into inaction has at least two other important impacts. First, there is "nowhere to hide" for companies; their products will be relentlessly judged by a growing global network of customers who vote (online) with their credit cards and relish sharing opinions, information, and experiences, positive and negative, about products, services, and service delivery. Second, when individual choice becomes too difficult because of the sheer amount of product information and the sheer number of competing products in certain product categories, customers will rely on sources other than companies, such as relatives, friends, or online acquaintances, to process comparative products and render buying recommendations. This is yet another reason that referral is becoming an increasingly important sales mechanism for companies today.

Loss of Privacy and Identity

To say that we all have lost some privacy by having most of our personal information freely available to whoever wants to mine it from the Internet is to understate the case by an order of magnitude. Information technology has completely redefined our concept of privacy, largely without our being aware of it until after the fact. Privacy used to be defined as the ability to be left alone, yet today it is defined as the ability to protect one's identity. Because we are all becoming more and more connected, despite the fact that we have all chosen to do so, protecting our identity is becoming more and more difficult.

Identity theft is talked about as being the fastest-growing crime in the United States—a new crime spawned by the Internet. Identity theft has existed for some time but has been greatly enhanced by the availability of private personal data on the Internet. What this means to individual service transactions is that customers now highly value their identities as a last frontier of control. Sales assistants who ask customers for their personal information at the checkout counter now put customers at risk. Automated customer service systems at most points-of-sale begin any sales or service transaction by requesting account numbers, dates of birth, and other personal information. Unfortunately, most points-of-sale are relatively vulnerable to security leaks. Many companies today do not even attempt to show good intentions in protecting customers' privacy, but even the ones that do cannot completely prevent wholesale identity piracy.

Spam Overload

Everyone with access to the Internet has been affected by some degree of spam overload and aggressive marketing, be it weight-loss products promising magic to desperate appeals from shady Nigerian government agents to the ubiquitous "male enhancement" products. With traditional broadcast and print media, we have always grudgingly traded off exposure to random advertising (wanted or not) as the price for valuable, and generally public "free" content. But we never anticipated the level of unwanted, offensive, irrelevant, and irritating advertising that now floods our e-mail in-boxes The difficult thing about spam is that it works for companies as a marketing tool (Gaudet, 2004). Customers say they hate it, but it is cost effective for corporations to use it because customers respond to it in sufficient numbers to warrant its relentless proliferation. The return on investment for spam remains high for many companies, as the cost of sending a million e-mails is close to the cost of sending a single one. And as the cost of customized and specific data on customers continues to drop, more companies can afford to spam more often. It is difficult to tell how much spam customers can handle ultimately, but recent legislation and emerging technology promise to stem the flow of junk e-mail to our in-boxes (Gaudet, 2004). When (or whether) these measures will be successful remains to be seen.

General Perception of Service Degradation

Information technology has made things easier for companies, but not necessarily for customers. Most seem to feel that, on balance, customer service is not improving (Weinberger, 2004). Whatever specific research and studies show about recent changes in customer service, there is certainly abundant anecdotal evidence of a general degradation of service across many different industries (Marye, 2004). Our own customer research at BrandSequence has indicated that many customers today perceive a considerable decline in the level of service they experience. In any case, part of the problem is that as far as the public is concerned, there is no universal standard for measurement beyond the Consumer Satisfaction Index:

> A current snapshot of consumer satisfaction by the University of Michigan Business School reveals a large group of unhappy campers. In its most recent American Customer Satisfaction Index, the average score for the specific issue of complaint handling is 57 (out of 100) for the 40 industries tracked by the index. "No one does a particularly good job in handling complaints," said David VanAmburg, managing director of the index, which measures consumer satisfaction with goods and services. There is one exception, though: supermarkets, which had a customer satisfaction score of 76 for [taking] care of complaints. The lowest score was recorded by local telephone firms (the index didn't measure wireless phone service).

Even more disturbing, VanAmburg said, is that a closer look at seventeen industries with enough data to measure satisfaction in great detail showed that fourteen, or 82 percent, field complaints in such a way that they are driving customers away [Mayer, 2004].

Depersonalization of Service

The ultimate result of information technology–induced externalities, both positive and negative, is the hyperstreamlining or even elimination of the traditional person-to-person service transaction. A typical amazon.com purchase can take less than fifteen seconds from start to finish, with no human intervention at all. A recent research project we did with eBay buyers indicated that a large percentage of users had no expectations of customer service quality from eBay whatsoever, because they had never had a problem and had never needed customer service. Indeed, the incentive of online businesses, and an increasing number of bricks-and-mortar businesses, is to "engineer out" customer service. This is both a cause and a natural consequence of increased efficiency, but the resulting negative externality is a loss of respect for the customer and a widespread depersonalization of service.

Depersonalization of service, however, can be desirable to customers and afford them a measure of control in many buying situations, such as booking airline tickets, when the presence of a service representative is counterproductive if customers want to search for the lowest price or change their minds ten times. Also, as Schneider and White (2004) point out in their book *Service Quality,* many products and services are better delivered with a minimum acceptable level of service quality. Too much service provided in the delivery of low-cost or commodity products may irritate customers, make them suspicious of a company's intentions, or make the company appear to be desperate for business.

The negative and positive externalities of information technology not only affect customer behavior; they influence how companies respond to this changing behavior in their marketing efforts.

The New Shape of Marketing

All the externalities detailed above add up to increased power for customers. With more choices, more product information, and lower prices, they have become more fickle, so loyalty is harder for companies to build. They are weary of being spammed and becoming more sensitized to mass marketing. They also talk to each other more and more about their positive and negative experiences with products, and this global conversation is becoming more important to brands as more products become harder to compare and evaluate in crowded categories. And there are more customers emerging in different markets: globalization is opening up the world to billions of new customers all the time, especially in China. Even with a low per capita income relative to the United States, China alone is projected to contribute 170 million urban middle-class customers to the world market in the next ten years (Zhigang, 2004). Lower-income people all over the planet will also command an enormous amount of spending power (Surowiecki, 2004b). Companies will have to develop new models of communication and service delivery in order to deal with the needs of these new kinds of customers as well as the changing needs of current customers. How do information technology–induced externalities affect marketing and service delivery? How can marketing and service delivery best evolve to deal with them?

Customer Quality Is Critical

The traditional model of mass marketing (blitz advertising in the service of raw market share) has reached a crucial turning point, where two things are happening: companies are finding that it is not the most effective or profitable way to market, and customers are overwhelmed with it. Mass marketing still works for most companies; available database technology that allows companies to blast identical messages to a wide market, albeit with a very small percentage return, is still profitable. But as customers become more fickle, gaining a large market share of them is not the same as a smaller share of higher-quality, more profitable customers. Powerful information and database technology can be used in the true purpose of marketing: to connect buyers with sellers. What is changing is an awareness of (and an increasing ability to optimize) the quality of the match-up. A brand is strong if it is highly differentiated; it cannot be all things to all people. Neither can a company, and some are realizing that certain customers may not be worth having in the first place. The service-profit chain model shows that focusing on the quality of customers makes more sense than focusing on quantity; profit per customer increases over time, the most profitable customers are the most loyal, and the lifetime value of a customer is a much more valuable measure of customer quality than most companies realize (Heskett, Sasser, and Schlesinger, 1997).

Continual Feedback Loops Are Critical

As customers become more demanding, product selection skyrockets, and product cycles compress, continuous feedback from customers and other diverse groups that have an impact on a brand is becoming more and more important to the success of service, product development, and marketing efforts. In order to be most effective, feedback needs to be based on a small number of factors that are most important to customers in the Brand-Expectations-Experience cycle: results. Measuring process quality is not the best investment of resources if deliverables are not being delivered. Feedback needs to be aggregated from a diverse, decentralized, and independent group of customers, both internal and external. The feedback must be consistently gathered in order to be relevant. And it needs to be properly aggregated and analyzed to deliver only relevant data to the company.

Roles Are Shifting and Becoming More Interdependent

As customer behavior changes, roles in companies are evolving to adapt to it. Service, marketing, and product development functions are becoming increasingly interdependent as feedback from customers and awareness of their needs and experiences become more crucial to companies' success. Feedback also gains value by being cross-referenced with data collected from many different departments and functions: sales, billing, manufacturing, and quality assurance, as well as marketing and service.

Referrals Are Critical

The cost of converting existing customers into more profitable ones is lower than that of acquiring new customers, so referrals from satisfied customers mean a lower cost of new customer acquisition, in addition to building brand equity. Also, customers are increasingly turning to sources other than companies (namely, each other) for product information and recommendations as products become less differentiated and more numerous. Some of the many marketing mechanisms that have evolved to amplify basic word-of-mouth are blogs, online product rating systems, and buzz agents. Buzz agents are a particularly intriguing phenomenon. Engaged by a word-of-mouth marketing company to promote a product or brand, many receive no monetary compensation for their services or activities, ostensibly being motivated entirely by the pleasure of the social interaction involved in making referrals to their network (Walker, 2004). The emergence of this trend sheds new light on what we know about referral marketing, the complex relationships between companies and customers, and the dynamics of social networks. Lest we harbor suspicions that buzz agents are a new form of brainwashing and that word-of-mouth is a newfangled marketing strategy, we are reminded by Ed Keller (2005), blogging on womma.com (the Web site of the Word of Mouth Marketing Association) that

> The first, and perhaps most important step, that brands can take to generate "buzz" is to ensure that consumers like them. Consumers who really like brands are far more likely to recommend them. In fact, being liked is more critical than being purchased in terms of getting good buzz.
>
> On the whole, an average of 34% of consumers who "really like" brands frequently recommend them, compared with 29% of those who "regularly use/own/watch" them.

In other words, companies are not off the hook when it comes to making good products. Good products and service lead to good customer experiences, which lead to increased expectations of good experiences, which lead to a stronger brand and better referrals, and the cycle repeats itself. Marketing activities are no substitute for product and service quality. What is more, in the new viral marketing word, bad word-of-mouth will damage a product much faster than before, and both companies and customers know it.

Transformation of Media and Advertising

One of the many factors causing the disruption of the advertising industry is the transformation of the media industry. The traditional forms of media that carry advertising are declining in relevance to customers. Traditional television networks have lost 28 percent of their viewers for nightly newscasts over the past decade, in part because of increasing competition from cable channels. Newspaper readership (and credibility) has declined continuously since 1990 (Agence France-Presse, 2004). Media markets are becoming fragmented, and the introduction of low-cost DVD recording devices threatens the basic business model of broadcast media. Global online advertising as a percentage of total advertising is projected to grow to 8.3 percent in 2005, a 415 percent growth since 1997. Comparatively, off-line advertising grew at a rate of only 129 percent in the same period. Although it is still a small portion of overall spending, online advertising is arguably a better investment for companies in part because it is more measurable. (Whether companies can make sense of what they measure is a different story.)

Search engine marketing is growing in importance, with a rapidly evolving array of new marketing strategies, services, and business models emerging, such as search engine optimization, pay per click, paid placement, paid inclusion, comparison shopping engines, contextual advertising, link optimization, and Web architecture optimization. These new marketing technologies have the advantage of showing instant or very rapid results to marketing communications, as long as the desired action is to drive customer traffic to a Web site to do business (as an ever-increasing percentage of desired marketing actions are). Finely grained metrics like cost per click, cost per lead, and cost per customer conversion can be employed to evaluate marketing and customer service strategies on an empirically verifiable basis. New forms of proactive online word-of-mouth marketing are also emerging, where companies or their Internet marketing agencies can monitor customers' online conversations and discussions in blogs and chatrooms and start product buzz by offering advice, asking questions, and gathering anecdotal data, all useful in product launch planning or other forms of marketing communication. This kind of engagement with customers can hardly be seen as advertising or marketing in any traditional sense, as it is highly interactive for customers (as opposed to passively enduring a blitz of hard-sell advertising), highly focused to niche groups (as opposed to mass messaging), and highly measurable, as opposed to most traditional methods, about which Viscount Leverhulme said, "Half the money I spend on advertising is wasted, and the trouble is I don't know which half" (Ogilvy, 1963).

As marketing needs in the twenty-first-century global economy become more complex and science and technology evolve, many companies are turning to brain-based research and new inquiries into the nature of thought in an effort to get closer to an understanding of customers' minds.

An Evolutionary View of Customer Thought

The past twenty-five years have seen the application of Darwinian thinking to a number of social problems. This has resulted in rapid growth in fields such as evolutionary economics, evolutionary psychology, evolutionary linguistics, evolutionary epistemology, and even evolutionary cosmology (Aunger, 2002). Signaled by the emergence of ideas like viral marketing during the mid-1990s, evolutionary marketing is joining the party. Efforts to understand customer behavior have led many researchers to inquiry into the fundamental mechanisms of thought itself. Indeed, thought is being seen as an evolutionary process, a view informed by observations and developments in computing as well as in biological sciences. Common to many current theories of thought is the idea that metaphors and symbolic systems such as language evolved as a way of conserving processing resources (to use a computing science term). The mind employs symbols or metaphors, as well as memory, as shorthand in order to use less energy in processing information and to keep it from overloading (Zaltman, 2003). Thus, a deeper understanding of how customers use metaphors in their thought processes can improve the validity of research into branding and service delivery, as well as the effectiveness of marketing communications that build brands and influence customer expectations of service delivery (Zaltman, 2003).

When viewing brands, organizations, or even thought itself from an evolutionary standpoint, one of the problems is that while evolution is a powerful and productive framework from which to view a wide range of systems and processes, it is a complex and persistently controversial theory. A complete understanding of evolutionary processes is probably beyond the grasp of most of us (including, as yet, this author). Because of this complexity, there is a tendency to isolate a single organism (or entity) for study, while ignoring other organisms in the environment that are co-evolving along with it. What this means in business terms is that it is not enough to focus on your brand alone. Factors important to the brand—service delivery, employees, company, and customers—are all moving targets for study, influencing each others' evolution to varying degrees. And so are all the factors that affect the evolution of competing brands, in their own respective "ecosystems." This is why seeing brands from the customer's viewpoint—that is, in their true competitive context—is vital.

If thought, then, is an evolutionary process, not only is it important to know how competing brands are evolving, it is important to understand how a single brand might evolve in a customer's mind, and how marketing communications and service delivery bear on this evolution. The brand or image of a product or company can be seen as the direct co-evolutionary result of messages that activate and reinforce existing internal metaphorical images in customers' minds. Messages generated from companies have their own evolutionary path, along with customer's internal images or perceptions (Aunger, 2002.)

There are many different theories of thought and brain function evolving today. Two that are useful in understanding customer thought processes are memetics and human universals.

Memetics

Memetic theory, or memetics, evolved from Richard Dawkins's coining of the term *meme* in *The Selfish Gene* (1976) to signify what he called a "cultural unit of information." Memetics has been used to explain *viral marketing,* a term that became popular in the 1990s as the Internet exploded (Aunger, 2002). Memetics is a theory of thought that has not yet gained widespread acceptance from the scientific community, partly because memes have yet to be observed empirically (incidentally, a status they share with, for example, many subatomic particles postulated by quantum physics).

Memetics has value, however, in furthering our understanding of customer thought and behavior. With respect to branding, one of the useful aspects of meme theory is that it suggests that information can be seen as exhibiting replicating behavior, like genes, prions, and computer viruses, and that the dynamics of this replication (and evolution) lies in the fact that they depend on preexisting materials and conditions in their hosts (such as DNA and RNA in the case of genes and prions): operating systems and executable applications in the case of computer viruses and "human universals" in the case of memes.

One of the ideas in meme theory that affects marketing and customer service is the notion that messages from companies to customers depend on activating preexisting mental constructs rather than creating them. In other words, in order to connect and communicate with customers effectively, companies must understand and work within the limits of customers' cognitive knowledge and, more important, their emotional responses, rather than attempting relentlessly to impose external, rational messages on them.

Human Universals

Donald E. Brown, in his book *Human Universals* (1991), postulates the existence of a discrete number of cultural traits and qualities common to human beings in all world cultures. Brown first proposed universals as a critique of cultural relativism, then the dominant paradigm in anthropology. Culture and nature were viewed as separate entities, and their interaction was not well understood. Brown identified approximately two hundred universals, including use of metaphors, systems of status and roles, fear of snakes, creation of art, use of numbers, standards of measuring beauty and ugliness, ethnocentricity, competitiveness, need for privacy, use of mood-altering drugs, and establishment of etiquette (Zaltman, 2003).

The theory of human universals offers a useful framework in which to base product development, marketing, and service delivery for global companies that must sell in diverse cultural markets. With information and database technology offering the capability to slice market segmentation ever finer, companies find it impractical or impossible to market to too many different segments, especially if they operate under an assumption (as did anthropologists for most of the nineteenth and twentieth centuries) that world cultures are fundamentally different. Companies attempting to deliver on the promise of mass customization or one-to-one marketing that surfaced as a result of artificial intelligence and other information technologies fell victim to the misconception that ever finer market segmentation was both possible and desirable. In product development today, while some mass customization experiments have been successful and demonstrated a feasible response to customer needs, many failed because they were too expensive, too complex, or too difficult to execute (Keenan, Holmes, Greene, and Crockett, 2002; Piller, 2000). In marketing now, the successful instances of one-to-one marketing do include things like tolerable, if marginally effective, purchase recommendations from amazon.com, but instead of effective, tailored offerings, customers still experience mostly more and more spam.

According to Gerald Zaltman, "Increasing market segmentation only worsens managers' tendency to focus on customers' surface differences rather than their similarities. Of course, consumers are both similar to and different from one another in various ways. Their similarities hold the key to understanding their thinking and influencing their buying behavior. The deeper we dig, the more we find that otherwise very different consumers share important thoughts and feelings about the same topic. These similarities powerfully drive consumer buying behavior and remain surprisingly stable over time" (2003, p. 137).

A keen understanding of human universals is particularly useful to companies that sell across many different cultural boundaries and in different global markets, as well as to companies with complex product lines or sales cycles. It also helps to focus branding and customer service efforts by emphasizing bottom-line and commonsense factors. On a basic level, all customers need to know is what your product is, how it gives them results, how it is different, and why they should trust it. They need to be greeted when they come into your store, helped when they need help, and thanked for their business. Far too many companies today fail to deliver on some, if not all, of these universal requirements in their branding and service delivery.

These theories (that thought evolves in a way that may be similar to the spread of computer viruses or genes and that humans may have a discrete, almost hard-wired set of common cognitive and behavioral characteristics) may still be incomplete, controversial, and not widely accepted in the scientific community. Although Brown (among others) was successful in repudiating many of the conclusions made by the groundbreaking anthropological studies of Margaret Mead and Bronislaw Malinowski, long held as gospel, human universals are not widely understood in business practice today. And while memetics is an utterly fascinating theory at the intersection of computer science, microbiology, neurobiology, genetics, and linguistics, it is highly controversial, not least because it is probably completely understood by only a small handful of academics, let alone by practicing professionals. (The word meme has survived, and has a certain metaphorical currency in business use, if largely limited to articles in *Wired* magazine.)

But scientific theories of thought or behavior do not have to be completely watertight or universally accepted in the scientific community to be useful in research and business practice, especially if they provide useful new ways to map or describe the customer mind.

Frontiers of Customer Research: Mapping the Customer Mind

Understanding customers' inner minds is crucial to any company today that cares about seriously competing in the marketplace, but few things are harder for companies to do. Research that directly asks customers what they want is usually flawed because most people do not know what they want or cannot articulate it so that researchers can gain relevant data (Trout, 1996). We literally do not know our own minds. It is estimated that as much as 95 percent of our awareness of the world is unconscious. Asking customers what they are likely to buy can also be a seriously flawed research technique, as the correlation between stated intent and actual buying behavior is generally low and negative, although consistent deviation between the two has been determined in some cases (Heskett, Sasser, and Schlesinger, 1997). Traditional customer research methods assumed that customers make buying decisions on the basis of a rational, carefully considered assessment of relative attributes and prices. Now some researchers claim that buying decisions are made emotionally, on the basis of sensory stimulation, and that rational thought often kicks in later only to justify the emotional decisions (Zaltman, 2003; Hill, 2003).

The interdependent relationship between marketing and customer service means that companies today need more sophisticated feedback mechanisms to measure customers' thoughts and experiences before, during, and after service delivery transactions. It is relatively easy to measure most technical service delivery variables, because they are based on observable behavior (things like speed of transaction processing, accuracy of data collection and payment information, number of transactions per hour or day, or number of leads or clicks that convert). It is equally important, but more difficult, to measure and manage the functional elements of service transactions (things like the attitude of frontline service staff, ease of use of interfaces, and customer-centric policies and processes). But today companies need to do much more than measure after-the-fact behavior; they must also determine the causal relationships between brands (which drive customer expectations) and results (customer perceptions of service and product experiences).

Customer research is traditionally divided into quantitative and qualitative methods. Quantitative methods often attempt to predict future behavior from past behavior or identify ranges of likelihood of future events as described by statistical models. Qualitative methods refer to ways of gathering data that cannot easily be measured but are often the most critical pieces of information in customers' minds, such as deeply held attitudes about sensitive subjects like feminine hygiene, teenage pregnancy, or erectile dysfunction.

As science and research methods evolve, this artificial dichotomy loses relevance: referring to factors as qualitative or intangible is often simply another way of saying that we have not discovered or widely agreed on an effective way to measure them yet. That does not mean that they are inherently resistant to quantification or understanding, or less important than quantitative data. Uncovering the inner logic of customer thought around difficult-to-quantify issues like being touched (or not) by a sales representative, dealing with the embarrassment of certain medical conditions, or supporting local products over those produced by the exploitation of labor in poor countries can have huge bottom-line implications in a wide range of industries. Effectively measuring and analyzing these kinds of data can make excellent use of both quantitative and qualitative data if research is designed appropriately.

Recent advances in many fields are useful in providing more accurate, embedded, and adaptive intelligence systems for improving marketing and service delivery. Forward-thinking companies today are looking outside traditional disciplines to find new ways to measure and understand human behavior in a commercial context and are benefiting from a best-practices approach, which in itself is a kind of Darwinian strategy. Many of the disciplines from which new learning comes are themselves influenced by a more interdisciplinary approach. Following are a few examples of thought-based research methods and techniques for understanding customer thoughts and behavior.

Behavioral Observation

Direct observation of how customers behave and interact with products, displays, and service personnel in retail environments yields valuable insights about branding, store design, and service delivery. One of the leading firms in this area is Envirosell, based in New York. Envirosell was founded in 1979 in New York City by Paco Underhill, a disciple of the sociologist William H. Whyte (1917–1999), best known for his seminal work in the study of human behavior in urban settings. Envirosell has adapted anthropological research techniques to retailing, basing its methodology on considerable empirical evidence: the measurements and observations accumulated by trackers and interviewers working on the floors and behind the scenes of retail establishments. Envirosell explores both similarities and differences in the shopping experiences of varied groups, including the distinctive ways in which men and women browse and make buying decisions, and it provides retailers with well-documented recommendations on details of store design, such as aisle width, lighting, signage, music, counter height, and seating specifications. Its research methodology combines direct observation, videotaping, interviews with shoppers and sales associates, and surveys:

Observation: On-site researchers record the movements and activities of customers in the act of shopping in the particular store. Data collection is unobtrusive and does not interrupt or influence the routine operations of the business day.

Video Recording: Several cameras are used concurrently, capturing virtually everything occurring in the area studied during the research day from individual areas of a store to heavily trafficked paths. Recording takes place continuously throughout the research day. The cameras are unobtrusive and have little impact on the normal course of business.

Exit Interviews: After completing their shopping and upon leaving the store, shoppers are intercepted and offered an incentive to complete a questionnaire. The actual number of interviews depends on the level of shopping incidence and interview acceptance. The survey lasts approximately five minutes. Our unique methodology enables us to interpret behavior patterns with respect to other variables such as customer profile information.

Sales Associate Interviews: We have incorporated a sales associate interview into some of our retail research. It has proven to be a good technique to provide valuable insights from the perspective of those who are on the floor each day. Interviews are about one hour in length and are tape recorded with the associates' permission.

[The following are typical interview questions:]

_ What are shoppers' most frequently asked questions, concerns, and needs?

_ What do shoppers most often complain about? What do they praise?

_ Can the store be changed to make it easier to shop/more efficient?

_ How does the store flow and layout work?

_ What do customers need the most help with (i.e. finding items, finding sections, etc.)?

_ What is most often the reason when customers decide not to buy?

_ What could be done to improve the store in terms of product mix/selection, store layout/design, etc.?" [Envirosell, 2004].

Metaphor Elicitation

Similar to the idea that memetic replication relies on preexisting conditions in the brain is the role of metaphors in communication and thought. Metaphoric images are efficient mechanisms for communication because they help the brain to process information symbolically (Zaltman, 2003). For instance a brand-building strategy like an ad that describes a product as "fresh as a spring breeze" can have the effect of imprinting the "fresh" construct in customers' minds in connection with the product, especially if conditions make customers receptive to the suggestion (no other products "own" the "fresh" concept in the category, and it resonates in the right way with customers internal associations with freshness).

Metaphor elicitation is useful in understanding customers' often unconscious reactions to products, environments, and service transactions and is done through carefully designed customer research and interviewing techniques. For instance, in a typical service transaction, a service provider may greet customers with the appropriate greeting, but with the wrong intonation. Customers unconsciously read insincerity or lack of commitment in the employee's voice and, when queried during research later, may choose to use a metaphorical image to describe their impressions of the transaction: "It was like she was on autopilot, talking like a friendly zombie. I got my latte on time, but I'd rather go to a place where the salespeople are not robots." This statement is quite typical of the kinds of comments we elicit in our customer research and contains three potent metaphors ("zombie," autopilot," and "robot"), each with significant potential to point to new, previously unrecognized problems (or opportunities), especially when *word use incidence analysis* or other methods indicate a broad consensus of "zombie" or "robot" perceptions among customers. Direct feedback like this is often gathered in conjunction with quantitative rankings of satisfaction or other factors. In this example, the customer could very likely have rated the service transaction favorably in terms of tangibles, such as "got order on time," "paid expected price," "service was friendly," or other measures that allow crucial observations to fall through the cracks.

Word Use Incidence

A customer research technique that we have employed at Brand-Sequence is word use incidence analysis. During customer interviews, we take written transcripts of each interview. We then process these transcripts and tally the frequency of use for certain words, which can have different meanings depending on the context of the interview and the context of the product category. Words with a high incidence of repetition across a diverse group of customers often indicate important relationships between customers' preexisting attitudes, thoughts, and feelings and those attributed to a product or service encounter. These key words often signal strong metaphorical images that can be useful in marketing communications or service delivery guidelines, such as conveying complex product information in simple ways to customers or solidifying key brand positioning concepts. Word use analysis is also quite valuable in determining key word recommendations for search engine marketing.

Psychophysiological Responses

Measuring and analyzing the emotional and physiological responses of customers in an effort to gain a deeper understanding of their thought processes has proven valuable to many researchers because of their shared observations of some key behavioral patterns: customers make buying decisions primarily with their emotions, and they use rational thought processes to validate the emotional decisions; strong sensory stimulation is more effective in engaging customers emotionally; and people are largely unaware of their unconscious responses to stimulation and therefore cannot be expected to articulate them consciously. Some of the main techniques in this category being used today are the Facial Action Coding System (FACS), biofeedback, and neuroimaging (Hill, 2003).

FACS, developed by Paul Eckman, a professor of psychology in the Department of Psychiatry at the University of California at San Francisco, and Wallace V. Friesen, his longtime collaborator, is the result of over seven years of intensive analysis and subsequent categorization of facial muscle movements and expressions (Gladwell, 2002). Consistent patterns of muscle movements have been found across diverse cultures; these patterns correspond to the basic emotions of happiness, sadness, fear, anger, disgust, and surprise. Forced smiles can be distinguished from genuine smiles, for instance. Using FACS as a tool in customer research, with frame-by-frame analysis of videotaped expressions and micro-expressions, companies can gain a new level of understanding of customer service transactions or responses to new products or marketing communications (Hill, 2003, pp. 112–114).

Biofeedback is a technique of monitoring signals such as brain activity, blood pressure, heart rate, and other bodily functions that normally are not controlled voluntarily. It has been used by psychologists as a treatment method and has the benefit of measuring immediate physiological responses to stimuli. Biofeedback has the advantage of being relatively inexpensive (compared with neuroimaging, for instance), and mobile versions of the technology are being developed for use in retail environments (Hill, 2003).

Researchers are using neuroimaging techniques to observe the brain while it thinks in order to understand the process. According to AC Nielsen (2003), "Neuroeconomics deploys brain scans such as functional magnetic resonance imaging (MRI) or positron emission topography (PET) to literally view neurological reaction to stimuli such as product photos or advertising messages. Unlike focus groups or other research methods, consumers cannot fake it or tell you what you want to hear, because brain activity doesn't lie."

Bright House Networks (2004), one of the leading practitioners of neuromarketing, describes its methodology thus:

> We are a novel form of consumer consultancy that leverages scientific knowledge about how the human brain motivates consumer behavior to deliver strategic insights that are intended to enhance the relationship between the consumer and the product, brand and company. Our goal is to define the neural basis of behaviors that are of specific interest to strategic business decision making, as well as of generic interest to the field of neuroscience. We are not interested in telling companies what people think about their products, but rather how they think. Our focus is decidedly from the consumer perspective with the direct intent to influence the behavior of companies, rather than consumers.

One might wonder exactly how scanning brains, counting words, measuring aisles, and dissecting potent poetic images teased from the depths of customers' minds help to sell cars, dog food, or cruise vacations. Different techniques have varying degrees of utility and relevance. Neuromarketing may vividly demonstrate correlations in brain activity with certain kinds of advertising images, but it is not clear that it can explain the underlying causality between neural activity and visual stimulation. Behavioral observation is highly effective at providing solid data on which to base store design and service delivery, but it cannot explain what gets new customers to the store in the first place or how they may behave when buying on the company Web site. Metaphor elicitation and word use incidence analysis provide key windows into customers' minds, but they must be translated into metrics for the ongoing collection and analysis of data. Customer minds have to be mappable in terms simple and practical enough to enable managers to build effective strategies to transform their marketing and service organizations.

A Cycle of Causality

Brands and customer satisfaction are often difficult to define and measure, especially when the measurements and definitions are expressed in terms suited to researchers, marketers, or analysts rather than customers. Both are attitude driven; they live inside customers' brains and therefore have resisted practical quantification. Brands tend to be measured with snapshot methods; few research methods track how brands change over time in customers' minds. Customer satisfaction is frequently measured for change over time, but the causal relationship between expectations, satisfaction, and loyalty is not well understood by many companies. The service-profit chain model also demonstrates causal links between customer satisfaction and employee satisfaction. Because customer loyalty is measured as behavior (frequency and volume of purchases), it presents an easier target for quantitative analysis. But customer loyalty is driven by things that are more difficult to quantify.

Many models that are designed to represent the underlying dynamics of the customer value "equation" or "calculation" are complex, because customer thoughts, behavior, and markets are all complex phenomena. Reducing customer brand perception to an equation or calculation is tempting, but it is usually useful only in analysis, as customers rarely make a linear sum calculation. Any one variable (such as results, price, service, or credibility) may tip the outcome in favor of one brand over those of competitors.

What is needed is a simple model that views a customer's relationship with a company and its products in terms of related causes. I call this model the Brand-Expectations-Experience cycle. Brands, customer expectations and needs, and customer experiences of products and service are all interdependent. Brands, as "reputations" of companies and products, influence customers' expectations of results from products. Expectations and needs influence buying behavior and subsequent experiences with products, which in turn influence expectations and brands. New customers are drawn into this cycle of experience with a company or product by referral from existing customers or by marketing (see Exhibit 4.1).

Many different factors contribute to each part of this cycle, but it must be viewed as a whole system, and successful companies must multitask and work on all parts of the system simultaneously. In today's global economy, any single element—quality products, excellent service, satisfied customers, great marketing, or customer referrals—is no longer enough to carry the whole system.

In this section I discuss the customer value equation, how brand equity affects customer expectations, how a shared vision of

Exhibit 4.1. Causal Relationships.

the customer experience can affect service delivery, and how diversity of viewpoints is essential to the understanding of brands. But first I address two persistent problems: defining *brand* and putting customer satisfaction into a more relevant context.

Toward a Working Definition of *Brand*

One of the difficulties in research and professional practice regarding brands is a considerable lack of consensus on the definition of *brand,* even within the circles of professional practice and academia. Client companies are also often confused about what is signified by the term *brand,* although most agree that it is something important and valuable. Just as much of the customer service literature is focused on defining the basic terms *customer* and *service,* probably far more ink and pixels have been devoted to a suitable working definition of *brand.*

Many researchers and practitioners choose to define a brand by examples and references to various intangible qualities. Definitions vary considerably from brand guru to brand guru. One of the most respected and widely published brand experts, David Aaker, states, "Brand identity should help to establish a relationship between the brand and the customer by generating a value proposition involving functional emotional or self-expressive benefits" (1996, p. 68). Other plausible definitions from the wide array of brand consultants are too numerous and widely varying to mention here.

The effect of a lack of clear understanding of the definition of the term has led to some distrust in the business community of branding and marketing experts, many of whom fail to deliver consistent, measurable results from their research and recommendations. Nevertheless, many do show valuable, measurable results. Consultants offer many analytical definitions and methods that can be successfully used to study different aspects of customer perceptions, behavior, and experience, but the methods and their results are often too complex for managers to grasp or implement. How can a brand be defined as an integral asset to a company, and a part of the evolutionary balance between companies and customers, in a practical way that gives companies and consultants a common language? And another question is most important to our era of measuring all customer activity and data on the Internet and everywhere else possible: Is it possible to quantify brand equity? If so, how do we do that reliably?

A brand is built on existing universal images common to all customers and uses metaphors as shorthand to unify the diversity of its individual attributes in customers' minds. For example, different attributes of the Nike brand may be "inspires me to do my best," "the original," "sleek and efficient," or "running shoes." But in the minds of customers, all of these are summed up in the brand positioning of "authentic athletic performance." In other words, at the root of all Nike products, service, and communication is a deep understanding of how athletes see the world in terms of performance (Bedbury, 2002). This is consistent with Nike's origins as a running shoe company, and hence its ownership of the "running shoe" category in customers' minds. Metaphorical images in Nike ads and marketing communications usually strongly convey "authentic athletic performance."

A brand is the aggregate, common experience that a diverse, independent, decentralized group of customers has with a product or service. It is the reputation of a product or company, and thus both drives and is driven by customer expectations. Expectations frame customer experience (and hence satisfaction), which influence the brand and customer loyalty.

Customer Satisfaction, an Elusive Metric

The concept of customer satisfaction on which many companies appear to base service measurement systems is like the way waitresses and waiters in restaurants virtually everywhere in the United States inquire, "Is everything okay here?" after delivering diners' orders to the table. This particular service transaction is driven by entrenched social norms and is dramatically flawed for several reasons. First, the burden of complaint is placed on the customer; the vast majority of customers refuse to send food back, out of deep embarrassment about making a fuss and by wanting to be polite to their guests by not making them wait to eat while their order is prepared. Second, Americans (and probably people of many other cultures) do not welcome conflict, however minor, at the table, especially in the highly public setting of a restaurant, and especially an expensive one. Third, and probably most crucial to the quality of customer feedback, most diners would rather respond, "Yes, everything's fine!" even if the meat is tough and the soup inedible and a slug is nested in the salad. Without a good awareness of possible nonverbal clues to the contrary, the waitperson thinks that the customer is "satisfied." He or she may never discover the truth, even after getting the tip, as diners may not blame their awful dinner on the service but on the kitchen. By making a very slight but qualitatively different inquiry, such as, "Is there anything here that isn't perfect?" a waitperson can get much more honest and useful responses from customers and rapidly improve the dining experience for those at the table and for future patrons. Restaurants never get second chances from customers who have had a bad experience the first time. And in an increasingly competitive global marketplace, neither do most other service businesses.

Many companies today continue to use customer satisfaction measurement systems that provide only part of the picture necessary to understand complex relationships between different aspects of customer behavior. Like the waitperson in the restaurant, inquiries that attempt to get relevant data on customer satisfaction with questions that require only yes or no answers or rating on a scale of 1 to 5 will never get at the core reasons for customers' real satisfaction, anger, disappointment, or ecstasy. Hence, in initial brand research with customers or in frontline service encounters, eliciting valuable feedback entails asking the right questions, giving customers more opportunities to give useful answers, aggregating and analyzing the results effectively, and sharing them throughout the organization on an ongoing basis.

In *The Service Profit Chain* (1997), Heskett, Sasser, and Schlesinger demonstrate a far more compelling and dynamic view of customer satisfaction because they show causal relationships between it and customer loyalty, employee satisfaction, growth and profits, and a number of other factors. In Brand-Expectations-Experience cycle thinking, whether customer expectations meet results is a strong indicator of satisfaction and a better predictor of loyalty.

The Value "Calculation"

Attempts to analyze discrete dimensions of customers' buying behavior often fail to take into account three factors: (1) different dimensions of a brand or a customer service experience may have widely varying effects on bottom line results; (2) despite many recent advances in technology and knowledge of brain function, many variables remain difficult to define or measure; and (3) it is not clear that customers always perform rational value calculations when making buying decisions, even though value equations can be useful for companies in determining areas for improvement of services delivery and product quality.

For Heskett, Sasser, and Schlesinger, the customer value equation is increased results from products and service quality combined with reduced price and costs of acquiring service. They convincingly demonstrate that companies that focus on process (service) quality as well as delivering results to their customers build customer loyalty and are profitable because loyal customers become more profitable over time. Loyal customers also lower the cost of new customer acquisition by making good referrals, thus building brand equity. In a well-reasoned argument that reflects the previously mentioned bias against marketers, Surowiecki (2004a) says, "Marketers looked at [successful] companies and said they were succeeding because their brands were strong. In reality, the brands were strong because the companies were succeeding."

The complexity comes when trying to determine the proportionate effect that any single dimension of a brand or service delivery experience is likely to have on buying behavior. In a rational value equation, what "results" mean may vary qualitatively and quantitatively from customer to customer, as can perceptions of process quality and service acquisition costs. That is not to say that devising accurate ways to measure each dimension quantitatively is not important and will not yield good data; it is and it can. It is just that the value equation needs to be tempered and correlated with qualitative and quantitative measurements of customer expectations and with a deeper and more practical understanding of customers' irrational, emotionally driven behavior. Lovelock (2001) shows that customer experience ratings become more valuable when gauged against customer expectations (which are brand driven). And our own research at BrandSequence has indicated that customers form impressions and images of a brand in a nonlinear, irrational way. In our customer research work, we used to think of a brand analysis as a process of breaking down customer perceptions into a formula, with a logical calculation, but we found that it did not work that way in customers' minds.

Brand Equity and Service Expectations

What does *brand equity* mean exactly? In the past, this term was often connected with attributes called "intangibles," which basically meant that nobody had quite yet figured out how to measure them. Because the stakes are so high, methodologies are now emerging that are up to the task. With the right set of metrics and methods for measuring customers' minds, brand equity may take its place along with cash flow, cost per unit, sales per square foot, or other standard business metrics.

Brand equity is connected to higher perceived product quality, with *perceived* being the operative word. An example is in the cola product category (beverages are particularly susceptible to brand influence). Blind taste tests indicate that customers usually prefer Pepsi, but they change their minds and say they prefer Coke after they are made aware of the true identities of the beverages they compared. Most beverage taste tests produce results like this that seem to indicate that people really do not taste the products at all or cannot tell the difference between them. The brand name and the label predetermine their expectations of the taste experience, and this appears to be all that matters, especially when there really is little difference among products.

Brand equity can also be expressed as a monetary value, as branded items command a higher price over undifferentiated commodity items in the same category. In this context, sometimes the entire value of the difference can be in superior customer service. Customers experience service with companies rather than with products. In fact, it is possible to argue that customers really experience service in the fullest sense only with *people* in companies, although the percentage of automated or impersonal service delivery is rapidly increasing. Improving service delivery thus presents important opportunities for building brand equity, as more and more service delivery is becoming ineffective and undifferentiated. Also, like taste expectations with cola, customers are more likely to experience better service from a company from which they expect to experience better service.

Shared Customer Experience

Service delivery can evolve effectively with and reinforce a brand if a deep understanding of the essential customer experience is shared throughout the company. At Starbucks, frontline service staff are referred to as baristas—Italian for "bartender." But bars in Italy are not like most bars in the United States; they are beautifully appointed neighborhood gathering places with elegant and elaborate coffee-making apparatus, frequented by patrons of all ages, that offer delicious and tastefully displayed food, drinks, and other sensory delights. In short, they are the perfect places to experience a wide variety of life's little pleasures.

All of Starbucks' efforts at building its brand stem from replicating a certain kind of experience found in Italian and European bars. They have become "America's living room," which is similar to the function that bars play in Italian cities and towns. Their staff deliver professional service to strict standards, their drinks are named after Italian coffee drinks, and their products are varied and high quality, but all relate to the ritual of coffee, tea, snacks, and informal neighborhood gathering. Say what you will about Starbucks: there are other vendors that make better coffee, and it is a huge global corporation that has put many real small bars and coffeehouses out of business across the Untied States—but it single-handedly dramatically reversed the steadily declining trend in global coffee consumption with the strength of its brand vision.

Impact of Diverse Groups on the Brand

Heskett, Sasser, and Schlesinger (1997) have demonstrated close multiple relationships between growth and profit, customer satisfaction, customer loyalty, customer value, employee productivity, employee loyalty, employee satisfaction, and employee capability. One of the values in documenting the positive effects on growth and profit of satisfied noncustomer "customers" (a group that includes employees, investors, and internal customers, to name a few) is that it validates efforts to gather feedback from them and direct communications to them. Many companies direct marketing efforts to customers only and neglect to give proper consideration to the decisive impact that noncustomer groups can have on a brand. In our customer research at BrandSequence, we carefully select sample groups to reflect an appropriate level of diversity of viewpoints, experiences, and opinions. Frontline service providers are particularly valuable in assessing customer attitudes, as they can often articulate customers' attitudes and preferences better than can customers themselves. Also, data and input that correlate across the widest sample segment tend to be more valuable.

Traditional customer service literature and practice largely address internal functions of service delivery, and traditional marketing literature and practice largely address the external image of products and services. But customers experience a company and its products or services as a single entity, and the Brand-Expectations-Experience cycle means that a simpler, more agile model of product development, marketing, and service delivery should be used to integrate previously separate functions in organizations. Our research methodology at BrandSequence was developed to provide feedback loops from all parts of a company with an impact on a brand.

Working with Brand DNA

Much as different dimensions of service quality were postulated in an effort to define what service quality was (Schneider and White, 2004), I have found it useful to isolate different dimensions of a brand for purposes of study and analysis, using a taxonomy from customer research and marketing trade practice. "Brand DNA" is a metaphor borrowed from molecular biology, used to convey the idea that a brand essence is simultaneously complex and simple, made up of several dimensions, but somehow reducible to one that replicates instantly in a customer's mind using existing thoughts and associations. In the development of our brand research methodology, we isolated five brand dimensions that appeared to recur throughout many systems of customer research and brand analysis: category, personality, benefit, difference, and credibility.

Exhibit 4.2 is a typical example of the results of a brand research project that determines a snapshot view of a digital asset management company's brand. It takes the form of a construct map, made to show relationships between the constructs most common to interviewed customers and the single construct that is at the center of all of them, which is the brand positioning. This essential construct is not arrived at in a necessarily logical way in customers' minds, but a careful analysis of interviews and customer surveys shows that the specific result that was most relevant to customers was providing complete documentation for legal purposes, something that was far from clear at the beginning of the research. All other brand attributes were important but served to support the brand positioning.

Exhibit 4.2. Brand DNA Construct Map.

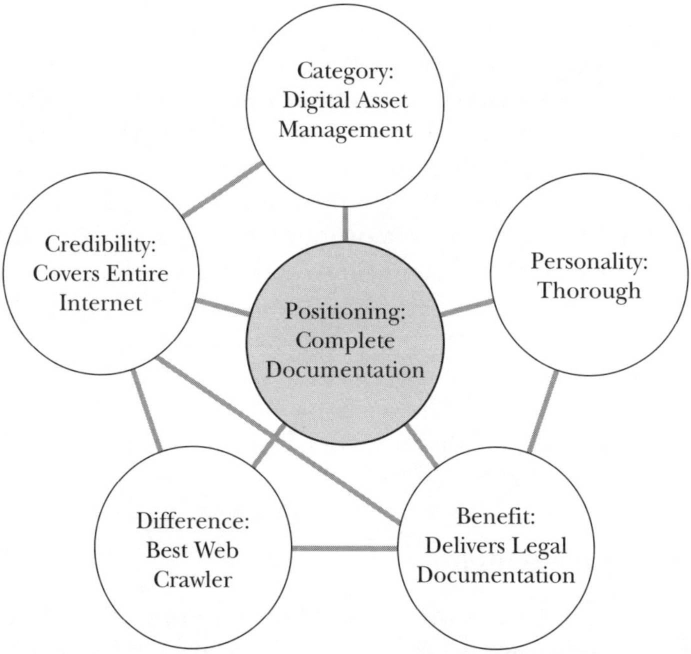

Category

If the brand is the organism, then category is its environment. Customers begin their cognitive awareness of the brand by placing it into a product category. For instance, in customers' minds, Nike's products are in the "athletic" category, not the "casual wear" category such as jeans. If Nike tried to sell jeans, it would fail because "jeans" and "athletic gear" are not readily compatible product categories in the brains of customers. Our brains work this way with product categories because they work this way with categories in general. In fact, a tried and true way to effect strategic brand differentiation is to reorient customer perceptions of a product by creating a new product category for it rather than trying to compete in a crowded one (Trout, 1996).

Personality

Personality (or character) is the brand dimension in which anthropomorphism comes into play and where metaphors are used effectively. Customers often think of brands as a person—as having a personality that is trustworthy, safe, inspiring, dependable, flaky, devious, imperious, or whatever else. Companies often use metaphorical characters like Charley the Tuna, the Jolly Green Giant, or the Snuggle Bear to embody specific personalities or attributes that customers will respond to emotionally. These characters are used to differentiate a product from competing offerings in commodity product categories where there is otherwise little room for differentiation.

Another aspect of this brand dimension is that in a very real sense, a company or brand's frontline service delivery personnel embody its personality. The quality of their personal interaction with customers, especially in service brands, is inseparable from the brand's personality.

Benefit (and Results)

In the past, companies often completely ignored the perceived benefits that customers received from products and focused on surface-level features—colors, flavors, or technology. This worked for a time in a commodity-based economy where offering slight variations on basic offerings was all that was needed to guarantee customers. Today, not only benefits but results are crucial to brands because customers not only expect results from everything they buy, they expect companies to know what they need and to deliver it to them at a competitive price. In marketing communications, practical product benefits, like "saves money," "cleans faster," or "smells good," are much more compellingly stated to the customer as delivering results (that produce desired feelings): "makes me feel young again," "makes me look like a good housewife," or "helps me get ahead in life."

Difference

Difference is a crucial brand dimension because all brands exist in competition with other brands or in competition with something else that may not even be in the same product category. A dramatic difference is preferable to a minor one, but an incremental difference can mean success in a tightly competitive and volatile market. Competitive context is crucial to a perception of a brand: customers tend to segment brands as either category leaders, near the top, or "also-ran" (undifferentiated). Assessing and effecting product or service differentiation is a complex endeavor because companies must assess competing products as well as their own products from the customer's standpoint, and not only are all products constantly evolving, they have an impact on each other's evolutionary trajectories.

Positive product attributes, as well as service delivery, are meaningless unless they confer a comparative advantage. All products and services are delivered in a competitive context. The world (and the global marketplace) is a vast, complex ecosystem of competing organisms. Often the competition for a specific product or service is not readily apparent. It may not be another similar product at all. When the Palm Pilot first entered the market, its competition was not other similar devices, because there were none to speak of at the time. It was paper and pencil: people's established, traditional method of keeping track of their personal contacts and appointments. So developing and delivering competitive products and customer service may require constantly observing and measuring not only your customers and how they think of your products and service, but also your competitors, and what their customers think of their products and service compared to yours.

Credibility

Credibility is the brand dimension built around customer trust. It allows the customer to understand a new offering in terms of a familiar concept or vendor and can come from association with celebrities, previous personal experience, or the experience of trusted friends or family. A brand with high credibility has an increased opportunity to build customer loyalty, as customers have high expectations of experiencing desired results. Credibility also allows customers to refer the brand to others with low risk of embarrassment.

The Irrational Calculation

A strong brand must have all five dimensions clearly defined in customers' minds in order to succeed, but not all dimensions are equally important. Individual attributes are crucial to the understanding of the brand because they are all interrelated, but some may perform more important functions than others. In the end, customers remember a brand consciously for only one differentiating attribute, which acts as shorthand for the other brand dimensions. Also, the brand dimensions are all interrelated and form different parts of the buying decision equation. For example, a customer may patronize Starbucks because it is the leader in the gourmet coffee category, has a relaxing yet stimulating atmosphere, offers a quick pleasurable break from a stressful workday, has a range of products and services that nobody else does, and has a long history of satisfying customers. Other coffee vendors may be better in terms of product quality, but they do not have the same atmosphere in their stores. Starbucks coffee may or may not win blind taste tests against other coffees, but it has succeeded because it understands its competitive differentiation very well: its brand is about providing customers with "rewarding everyday moments" (Bedbury, 2002).

Redefining the Partnership with Customers

What are some of the areas in which companies can address service and marketing issues and implement the findings from new customer research? How can researchers be more responsive to the needs of companies and vice versa? What kinds of widespread systematic changes are necessary for companies to evolve and thrive in the new global economy?

Diversity of Opinion and Viewpoints

The culture clash between business and science in the United States is pervasive and entrenched. One reason for this is that scientists and researchers have very different incentives from corporations regarding the flow of information. Scientists (and science in general) benefit from the sharing of information because it enables decision making and problem solving. Corporations, in contrast, want to own and protect proprietary information, but they need the innovation and technology that is the result of scientific inquiry as much as scientists need the funding and other resources that are increasingly provided by corporations. Both corporations and scientists, however, benefit from a diversity of opinions and information, even if the information is sometimes conflicting or incoherent. And researchers can benefit from looking beyond their own specialized disciplines for information that correlates with or contradicts their findings.

Companies that are interested in improving service delivery and marketing can benefit from gathering feedback from as many diverse, independent sources as possible—from competitors, employees, stockholders, and customers. For instance, Southwest Airlines regularly includes its top frequent flyer customers on employee selection panels. Who could do a better job of seeing employees from a customer's perspective than your best customers? Some companies even enlist the services of volunteer "buzz agents," who not only promote the products through their own social networks, but can act as informal customer service representatives, helping customers with problems and reporting back to the company with feedback and customer evaluations.

Facilitating Better Customer Communication Mechanisms

Marketing practices and customer feedback mechanisms in many U.S. companies today are ineffective, inefficient, redundant, or irrelevant. In many industries, such as advertising, this is the case because existing practices are either too expensive to change, or compelling alternatives simply have not yet appeared on a widespread basis, despite many promising technological advancements.

New communication technologies quickly mutate into faster, cheaper ways for companies to deliver the same ineffective communications to customers. The widespread availability of cheap database technology, together with wholesale sharing of customer lists, has fostered more and more relentless telemarketing, especially by national telephone companies dueling for market share. E-mail marketing emerged many years ago, with great predictions of "one-to-one" marketing, but it rapidly evolved into global spam overload. "Personalization" promised wonderful returns based on artificial intelligence technologies—predictive algorithms that suggested related products to customers based on past purchases. To be sure, amazon.com has experienced some success with this technology, but it can hardly be called a rich and sophisticated way of communicating with customers. And the entire Internet rapidly transformed itself into simply another media channel, cluttered with pop-up ads and more and more links to e-mail spam.

The basic traditional push model of marketing in the United States, where companies seek to manipulate customers by pushing information to them about products and their features and benefits, is gradually evolving into a more sophisticated model. In this model, marketing and customer service begin with a deep understanding of the universal and specific emotional and cognitive constructs that live inside their customers' minds. These constructs, thoughts, feelings, and behaviors are then activated from within rather than imposed externally. Rational evaluation of a product's price, features, and benefits is important, but in the new model of marketing and customer service, it comes *after* the customer is engaged on an emotional level.

Effectively gathering and using customer feedback does not necessarily mean using new information technology, but instead can rely on decentralized decision making, as is the case with the specialty retailer Trader Joe's. Customer service representatives in these stores are in fact the salespeople on the floor, the "captains" (managers) and "crew members" (sales staff) who are allowed a considerable amount of freedom to develop product programs that are responsive to local customer needs. This means that inventory decisions are strongly influenced by customers' feedback (McGregor, 2004).

Redefining Service Models

If you were to ask most customers what the term *customer service* brings to mind, the following five basic constructs or mental models would probably dominate the answers. Replacing these models with more relevant ones involves seeing service delivery from the customer perspective first:

Old model: Service with a smile. Companies frequently compel frontline service providers to undergo "smile training," adopt gratuitous and artificial "happy faces" or follow rigid service "scripts" regardless of the specific service delivery context. While smiling service people are certainly preferable to scowling ones, this often has a counterproductive effect, as customers resent insincere, forced smiles and being treated as transactions rather than as individuals. Many companies are not effective with these "be happy" policies, as they give employees instructions to appear happy, but little incentive to actually *be* happy.

New model: Service with authority. Heskett, Sasser, and Schlesinger (1997) found a high correlation between employee satisfaction and many other measures, such as growth and profitability, and customer satisfaction and customer loyalty. They also found that the most important factor affecting employee satisfaction was capability: employees are happiest when they feel effective and capable in their jobs. Giving employees latitude in dealing with customers, while maintaining reasonable guidelines and limits, is probably the best replacement model for ineffective "smile training" strategies.

Old model: The customer is always right. Ultimately the customer is always right in the sense that if a company ignores customers' basic needs for too long, customers will put it out of business at the first available opportunity. But there is a danger in companies' pandering to customers too much or too blatantly. This aphorism oversimplifies customers' expectations and seems to imply that the company is always wrong. Perhaps this phrase persists because historically, companies have so often been wrong and need to be reminded that customers' needs are important. Customers ultimately do not care as much about who is right or wrong if there is a problem as they care about how it is handled. Customers who are dealt with fairly and consistently when there are problems are far more likely to become loyal in the end.

New model: Focus on the right customers. In service-profit chain thinking, the customer groups with the highest return on investment appear to be those at the extreme ends of the satisfaction spectrum. The most loyal customers are typically the most profitable, and that seems logical. But what is counterintuitive about this finding is how profitable dissatisfied customers can become with the correctly leveraged investment in their satisfaction. Basically, it makes more sense to invest in pleasing the customers who are most engaged with your company and not to worry too much about the ones in the middle of the satisfaction spectrum because they are the least profitable (Heskett, Sasser, and Schlesinger, 1997).

Old model: Customer satisfaction at all costs. This appears to be obvious: certainly companies want satisfied customers. But customer satisfaction is often measured in inaccurate or irrelevant ways. It is also not a particularly reliable indicator of future customer loyalty. Furthermore, many customer satisfaction measurement systems suffer from participator bias—in other words, customers who are inclined to participate in "How are we doing?" types of surveys may be far more likely to be satisfied in the first place. They are also usually a tiny fraction of the overall customer base and not likely to be representative. Companies need to look beyond stale definitions of customer satisfaction and look for opportunities to increase the quality of service delivery in ways that differentiate the company and its products.

New model: Build the brand-service-profit chain. The relationships between all the different parts of customer-company relationships are complex, interdependent, and constantly evolving. Satisfaction itself is an elusive quality to measure. Customer loyalty is a more reliable indicator of profitability, and although there is a strong relationship between satisfaction and loyalty, many other parts of the chain must be considered besides customer satisfaction. Brand positioning, customer value, employee capability, employee productivity, employee satisfaction, employee loyalty, and process quality can all equally affect a company's ability to grow and be profitable (Heskett, Sasser, and Schlesinger, 1997).

Old model: Complaint department. Many customers think of customer service as the place to go only when they have problems or complaints.

New model: Seek and reward feedback. Many successful companies today are learning to see customer complaints as valuable opportunities for quality improvement. Customers who take the incentive to complain may be difficult to deal with at times, but they are likely to feel more connection with an investment in the company than ambivalent customers, and they can offer valuable insights and data that other customer groups would not. The same holds true for employees: when they are encouraged to send negative feedback upstream to higher management levels without fear of retaliation, they can make valuable contributions that aid fact-based decisions.

Old model: We don't care. We don't have to. This model of service delivery is defined largely by the absence of effective or considerate customer service and is unfortunately the norm with monopolistic types of corporations like telephone companies, but it is by no means limited to them. Customers of these kinds of companies are often referred to as "hostage" customers: they do business with the company only because they are forced to by a lack of viable alternatives and will defect en masse at the earliest opportunity.

New model: We care because it's good business. Companies today ultimately cannot afford to alienate customers and employees with ineffective marketing, inefficient (or nonexistent) customer service, or deficient strategic brand and service vision. Caring about customers and employees does not mean focusing on extended process-centered initiatives if customers do not get the results they want, and it does not mean losing profit. Happy employees generally mean happy customers, and happy long-term customers generally become more profitable over time.

Intangibles and Emotional Labor

Companies need to reevaluate the elements of customer interactions that are traditionally thought of as intangibles. Much of the customer service literature refers to intangibles as distinct from goods, meaning literally that they cannot be touched. As an academic construct, this is useful in developing a more sophisticated understanding of service delivery as being only marginally responsive to total quality methodology that works well for controlling the quality of manufactured products. But in common business use today, *intangible* has developed a totally different meaning. Many "intangible" elements of service delivery are in fact quite "tangible" or measurable, but they are sometimes neglected largely because accurate and widely accepted methods for measuring them do not exist yet. Furthermore, as the global economy evolves into a service and information economy, "intangibles" become increasingly crucial to every customer transaction. Interestingly enough, one of the most compelling "intangibles" involves physical touching by service providers. Whether customers are physically touched during service transactions appears to have a strong influence on their positive perceptions of the transactions. In several studies, service employees were instructed to make subtle but polite physical contact with customers, like touching their arms or shoulders lightly while talking to them. Customers tended to report these transactions later as warm or positive compared to identical transactions where no touching was experienced (Zaltman, 2003).

The evolution to a service economy involves a large number of new jobs that place a premium on "emotional labor," where employees' ability to present themselves well and deal with difficult customers is paramount. New measurements of these abilities (or, perhaps, emotional intelligence) are crucial to employee assessment, training, and placement.

Monitoring Results

Most managers today track a small number of vital signs of their business daily in order to make effective strategic decisions. These indicators tend to be things like total sales, cost per unit, volume per location, or sales per square foot. But since customer expectations and perceived results are also vital, they too need their own systems of metrics, with the fewer variables the better; it makes it easier to collect data consistently over time. Assuming that an effective, unbiased system for measurement is in place, companies can learn a great deal about their brands and customer service by tracking a few key factors that focus on the Brand-Expectations-Experience cycle, such as: Did you get the service you expected? Did you wait too long in line? Did you pay the price you expected? The specific questions vary with the business, but these service metrics track the most important data: customers' actual results compared to expectations.

Similarly, querying new and current customers periodically about how they think of a brand (getting a reading on its category, personality, expected results, competitive differentiation, or credibility) may be a better indicator of how they are likely to behave than traditional measurements, such as awareness or intent to purchase. Ongoing monitoring of new and current customers' brand perceptions and expectations helps to optimize the return on investment for marketing expenditures, traditionally a difficult projection to make accurately.

Companies with a robust system for collecting ongoing and accurate customer feedback can also enjoy a tremendous strategic advantage by anticipating customer needs for services and products, enabling more efficient just-in-time supply chain delivery. When any employee who has contact with customers can effectively send customer feedback upstream to management and production, companies can reduce the risk of guessing wrong about future product and service preferences.

Global Commerce Necessitates Understanding of Universals

Daily evidence for the emergence of the global economy can be found in our lives in many places. In your local grocery store, more and more food packaging bears labels in three or more languages. When your telephone service has a problem, you are likely to be talking to a technical support person in Mumbai. The company you work for may be exploring market opportunities in Ireland,

Pakistan, or Malaysia. Although the initial stages of globalization have been characterized mainly by richer countries' exploiting the cheap labor sources of poorer ones, expanding markets for companies all over the planet, large and small, seem to be an inevitable development.

With new global markets will come more complex marketing communications and service delivery challenges. These are best met by locating the common intersection points from many cultures for behavioral and cognitive factors that affect buying patterns. Diverse cultures may have differing surface expressions of underlying universal behavioral qualities, and companies need to have a keen understanding of this dynamic, in order to adapt their offerings successfully and efficiently to many different cultures (Zaltman, 2003).

Humanizing Marketing and Customer Service Technology

Communications technology has made great strides in the past generation, but most of our communications are still relatively poor in terms of sensory stimulation. E-mail is fast and efficient but poor for conveying vital emotional signals. Customers who receive even instantaneous response from a company only from e-mail still feel a loss of connection. When the Internet was introduced many years ago to the Inuit in northern Canada, their first question was, "When can we see the faces and hear the voices of people we want to communicate with?" They immediately understood that communication without the value of being able to read facial expressions or parse subtle changes in voice tone was seriously compromised. Video telephony is still not a widespread technology, despite its obvious advantages to all levels of information sharing, including marketing and customer service.

On some level, customers cannot help resenting the relentless depersonalization of service transactions. Some companies may eventually discover that many of their service solutions can become much more efficient with a return to true one-on-one real-time conversations between customers and service representatives. This may be aided by the advent of new technologies like cheap, accessible videoconferencing, for instance.

The interfaces—such as Web forms, content-rich e-mail, automated telephone answering systems, and voice-activated search functions—that are used to deliver service and marketing communications are fraught with frustrating and counterproductive designs. For example, when you call your bank, you are prompted by an automatic voice answering system to enter your account number, so that you can be routed to the appropriate customer service representative. When you finally reach a live human being, you are asked to repeat your account number again and may be asked to enter it on the telephone keypad or repeat it yet again if you get transferred again, which is likely. Small details like this illustrate the fact that most technology-driven service transaction mechanisms appear to be designed completely for the benefit of the company, not the customer. From the customer's standpoint, many basic service transactions that are delivered live, person-to person, are much more efficient than protracted battles with incomprehensible, even hostile automated systems that ultimately may require more, not less, expense for the company as well, especially when you consider the value of lost customers. What the customer often experiences is a defective service and communications process exacerbated by technology. Companies can and should use technology to enhance the quality of service transactions.

To be sure, developing good information technology interfaces is a pervasively difficult process. Interfaces are not as well understood as they need to be. Little progress has been made, for instance, in alternatives to the WIMP (windows, mouse, pointer) computer interface, despite its clumsiness. It is also unclear exactly how voice-activated technology will evolve, largely because humans may have deep aversions to using human language to communicate richly with nonhuman devices. At the moment, getting a telephone number from the national voice-activated 411 system can be a ridiculous waste of time. After the current phase of impersonal service automation passes, customers may ultimately demand a more meaningful, and human response to service delivery.

The Politics of "Customerization"

All of us are customers, and all of us have had nightmare service delivery experiences, where simple problems turn into time-consuming, frustrating, and alienating encounters with arrogant, disorganized, and overly bureaucratic companies. These stories seem to be increasing in frequency, intensity, and absurdity, like the case where a cell phone company denied a woman a credit on her husband's cell phone contract when he died before his contract expired. It is beginning to dawn on us that service delivery is not just an added benefit; it can become a basic necessity. And when it is denied or delivered in a way that makes our lives increasingly difficult, seeking recourse can begin to acquire a political dimension. If our basic necessities are increasingly controlled by corporate interests that have no responsibility to the public good by their very definition, clearly customers feel betrayed on some deep level beyond disenchantment with any one particular company.

The absence of service delivery that is truly responsive to customer needs can be seen in part as the result of undue concentration of power, absentee ownership, and an overriding concern for profit over people. When corporations become monopolies, they can lose their incentives to provide adequate customer service (the "We don't care, we don't have to" syndrome). This is the case with many service sectors, notably telecommunications, where innovative technologies like the Internet or cellular telephones are too new to be fully understood by government representatives, let alone adequately regulated by them. Yet their widespread use and rapid adoption as basic standards make them basic necessities, and inherently in need of government regulation and protection in order to facilitate economic and social stability. As these technologies mature, government can step in and force corporations to engage in fair trade practices, as California did recently with the Telecommunications Consumer Bill of Rights, clearly a case of service delivery becoming a political issue (California Department of Consumer Affairs, 2004).

In the wake of the shocking exposés of the criminal activities of companies and CEOs such as Enron, Tyco, WorldCom, and Martha Stewart, corporate ethics has become a political issue, as it does periodically when egregious abuses of power and of customers' trust become unconscionable. Doing the right thing for customers is good business, and most businesses realize it most of the time. But one of the problems with capitalism is that occasionally corporations get out of control, and government needs to intervene with mechanisms like antitrust, pollution, and consumer safety legislation.

Brave New World

How can companies use technology to communicate with and serve customers better? Will customers be able to understand the trade-off between privacy and improved service yet feel that they still have control of their personal information? Can a world exist where advertising is not obnoxious, acceptable service is extended to most customers, and service nightmares are relatively rare?

Contemplating a future where advertising offerings are not irritating is difficult, if not impossible, but ultimately customers determine the market: companies cannot exist without them. Improved and more embedded customer feedback loops can improve products and service delivery and ultimately provide some measure of balance in markets by lowering the risk for companies of inaccurate product predictions and customer attrition. Improving the relationship between marketing communications and service delivery will improve the relationships between customers and companies and help to mitigate some of the economic dislocations of globalization.

References

Aaker, D. *Building Strong Brands*. New York: Free Press, 1996.

AC Nielsen, "Trend Watch—Neuroeconomics: A Brainy Approach to Brand." *Consumer Insight Magazine,* 2003 [http://www2.acnielsen.com/pubs/2003_q4_ci_trendwatch.shtml].

Agence France-Presse. "U.S. Traditional Media in Steep Decline: Study." *Manila Times,* Mar. 16, 2004.

Aunger, R. *The Electric Meme*. New York: Free Press, 2002.

Bedbury, S. *A New Brand World*. New York: Penguin, 2002.

Bright House Networks. "Practice Areas," 2004 [http://www.bright-house.com/neurostrategies.html].

Brown, D. E. *Human Universals*. New York: McGraw-Hill, 1991.

California Department of Consumer Affairs. "The Telecommunications Consumer Protection Bill of Rights," 2004 [http://www.dca.ca.gov/r_r/telecommunications_rights.htm].

Dawkins, R. *The Selfish Gene*. Oxford: Oxford University Press, 1976.

Envirosell. "Research Methodology," 2004 [http://www.envirosell.com/method.html].

Gaudet, G. "Email Regulatory Impact of Email." *Email Marketing News,* 2004 [http://www.optinnews.com/email_marketing_regulation .html].

Gladwell, M. "Annals of Psychology, The Naked Face: Can You Read People's Thoughts Just by Looking at Them?" *New Yorker,* Aug. 5, 2002 [http://www.gladwell.com/2002/2002_08_05_a_face.htm].

Heskett, J. L., Sasser, W. E. Jr., and Schlesinger, L. A. *The Service Profit Chain.* New York: Free Press, 1997.

Hill, D. *Body of Truth.* New York: Wiley, 2003.

Hurlbut, T. "The Dreaded Assortment Creep," 2004 [http://www .hurlbutassociates.com/DreadedAssortCreep.html].

Keenan, F., Holmes, S., Greene, J., and Crockett, R. O. "A Mass Market of One." *Business Week,* Dec. 2, 2002 [http://www.businessweek .com/magazine/content/02_48/b3810088.htm].

Keller, E. "Getting Good Buzz: What Can a Global Brand Do?" Jan. 12, 2005 [http://womma.org/pages/2005/01/getting_good_bu.htm].

LeClaire, J. "Online Shopping Surged 26 Percent This Holiday Season." *E-Commerce Times,* Dec. 29, 2004 [http://www.ecommercetimes .com/story/ebiz/online-holiday-shopping-39296.html].

Lemon, C. "The eBay Brand Interview." BrandSequence, 2004 [http:// www.brandsequence.com/pdf/c2e_whitepaper.pdf].

Lovelock, C. *Services Marketing, People, Technology, Strategy.* (4th ed.) Upper Saddle River, N.J.: Prentice Hall, 2001.

Marye, B. "Customer Service: Your Advantage," Nov. 2, 2004 [http:// developers.evrsoft.com/article/Internet-marketing/customer-service-your-advantage.shtml].

Mayer, C. E. "Customer Disservice." *Washington Post,* Mar. 27, 2004, p. F1 [http://www.washingtonpost.com/ac2/wp-dyn/A28784-2004Mar27 ?language=printer].

McGregor, J. "Leading Listener: Trader Joe's." *Fast Company,* Oct. 2004, p. 82.

Ogilvy, D. *Confessions of an Advertising Man.* New York: Scribner, 1963.

Piller, F. T. "Mass Customization and Customer Relationship Management," 2000 [http://www.mass-customization.de/engl_infocycle .htm].

Schneider, B., and White, S. *Service Quality: Research Perspectives.* Thousand Oaks, Calif.: Sage, 2004.

Sewell, C. *Customers for Life.* New York: Doubleday, 2002.

Surowiecki, J. "The Decline of Brands." *Wired,* Nov. 2004a [http:// www.wired.com/wired/archive/12.11/brands.html?pg=1&topic= brands&topic_set=].

Surowiecki, J. "Penny-Wise." *New Yorker,* Sept. 27, 2004b.

Trout, J. *The New Positioning.* New York: McGraw-Hill, 1996.

University of Michigan Business School. *American Consumer. Satisfaction Index,* 2004 [http://www.theacsi.org].

Walker, R. "The Hidden (in Plain Sight) Persuaders." *New York Times,* Dec. 5, 2004.

Wal-Mart. *2003 Annual Report* [http://www.walmartstores.com/Files/annual_2003/ar2003_pg16.htm].

Weinberger, J. "Customers Feel a Decline in Quality of Service." *DestinationCRM.com,* June 15, 2004 [http://www.destinationcrm.com/articles/default.asp?ArticleID=4191].

World Bank. *World Development Indicators.* Washington, D.C.: World Bank, 2004.

Zaltman, G. *How Customers Think.* Boston: Harvard Business School Press, 2003.

Zhigang, X. "Dissecting China's Middle Stratum." *China Daily,* Oct. 27, 2004.

PART 2

Employees and Customer Service

Chapter 5

Customer Service Quality
Selecting Valued Performers
Jerard F. Kehoe
David N. Dickter

The purposes of this chapter are to map attributes of service employees onto components of service performance and, based on this mapping, describe key considerations in the design of selection strategies for service work. To develop this mapping, we introduce a new taxonomy of service performance components, described in the first section of this chapter, and rely on an existing taxonomy of employee attributes, described in the second section of the chapter. The new taxonomy of service performance is based on a broad conception of performance that includes the full range of service provider behaviors that are valued by the employer who owns the employment decision. This conception acknowledges that employers are likely to value many different facets of service provider behavior that affect customers, supervisors, the employing organization, and the employee.

The design of an effective selection strategy is discussed in the third section. Design decisions require a number of considerations. Certainly the employer must identify not only the most important service behaviors but also those valued behaviors that selection strategies can effectively influence. Generally selection strategies

We express our special appreciation to Eric Braverman for the many insights he provided in helping to shape the content of this chapter.

are designed in consideration of other human resource processes and systems the employer also uses to optimize service provider behavior. For example, in virtually all service jobs, accurate job knowledge is highly valued. In work and organization contexts in which job knowledge changes rapidly and is relatively easy to acquire such as telemarketing, the employer is likely to rely more heavily on training than selection to ensure accurate job knowledge. In contrast, in different work and organization contexts in which job knowledge is highly complex and requires substantial education and development, such as professional health services, the employer is likely to rely far more heavily on selection than training to ensure mastery of job knowledge. Finally, the employer must identify the organization context and constraints that will necessarily shape the most suitable selection design. We address the role of work context in influencing the importance and expected validity of selection procedures in the third section of this chapter.

Valued Performance Behavior

To paraphrase the old song, the successful service provider is a "many splendored thing." The point of view of this chapter is that the range of service performance behavior is best described as a mix of categories of performance behavior and, within each category, dimensions of behaviors relating to that category. We define the categories based on the perspectives of four key stakeholders in service performance who may value different, sometimes even conflicting, behaviors: the customer, the supervisor, the organization, and the service provider.

For our purposes the customer, whether internal or external, is the intended recipient of the service behavior. Ultimately it is the customer's perceptions and outcomes resulting from the service behavior that determine whether the behavior is effective. At the same time, it is the supervisor who usually has the most direct influence over the service provider's job behavior. Of course, a major dynamic in many service jobs is the degree of consistency between the customer and supervisor demands on the service provider's performance. For the purposes of this chapter, we distinguish the organization's stake in the service provider's performance from the supervisor's direct and immediate stake. Admittedly this can be a fuzzy distinction. However, this chapter defines the supervisor's stake as relating to the day-to-day task performance and other workplace behaviors that are measured and directly managed, coached, or influenced by the supervisor. In contrast, the organization's stake in the service provider's behavior relates to the range of behaviors that have an impact on broader organization interests at the group or organization level. For our purposes, the organization can also be thought of as the set of managers and executives who are above the supervisor hierarchically and those who have other functional responsibilities relating to the service provider's behavior. These supra-supervisor interests include, for example, the health, safety, and security of employees and the quality of the work environment and the organization culture. This distinction between the supervisor's and organization's stakes is commonly reflected, at least in part, by the metrics each manages. Finally, the service provider has a significant stake in her own performance behavior. For example, pay progression, career advancement, job satisfaction, and organization commitment are, in part, valued consequences of the employee's own work behavior. We make the fundamental assumption that the employer has an interest in each of these stakeholders and the extent to which the service provider's performance behavior affects each of them.

A Brief Background on Service Performance

Before describing the dimensions of performance relevant to each of the four stakeholders, we provide a brief summary of research on the dimensions and complexity of service performance. This summary describes the research foundation for the dimensions we will subsequently identify as related to each of the four stakeholders' perspectives about service performance.

Complexity of Job Performance

All jobs can be said to have multiple performance dimensions, and job performance clearly depends not only on the employee, but also on organizational, managerial, situational, and other factors that encourage or inhibit performance. Thus, industrial-organizational psychology has traveled a long road in its attempts to understand, classify, and predict performance (Austin and Villanova, 1992).

Along the way, researchers have identified a variety of taxonomies and dimensions of performance (for reviews, see Austin and Villanova, 1992; Viswesvaran, 2002). As there is no empirically derived consensus on an overall model of performance, we offer a general taxonomy of service performance that highlights major considerations pertaining to selection, so that hiring managers and other practitioners will be able to better define and understand what they are attempting to predict when they are choosing among various employment selection strategies.

Industrial-organizational psychologists have devoted considerable effort toward understanding customer service performance, though attempts to discover the dimensions of service performance through large exploratory analyses are rare. An exception is Hunt's research (1996) on a database of over eighteen thousand entry-level jobs (mostly service oriented), in which performance dimensions identified included industriousness (effort), thoroughness (quality), flexibility to accommodate work schedules, attendance, adherence to rules that require confronting a customer, and negative behaviors (for example, nonwork behavior, improper behavior, and theft). More typically, the management literature on customer service attempts to understand the service process, including facilitators and inhibitors, and to categorize the varieties of customer expectations and how to meet or exceed them. Total Quality Management, for instance, involves measurement and continuous improvement of processes, products, and culture to satisfy external and internal customers (Chowanec, 1993). It and other approaches acknowledge that company performance depends on more than focusing on what behaviors the service provider is performing.

Service Is More Than Task Performance

Industrial-organizational psychologists have written about the distinction between task performance (formal activities required as part of the job) and contextual performance (activities that often extend beyond the formal job description yet contribute to an organization's success) (Borman and Motowidlo, 1993). Contextual performance includes organizational citizenship behaviors (OCBs; Smith, Organ, and Near, 1983) and prosocial behaviors (Brief and Motowidlo, 1986), which may include cooperating, helping, and volunteering in situations not mandated or expected in the job role. Serving customers typically involves both a task and a contextual component. Successful service may depend on contextual performance and extra-role behaviors because service employees are typically beholden to multiple stakeholders even in entry-level, individual contributor (nonmanagement) positions, and each type of stakeholder may have different requirements, needs, and preferences.

The difference between bare minimum and exemplary performance might be described as the number and frequency of contextual behaviors relative to some threshold of task-oriented performance. Often performance of the task is taken for granted, as if, in customers' minds, it is the analogue of a "hygiene" motivational factor (Herzberg, 1966), a minimum that itself does not inspire (or in this case, satisfy). Indeed, customer satisfaction frequently depends on not only delivering the service on time and without error, but also on providing more than technical competence and basic fulfillment of the service. An example is the telephone service representative who not only answers a billing question but also, after listening carefully to the customer while reviewing the customer's transaction history, chooses to apply a discretionary, unprompted discount to reward the customer's loyalty. The distinction between what the employee can do (capabilities) and will do (motivation) is especially important for distinguishing adequate from superior customer service performance. We return to the task versus contextual performance distinction in our discussion of the attributes that are most closely associated with successful customer service providers.

Dimensions of Service Quality

In service and marketing fields, researchers who have focused on parsing the meaning of quality have been especially influential (see Schneider and White, 2004, for an update of dimensions of service quality). Parasuraman, Zeithaml, and Berry (1985) identified ten dimensions of service quality and narrowed these to five general, measurable dimensions. On closer inspection, one can see that the dimensions include both task performance and contextual, motivational performance. The original ten were access to services, communication with the customer, competence, courtesy, credibility, reliability, and the "tangibles" (physical appearance) of company materials, facilities, and people. Zeithaml, Parasuraman, and Berry (1990) refined a service quality survey that includes the following dimensions: reliability, responsiveness, assurance, empathy, and tangibles. Reliability is the ability to perform as promised and to be dependable. Responsiveness is the willingness to be prompt and to help. Assurance includes both knowledge and courtesy, engendering the customer's trust. Empathy includes individualized attention and caring. Tangibles are the physical qualities (for example, appearance) of the organization (Zeithaml, Parasuraman, and Berry, 1990).

The Four Stakeholder Perspectives About Service Performance

This section describes key dimensions of valued service performance for each of the four perspectives: the customer, the supervisor, the organization, and the service provider. Because this is a new taxonomy, previous research on service performance does not provide an unambiguous description of the performance dimensions most important to each perspective. The taxonomy we offer is based on a combination of previous research and our own experience working with service jobs. Exhibit 5.1 shows the four perspectives and the dimensions constituting each.

The Customer Perspective

Management research on service quality tends to focus on the customer's perspective about service. While some features of service quality reflect process or system characteristics such as access to services and the tangibles of service (see Zeithaml, Parasuraman, and Berry, 1990), other features represent the contribution of the service provider to the customer's experience of service (in particular, Zeithaml, Parasuraman, and Berry, 1990), dimensions of reliability, responsiveness, assurance, and empathy. Although these dimensions can be parsed into subfacets, we propose that they represent a meaningful summary of the key features of service provider performance with an impact on customers' evaluations of their service experience.

Interestingly, these four dimensions of the customer's perspective can be further divided into what service the employee pro-

Exhibit 5.1. Stakeholders in Service Performance.

Stakeholder Perspective	Components of Valued Service Performance
Customer perspective	Reliability
	Responsiveness
	Assurance
	Empathy
Supervisor perspective	Administrative task performance
	Customer-oriented task performance
	Job knowledge
	Organization citizenship behaviors
	Attendance behaviors
Organization perspective	Safety, security, and code of conduct
	Health and welfare
	Tenure and turnover
	Culture and climate
	Workforce flexibility
	Organization-level citizenship
	Organization service strategies
Service provider perspective	Job/career progression
	Self-management
	Job satisfaction
	Organization commitment

vides and how it is provided. The "what" is resolving the customer's basic need (for example, answering an inquiry about service policies, resolving a billing dispute, and entering the information into the computer system). Accuracy and completeness are examples of metrics of "what" success. The assurance dimension depends in part on "what" service is provided in that accurate, effective solutions are likely to lead to a customer's perception of assurance. In contrast, reliability, responsiveness, and empathy are largely a function of "how" the service is provided. "How" includes efficiency, timeliness, consistency of behavior, and a quality of social interaction that addresses the customer's interest in being understood and valued.

Customers of services may be external or internal to the service provider's own organization (for example, other service delivery employees, coworkers, or vendor partners). In many situations, service employees are accountable to each of these groups as recipients of some form of service behavior. A key distinction between internal and external customers is that internal customers are frequently subject to the same work performance metrics or standards as is the service provider, whereas external customers are not typically subject to any interests except their own. Given the often high expectations for customer service, satisfying external customers can be difficult because customers can occasionally make unreasonable demands or become verbally abusive (Grandey, Dickter, and Sin, 2004). Maintaining positive affect during harsh treatment requires considerable effort and can take its toll on the customer service provider, resulting in dissatisfaction and burnout (Grandey and Brauburger, 2002).

Supervisor Perspective

The supervisor's perspective about service performance is largely a function of the objectives, metrics, and day-to-day performance issues that define the interaction between the supervisor and individual service providers. We propose that five major dimensions represent the supervisor's perspective about service performance. As shown in Exhibit 5.1, supervisors typically engage service providers in:

- Administrative task performance
- Customer-oriented task performance
- Job knowledge
- Organization citizenship behavior
- Attendance behavior

Administrative task management includes the performance of a wide range of work rules and procedures such as task speed and accuracy, schedule adherence and management, prioritization of work activities, team functioning, and role specification.

Customer-oriented task management includes the supervisor's role in managing aspects of the service provider's interaction with customers. We make no assumption that the supervisor's interest in customer-oriented task management is consistent with the customer's interest in responsiveness, reliability, assurance, and empathy. Presumably in an effectively managed service organization, the supervisor's managed interest would be closely aligned with the customer's interests. However, it is virtually always the case that a natural tension exists between the supervisory requirements for efficient, low-cost, profitable customer management strategies that seek to minimize resource requirements for time and effort and the customer's interests in responsive, assuring, and empathetic service that can frequently demand time and effort. Customer-oriented task management includes specific activities such as frequency of contact, length of contact, outcome of contact (for example, sales, orders, schedule agreements), and less objectively managed activities such as quality of communication and customer handling. Certainly customer-oriented task management also includes customer satisfaction where supervisors have such information available as feedback to service providers.

We choose to separate job knowledge management from task management because the activities of job knowledge management tend to emphasize learning, whereas the activities of task management typically emphasize motivation ("answer quickly, or receive a lower performance appraisal") and learning ("say this in response to the customer's first objection"). This distinction relates to decisions about selection design in that learning behavior will be enhanced by selection based on general mental abilities, whereas motivated behavior is likely to be enhanced by selection based on dispositions, temperaments, past achievements, and interests.

In many service organizations, supervisors have a management interest in certain types of OCBs. Of the three major categories of such behaviors—loyalty, helping, and participation—supervisors are likely to have a direct interest in helping and participation behaviors that are directly related to service delivery. Such helping behavior may include providing just-in-time information or advice to fellow service providers who are handling pressing customer issues. Participation behavior of likely interest to supervisors includes participation as a local team leader or member or completion of quasi-supervisory roles such as schedule maintenance. These OCBs are directed toward the immediate work group or have direct impact on the delivery of service by other service providers.

Finally, supervisors typically have a strong interest in the range of behaviors relating to service providers' attendance management. Primarily this includes absence and tardiness, which are directly managed by supervisors in most cases. While it is certainly true that supervisors can cause and prevent turnover, we are excluding turnover management from this category of supervisor interests because turnover issues are frequently managed at the organization level rather than at the supervisor level. (This distinction assumes moderate to large service organizations; in small service organizations the distinctions we describe here between supervisor and organization interests may be completely blurred.)

Organization Perspective

The organization's perspective about service performance is defined largely by the organization-level consequences of service provider behavior that are overseen by managers and executives above the immediate supervisor level and that have an organization-wide scope. At the same time, it is important to acknowledge that organizations value both the customer and supervisor perspectives. Indeed, as a practical matter, organization-level decisions determine the supervisory roles, responsibilities, objectives, and metrics used to define the supervisor's perspective about service performance. The organization's interest in the performance of service providers includes behavior that affects:

- Safety, security, and code of conduct
- Health and welfare
- Tenure and turnover
- Culture and climate
- Workforce flexibility
- Organization-level citizenship
- Organization service strategies

Safety and security include a wide range of employee behaviors encompassing dishonest, criminal, or violent behavior, and other counterproductive or risky behavior such as drug- or alcohol-related problems.

Health and welfare include behavior that affects the health or well-being of employees in the workplace. These are mentioned here in the interest of comprehensiveness even though employment regulations restrict employers' ability to use employment selection as a tool for managing these interests.

Tenure and turnover are organizational issues that in many cases are particularly relevant to service work. Entry-level service jobs with little education or experience requirements are particularly prone to high turnover rates. Subsequently, organizations frequently structure these jobs to accommodate and manage the high turnover using part-time or temporary work strategies and other alternative work arrangements, such as telecommuting and virtual office strategies.

Some, but certainly not all, organizations have a strong interest in deliberately managing the culture and climate of their organization to facilitate pro-service behavior. We include this interest even though a focus on culture and climate may not imply any different employee behaviors than would be implied by a focus on those service-specific behaviors directly related to the customer or supervisor perspectives. However, a deliberate focus on an organization's culture and climate can provide direction about the relative importance of the many categories and dimensions of service provider behavior that determine whom the organization wants to hire.

An organization's interest in workforce flexibility may take many forms and have different implications for its service selection strategy. Some organizations may value having all employees achieve a certain level of education, say, a four-year college degree, to support a promote-from-within strategy. Other organizations may foster employee training and development to enable a larger proportion of employees to have the skills and knowledge to perform a wider range of functions. In any case, the organization's strategy around workforce deployment may have implications for the selection of service providers.

Like supervisors, organizations may have an interest in certain types of OCBs. The organization's interest would be in citizenship behaviors that drive organization-level outcomes, such as loyalty to the company and participation in organization-oriented programs or activities.

Finally, we identify service strategy as yet another service dimension from the organization's perspective. Service strategies are the specific interests an organization may have in directing decisions about the design of jobs and the embedded service delivery tactics, work management processes and systems, and the types of people to be hired into service positions. Our own experience has been that there is not always a clear, complete alignment between the organization's service strategy and the operationalization of service delivery. For example, an organization may have developed a strategy by which its telephone-based account representatives should seek to bridge incoming account inquiry calls to sales opportunities. Yet for many reasons, the account inquiry operation may not have implemented that strategy. In such a case, the organization's design of account rep selection systems may include an evaluation of sales skills and experience that would not be detected based on a job analysis of the work as it is actually performed. This phenomenon that the organization designs selection strategies that are not consistent with the work as it is currently designed may also occur where an organization seeks to use a selection strategy to implement new service behaviors that are not prevalent in the current work setting. The general point is that organization-level strategy planners may intend different service behaviors or tactics than are currently in place and seek to use selection to promote that desired change.

Service Provider Perspective

It may seem that the service provider perspective should not be relevant to the organization's design of the selection system. After all, the organization owns accountability for its own selection process. Nevertheless, organizations are likely to value selection strategies that help to improve outcomes for its service providers. For this reason, we choose to identify certain key outcomes for service providers as dimensions of the service provider perspective that may influence the design of effective selection strategies. These represent outcomes that have value for the service provider in addition to the value they may also create for the customer, the supervisor, and the organization. These include job or career progression, self-management, job satisfaction, and organizational commitment.

In addition to the workforce management benefit it creates for the organization, job or career progression represents a valued outcome for the service provider. For organizations that recruit based on an "employment deal" promoting job progression, the selection of service providers who experience such success is a desired outcome.

Effective self-management is particularly salient in many service jobs. As described above, stressors uniquely associated with service work often create burnout and dissatisfaction. Potentially competing demands from customers, supervisors, and organizations can require that service providers exert considerable psychological effort and energy to maintain the quality of service behavior in the face of such competing demands. Service providers who are capable of or disposed toward successfully managing such stressors are likely to suffer fewer ill effects of such stressors.

Closely related to self-management is the general outcome of job satisfaction. While many hundreds of studies have investigated the antecedents and consequences of job satisfaction, it is self-evident that it represents a positive outcome for service providers. Research typically represents job satisfaction as a causal variable leading to the types of outcomes that selection systems are designed to predict, such as turnover, task performance, and citizenship behavior. We also propose that job satisfaction is its own outcome for service providers and can be considered a dimension of valued service provider behavior to be optimized by effective selection systems.

Like job satisfaction, the service provider's commitment to remain in and act on behalf of the organization, which is frequently modeled in work research as a predictor of employee outcomes, can also be regarded as its own outcome that has value for the service provider.

Employee Attributes for Service Performance

In order to capture the full scope of employee attributes, the taxonomy described here is heavily influenced by the general work performance model described by Pearlman and Barney (2000) in their discussion of the impact of the changing workplace on selection strategies (see also Pearlman, 1997). The model represents the major categories of employee attributes that relate to both contextual and task performance as well as other outcomes of workplace behavior, including specific work outputs and other value-added benefits. This taxonomy is based on five broad domains of employee attributes: (1) life experience, (2) aptitudes and abilities, (3) acquired skills and knowledge, (4) personality, and (5) values, interests, and attitudes.

These domains are general and apply to performance and behavior in all work settings. However, the attributes within each of these domains were chosen to be relevant specifically to service work, as shown in Exhibit 5.2. This identification of attributes represents our attempt to reflect the research in a wide variety of domains, including person-organization fit (for example, Cable and Judge, 1997; Schneider, 1987; McCulloch and Silverhart, 2000), organization citizenship behaviors (for example, Organ and Ryan, 1995; Bettencourt, Gwinner, and Meuter, 2001), service climate (for example, Schneider, Salvaggio, and Subirats, 2002), the prediction of individual differences in job and training performance (for example, Schmidt and Hunter, 1998), personality (for example, Hogan, Hogan, and Busch, 1984; Hough and Schneider, 1996; Frei and McDaniel, 1998; Hogan and Holland, 2003), and attitudes and service outcomes (Schmit and Allscheid, 1995).

Life Experience

This domain of attributes refers to accomplishments in work, academic, and personal contexts that are indicative of similar future accomplishments. The distinction between life experience and acquired skills and knowledge, which generally are acquired through life experiences, is that Life Experience attributes are measured by assessing the event of the experience itself rather than the skill or knowledge produced by the experience. Life experiences can be assessed in a variety ways, including biodata instruments, résumé keyword searches, background checks, drug tests, behavioral accomplishment records, scored application blanks, and employment interviews.

Life experiences are relevant to service work on several dimensions. First, with respect to equal employment regulations, life experiences (other than convictions and drug use screens) are generally understood to be the types of information that organizations may use to determine whether a candidate satisfies the basic qualifications necessary to be considered an applicant as prescribed by

Exhibit 5.2. Mapping of Employee Attributes to Components of Service Performance.

Domain	Service-Related Attributes	Relevance to Components of Service Performance

Life Experience	• Employability factors
	  • Drug use
	  • Convictions
	• Education/training accomplishments
	• Work/life accomplishments
		• Administrative task performance
		• Safety, security, code of conduct
		• Tenure and turnover
		• Organization citizenship behavior
		• Organization culture and climate
		• Health and welfare
		• Self-management

Aptitudes and Abilities	• Problem solving • Perceptual speed • Verbal reasoning • Following directions • Multitasking	• Job knowledge acquisition • Administrative task performance • Turnover (performance related) • Customer assurance • Organization culture and climate • Workforce flexibility • Job or career progression • Health and welfare

Acquired Skills and Knowledge	Service-Related Attributes	Relevance to Components of Service Performance
Workplace	• Reading • Vocabulary • Writing • Arithmetic • Computer keyboard skills	• Job knowledge acquisition • Administrative task performance
Cross-Functional	• Oral communication • Interpersonal skills • Negotiation skills • Organizing and planning skills	• Workforce flexibility • Customer-oriented task performance • Administrative task performance • Customer empathy • Customer assurance

**Exhibit 5.2. Mapping of Employee Attributes
to Components of Service Performance, Cont'd.**

Domain	Service-Related Attributes	Relevance to Components of Service Performance
Occupational	• Trait richness • Strategy richness • Job data systems knowledge • Job content knowledge	• Customer-oriented task performance • Organization citizenship behavior • Job knowledge • Organization culture and climate
Personality	• Conscientiousness • Agreeableness • Emotional Stability • Extraversion • Service orientation • Integrity • Resilience • Empathy • Control (dominance) • Affiliation	• Tenure and turnover • Organization citizenship behavior • Self-management • Customer reliability • Customer responsiveness • Customer empathy • Administrative task performance • Customer-oriented task performance • Organization culture and climate • Job satisfaction • Safety, security, and code of conduct
Work-Related Values and Interests	• Job-specific interests and needs • Work satisfaction • Conventional • Social • Not realistic • Customer oriented • Detail oriented • Structure	• Tenure and turnover • Organization citizenship behavior • Job satisfaction • Organization commitment • Customer-oriented task performance • Job satisfaction • Organization culture and climate

the Equal Employment Opportunity Commission and the Office of Federal Contract Compliance Programs. Although as of this writing, these regulations are ambiguous particularly with respect to Web-sourced candidates, employers generally understand that previous work experience, training, and education are the types of factors that can be used to determine whether a candidate is basically qualified to be considered an applicant.

Second, by law, drug use and prior convictions may be used to screen applicants to support an employer's interest in a safe, secure, and drug-free work environment, regardless of their relevance to individual-level work outcomes. The employer's choice regarding these considerations will help shape the employer's culture and climate.

Third, research has demonstrated that life experience, particularly as assessed by biodata and interviews, is predictive of a wide range of work behavior, including sales, retention, and citizenship behavior.

Aptitudes and Abilities

Aptitudes and abilities are general attributes that represent the "capacity to perform particular classes or categories of mental or physical functions" (Pearlman and Barney, 2000, p. 22). The aptitudes and abilities likely to be relevant to service work are mental abilities, including cognitive abilities, primarily, and, where speed and volume metrics are important, perceptual speed. Abilities relating to psychomotor, spatial, or physical performance are far less likely to be relevant to service work. Extensive validation research (for example Schmidt and Hunter, 1998) has demonstrated the broad relevance of cognitive abilities to performance in a wide range of jobs, including service work. Because mental abilities are general, they enable work behavior across the full spectrum of work situations, settings, and types. Mental abilities are particularly relevant to work behavior that is dependent on learning and information processing. In service work, mental abilities are relevant to training mastery, administrative task proficiency, and overall performance. Such general abilities also are expected to contribute to successful progression and retention of employees where those depend on demonstrated performance success.

Acquired Skills and Knowledge

Acquired skills and knowledge refer to work-related, learned skills and knowledge that range from basic workplace skills and knowledge (relevant to virtually all work settings), to cross-functional skills and knowledge relevant to groups of occupations that share similar features (for example, fields of work), to occupational skills and knowledge that are specific to particular jobs. These three levels of acquired skills and knowledge are hierarchical in the sense that the acquisition of the most job-specific level of skill and knowledge implies that more general forms of skill and knowledge have also been acquired. For example, mastering a job-specific customer data management system, an occupational knowledge, implies mastery of reading skills, a basic workplace skill.

The basic workplace skills and knowledge most relevant to service work relate to the skill requirements of written and verbal information processing, communication skills, and computer use skills. Basic language skills such as vocabulary, writing skills, and reading skills are relevant to virtually all service work. Similarly, basic arithmetic and computing skills are likely to be relevant to a large proportion of service jobs that engage the customer in quantitative transactions relating to cost amounts, time periods, order volumes, and the like. However, these workplace skills are not distinctive to service work.

In contrast, cross-functional skills and knowledge are more specific to the requirements of work that involve customer interactions. These include oral communication skills, interpersonal skills, and more specific negotiation skills. In addition, because service workers typically are required to exercise some degree of decision making based on real-time information processing, skills related to information management such as organizing and planning are likely to be relevant. A case can be made that complex, real-time information management is becoming more characteristic of service work. For better or worse, technological advances are producing increasingly automated customer interactions where the nature of the information exchange is reducible to finite systematic algorithms that control automated voice response systems. The result is that the remaining customer interaction work staffed by people tends to be for interactions that are more complex and more demanding of human judgment or human interaction that goes beyond the mere application of precise rules.

The relevance of workplace and cross-functional skills and knowledge focuses on work behaviors and outcomes that result from learning rather than dispositions or interests. At the level of the individual employee, these include training mastery, administrative task proficiency, communication effectiveness, and the fit between the customer's need and the solution provided. At the organizational level, workplace and cross-functional skills enable workforce flexibility by providing employees with relatively interchangeable skills.

Finally, occupational skills and knowledge are specific to service work. They can take many forms, ranging from knowledge of work management systems and software to skill with techniques for managing customer interactions. Of particular interest are two service-specific knowledge domains defined by Sujan, Sujan, and Bettman (1988): trait richness and strategy richness. Trait richness refers to the knowledge of customer types or categories (traits) that are diagnostic of appropriate methods and techniques for effectively addressing the customer's need. Strategy richness refers to the knowledge of strategies, methods, and techniques for responding to customers' needs and the repertoire of behaviors for effectively interacting with different types of customers. Bettencourt, Gwinner, and Meuter (2001) showed that these customer knowledge categories are predictive of organizational citizenship behaviors particularly relating to group participation in developing service improvements and promotions and to delivering effective service to customers. The implication of this relationship between work knowledge and organizational citizenship behaviors is that organization-level attributes such as culture and climate are also likely to be affected by the levels and types of employees' acquired work knowledge. As noted below, a number of authors (see, for example, Schneider, 1996; Hogan and Blake, 1996; Hogan and Holland, 2003) emphasize the link between employees' interests and organization-level characteristics. Bettencourt, Gwinner, and Meuter's results (2001) suggest that organization-level characteristics such as customer orientation are likely to be influenced by employees' acquired knowledge that is specific to the service aspects of the work and organization.

Personality

Personality refers to personal traits representing behavioral patterns that are consistent across situations. As applied in employment selection settings, the assessment of personality traits is generally accomplished by self-report scales that are not specific to work behavior. Considerable research has demonstrated that the Big Five Factor model of personality (Conscientiousness, Agreeableness, Openness, Neuroticism, and Extraversion) fits most personality measures reasonably well (Digman, 1990), although some argue that this model is in need of refinement (Hough and Schneider, 1996). In any case, it certainly is well understood that facets of each of the five factors can be meaningfully distinguished and described. The relationship of personality to work behavior in service jobs can be understood by considering three levels of description of personality. First, at the five-factor level, the general result that Conscientiousness predicts several aspects of work behavior in a wide variety of jobs (Barrick and Mount, 1991) indicates that Conscientiousness is related to a variety of work behaviors in service work, including task proficiency, customer service, retention, absenteeism, and tardiness.

At the second level of analysis, two compound personality variables (composites of more unitary personality variables) also have received considerable attention: Integrity and Service Orientation. Like Conscientiousness, Integrity has been demonstrated to consistently predict counterproductive behaviors across a wide range of types of jobs (Ones, Viswesvaran, and Schmidt, 1993; Schmidt and Hunter, 1998). Integrity has been assessed in a variety of forms, including direct assessments of respondents' reports of counterproductive behavior. The unitary personality variables comprising Integrity are less than clear-cut. However, where Integrity has been assessed as a composite of general personality traits, it has been shown by some researchers to depend on facets of Conscientiousness and Emotional Stability (Hough, 1992; Ones, Schmidt, and Viswesvaran, 1994). There is mixed evidence from the same authors that Achievement and Agreeableness are linked to Integrity.

Service Orientation also has been measured as a composite of personality factors pertaining to an individual's propensity to perform customer service work (Hogan, Hogan, and Busch, 1984; Costa and McCrae, 1995; Frei and McDaniel, 1998). In a meta-analysis of forty-one validities involving Service Orientation predictors, Frei and McDaniel (1998) reported an average observed validity of .24, which increased to .50 when corrected for criterion unreliability and range restriction. More recently, Bettencourt, Gwinner, and Meuter (2001) reported two studies showing substantial observed correlations ranging from .37 to .63 between Service Orientation and three types of service-oriented organizational citizenship behaviors: loyalty, service delivery, and participation. It is important to note that the available published research on measures of Service Orientation has largely been the work of a few major consulting houses. And like Integrity, Service Orientation is defined differently in different published scales. Interestingly, as reported by Costa and McCrae (1995) and Frei and McDaniel (1998), some instruments have defined it to include some of the same high-level traits that Ones, Schmidt, and Viswesvaran (1994) concluded underlie Integrity: Emotional Stability, Agreeableness, and Conscientiousness.

At the third level of analysis, facets of personality traits may also have specific relationships with service work behaviors beyond their association with Conscientiousness, Integrity, or Service Orientation. One possibility is worth brief consideration here, in spite of the small amount of empirical evidence. Bettencourt, Gwinner, and Meuter (2001) report evidence that affective empathy (sympathetic and emotional association with customers) had little relationship with service performance in call center representative jobs and customer contact library jobs. Furthermore, it is notable that commonly used Service Orientation measures tend not to weigh Sociability heavily but rather focus on Emotional Stability, Agreeableness, and Conscientiousness. The implication is that successful customer service, particularly in high-volume problem-oriented settings, may depend more on the ability and willingness to sustain energy in the face of demanding interactions than on the ability to affectively empathize with customers. An irony of this observation may be that the climate of successful customer service organizations may be defined less by affiliative, affectively sensitive employees than by friendly, good-natured, resilient employees.

Values and Interests

A basic question about values and interests is, "How are they different from personality traits?" Values and interests might be described as the objects of an individual's behavior, whereas personality traits might be described as characteristics of an individual's behavior. As Hogan and Blake (1996) note in summarizing Strong's view (1955), values and interests are about motives; they are about the directedness of our actions—our likes and dislikes, the things we seek and those we avoid. In contrast, personality traits are descriptions of our typical behavior: what is characteristic of the behavior, not what drives it. In this discussion of customer service work behavior, however, we make the assumption that, at least as they are operationalized, values and interests are motivational in description, unlike personality traits, and are usually measured in more work-related contexts than personality is. Certainly they are connected in meaning but not completely. Typical correlations between Holland's six vocational interests—Realistic, Investigative, Artistic, Social, Enterprising, and Conventional—and the five-factor model personality traits most similar in meaning range from the low .20s to the low .40s (Hogan and Blake, 1996). Notably, Emotional Stability does not correlate with any of the six interest types. Conscientiousness tends to correlate with Conventional, Extraversion with Social and Enterprising, Agreeableness with Social and (negatively) Realistic, and Openness with Artistic and Investigative.

In addition to Strong's vocational interests, work and organization values have been identified as the basis for evaluating the fit between individuals and organizations. One model in particular, developed by O'Reilly, Chatman, and Caldwell (1991), has been used by LIMRA International, an insurance industry research and development organization, as the basis for a culture fit assessment tool that has been validated in customer service contexts (see Exhibit 5.3). O'Reilly, Chatman, and Caldwell's culture fit model is based on a set of nine features of work and organizations: innovation, structure, pace, stability, achievement orientation, customer orientation, coworker orientation, detail orientation, and professionalism. Fit is measured by first having subject matter experts describe the organization on these nine features and then having

Exhibit 5.3. Service Culture Types Based on LIMRA's 2003 Analysis of Call Centers.

Culture Type	Distinctive Culture Features	Organization Characteristics
"Fast and Friendly"	• Very high achievement orientation • Very high customer orientation • By-the-book rules and directives • High predictability or repetition	• Quick help, high call volume • Fast pace • Highly defined structure • High turnover (26 percent) • High customer satisfaction • Health care and pharmaceutical call centers
"Concierge Level"	• High warmth, low burnout • Very high customer orientation • High urgency • Low "by-the-book" • Low predictability or repetition	• High-end, expert service • Complex and varied interactions • High autonomy • Low turnover (12 percent), high morale • Moderate customer satisfaction • Computer, software, and information technology centers • Retail industry centers
"Frenzied"	• Low stability • High urgency	• Low call volume • Short-term employment • Moderate turnover (22 percent) • High morale • Average customer satisfaction • Professional services centers • Business advisory centers

**Exhibit 5.3. Service Culture Types Based on
LIMRA's 2003 Analysis of Call Centers, Cont'd.**

Culture Type	Distinctive Culture Features	Organization Characteristics
"Quick and Slick"	• High entrepreneurship and opportunity • Low customer orientation • Low warmth, high burnout • High predictability and repetition • Low urgency	• Low education levels • Low customer satisfaction • High turnover (31 percent) • Various industries
"Stuck in Low Gear"	• Low achievement orientation • Low customer orientation • Low entrepreneurship • High predictability and repetition • High stability	• Low education • Low customer satisfaction • Low morale • Low turnover (14 percent) • Nonprofit organizations • Product and manufacturing centers

individuals describe their work and organization values using the same features. For each individual, fit is assessed as an index of profile match between the individual's value profile and the organization's feature profile.

Both vocational interests and culture fit values may be expected to influence work behavior through their impact on job satisfaction and affective organization commitment. Barge and Hough (1988) reported eighteen studies showing a median correlation of .31 between vocational interests and job satisfaction. In turn, Organ and Ryan's meta-analysis (1995) showed correlations in the .20s and .30s between organization citizenship behaviors and job satisfaction and affective organization commitment. McCulloch and Silverhart (2000) showed correlations in the low .30s between culture fit and tenure specifically in call center representative jobs.

Overall, less research has evaluated the relationships between values and interests and subsequent work behavior than has evaluated the relationship between aptitudes and personality and work behaviors. Nevertheless, the emerging picture is pointing to a causal chain between values and interests influencing job satisfaction and affective organization commitment, which in turn influence key work behaviors including tenure and organization citizenship behaviors such as loyalty, participation, general workplace compliance, and effective delivery of customer service.

Designing Selection Strategies for Service Work

The previous sections have described the basic building blocks of a selection strategy for service work: the various components of service behavior and the employee attributes that lead to those behaviors. In order to make decisions about which attributes to target for which service behaviors, it is necessary to consider what is important to the organization and what is possible given organization contexts and constraints. This section integrates these considerations into a description of methods for designing selection strategies for service work.

Work Context

To understand the relative importance of the range of possible service behaviors, it is important to consider the work and organizational context in which they are performed. The work context not only acts to facilitate or inhibit service performance, but can determine what performance aspects are perceived as important by the organization's employees and what aspects are in fact important.

As with all other selection development work, an appropriate analysis of the work itself is central to the decision about which candidate attributes should be assessed. In our experience, four major features of service work are important in determining the relative importance of experience, abilities, acquired skills and knowledge, personality, and values and interests in the selection of service workers: work complexity, work structure, customer engagement, and customer influence.

The information complexity of service work varies from low (for example, ticket takers, parking attendants) to very high (for example, high-tech troubleshooters, nurses), which determines the relative importance of cognitive abilities (Hunter and Hunter, 1984). In most service jobs, it is likely that cognitive ability will have substantial utility. The degree of complexity will help guide decisions about the relative weight placed on cognitive ability in a compensatory strategy or the minimum level of cognitive ability required to meet minimum qualification requirements, if used.

There can be several dimensions to the structure built into service work, including system and process rules for administrative tasks, guidelines or scripts governing the tactics of customer interaction and establishing boundary conditions for problem resolution, and metrics or objectives by which performance is managed. Although structure can influence the information complexity of work, thereby affecting the importance of cognitive abilities, it can also have a substantial effect on the range of opportunity for other personal attributes of the service worker to influence work outcomes. High structure can reduce autonomy, which has been shown to moderate the influence of the "big five" personality factors on performance (Barrick and Mount, 1993). In addition to moderating the validity of individual difference variables, structure can constitute an element of organization climate that influences psychological processes such as satisfaction, coping, commitment, and work motivation leading to outcomes including turnover, stress effects, and proficiency. In general, high structure that creates a strong climate is likely to decrease the relative importance of personality attributes relating to dependability, achievement, and extraversion and increase the importance of person-organization fit based on candidates' work-related values and interests.

By definition, service work entails interaction with customers or others. These interactions can vary considerably with respect to the degree of personal engagement required of the employee. High-engagement interactions require interpersonal skills for sustaining an effective interaction and may also require deliberate, effortful responses that in many cases are inconsistent with the employee's current affect. Acting friendly when feeling hostility, remaining calm when angry, and responding energetically when discouraged by rejection all require behavior that is inconsistent with affect. Similar to the dual effects of work structure, customer engagement not only influences the relevance of interpersonal skills and knowledge such as strategy richness but also influences the importance of self-management skills such as coping skills (Grandey, Dickter, and Sin, 2004). In general, higher levels of customer engagement tend to increase the relative importance of personality attributes and values and interests relating to interpersonal behavior.

Separate from customer engagement is the extent to which employees' behavior can influence the customer's desired response. This aspect of service work is distinct from customer engagement in that high-engagement service work may be associated with either high-influence or low-influence work. It seems highly likely that low-engagement work will also be low-influence work. An example of high-engagement, low-influence service work might be certain types of account inquiry jobs in which, once the relevant information is known, the range of response options is highly prescribed. In such work, customers call with billing or account questions or problems that may require considerable fact finding and possibly considerable interpersonal effort to behave empathetically. However, once the customer's information is gathered, the service provider may have few options for resolution, which may or may not be satisfactory to the customer. The ultimate desired customer behavior is to remain a customer of the service provider. The service provider's behavior may be much less relevant to the customer's choice than the features of the prescribed resolution to the original inquiry. In contrast, other high-engagement service jobs are also high-influence jobs. Frequently these types of service jobs share many features with sales jobs. For example, associates in home repair department stores engage in substantial information exchange with customers and frequently are expected to offer advice about the best methods, approaches, tools, and equipment to accomplish the home repair activity. These positions may be considered service jobs rather than sales jobs because they are not measured or compensated on individual sales results. However, the desired customer behaviors include purchase behavior and loyalty, which may be influenced to a great extent by the service provider. The degree of customer influence is likely to affect the relative importance of acquired customer handling skills, cognitive ability, and personality facets related to attributes such as achievement, dependability, and resilience.

Business Constraints and Priorities

The traditional starting point regarding the design of selection systems is a careful analysis of the work itself to understand the tasks and context and the worker attributes associated with success. This certainly is a necessary, but not sufficient, step. This chapter's perspective is that another step—understanding the business constraints and priorities relating to the management of the service workforce—is necessary and frequently precedes and directs any useful analysis of the work itself.

Business Priorities for Service Workforce Management

A wide variety of business priorities for workforce management may exist across the diversity of service organizations. For example, large call centers with highly prescribed work and effective training may place more importance on vacancy management—minimizing the daily average of unfilled seats—than on any other single feature of their workforce. Other service organizations that support complex, but seasonal, service work may require trainability more than anything else. Others may emphasize schedule flexibility, or teamwork, or something else.

These business priorities should be viewed as separate from information about the work itself even though they may be related. In part, this is because these may be the priorities of individual managers who are responding to their most pressing needs, which may be a function of the manager's job more than the service representative's job. Managers' priorities may be based on other considerations in addition to the requirements of effective task performance and contextual behavior that presumably would be identified by analysis of the work itself. For example, vacancy management may well be the most pressing administrative problem that call center managers face day in and day out, particularly in tight employment markets or in periods of rapid business growth. As a result, managers in such situations may place more emphasis on managing the employment pipeline than on the skills of the newly hired employees. The task performance and contextual behavior of an empty seat contribute little to a manager's business objectives.

In our experience, the business requirements most likely to influence the design of selection strategies for service work are:

- Salience of speed and cost of employment
- Volatility of hiring volume
- Role of hiring manager in hiring decisions
- Use of part-time or temporary service workers
- Salience of local employment competition

Speed and Cost of Employment

It may seem obvious to make the point that the importance of employment speed and cost will influence the design of a selection process. However, service organizations may be quite different with regard to the importance they place on both issues. For example, service organizations that experience high turnover and follow a management strategy that emphasizes fully staffed workforces may place an overriding importance on rapid employment processes that minimize vacant positions. In this type of environment, selection procedures will be highly valued that can produce job offers on the same day that candidates go through the employment process. As a practical matter, this requirement would eliminate live, telephone-based work samples that may require advanced scheduling and screening. In contrast, service organizations that experience low turnover and highly predictable work volumes may have much less need for one-day turnaround of candidates. In this business environment, there may be more tolerance for multiple event screening processes that required candidates to return for a second round of assessment. The source of employment efficiency in such an environment may depend more on the continual maintenance of a pipeline of interested, qualified candidates than on rapid turnaround of newly recruited candidates.

The issue of cost also has nuances. The first facet of this issue is, "Whose money is paying?" If corporate funding is paying for employment processes, the managers of the hiring organization may have little concern about the cost of the selection process. But if operational budgets are funding the local employment process, cost is likely to be a far more significant issue. In this case, the second facet of this issue is likely to emerge. A basic principle of operational business economics is likely to influence managers' support of selection processes. Put succinctly, this principle is that a dollar of an operations budget is worth much more than a dollar of human resource value.

Managers almost always attach more importance and worth to dollars in their budget than to dollars associated with the value of human resource programs. Budget dollars are tangible; they can be spent. Usually human resource–value dollars cannot be spent. Managers are held directly accountable for budget dollars but only indirectly, if at all, for human resource–value dollars. Budget dollars are usually a very finite resource, whereas human resource–value dollars frequently seem to multiply beyond credible amounts. For many reasons, the issue of cost is usually not a simple matter of demonstrating higher human resource value than required budget dollars. It is important to understand the importance of budget dollars to operations managers to understand their willingness to invest in selection processes. To be sure, this issue is not unique to managers in service organizations. However, compared to other work outputs, the value of service is frequently far less tangible than the value of budget dollars.

Volatility of Hiring Volume

The demand for employees can be highly volatile for service organizations. Certainly variability in high turnover rates can be one reason. In addition, sudden changes in business conditions can have a dramatic and quick impact on hiring volumes. Service organizations such as telemarketing and order processing centers that are driven by an organization's marketing strategy can experience unpredicted and large changes in work volumes. For example, an organization's competitor may introduce a new marketing strategy, which may drive that organization to unexpectedly introduce a new business offer that triggers a large number of new incoming calls from interested customers. The travel industry is notorious for just this type of marketing volatility. One airline's announcement of new fares frequently triggers similar responses from competitors. Such marketing is intended to suddenly increase the number of customer calls, which may require a sudden increase in the number of service workers. Also, seasonal changes, even if predictable, may require rapid increases in employment volume.

This volatility in employment volume suggests at least two types of selection strategies. One is to design a regular selection process that is simple and rapid enough and with sufficient capacity that it can be quickly accelerated or decelerated on short notice. Selection processes that rely on Web-enabled tools with relatively low security requirements may satisfy this requirement. An alternative approach is to design a regular selection process that supports steady-state employment volumes and an alternative version of that process for high-volume periods. A common example would be to have paper-and-pencil testing materials available for mass testing to replace computer-based testing at a limited number of stations. In this example, the requirements remain the same, but the methods of delivery are changed. A third alternative is to change the requirements either by suspending time-consuming requirements such as work sample exercises or extensive background checks or by reducing the minimum qualification requirements, thereby increasing the yield of the regular process. This third alternative is likely to be easier to implement but also riskier because it may change the degree of adverse impact and reduce the skill levels of new employees.

Role of the Hiring Manager

A key element in all selection processes is the role of the hiring manager. Our experience has been that hiring managers, for any of several reasons, may take on any one of three distinct roles: receiver of new employees, decider among qualified candidates, or owner of the whole decision process. In general, selection processes designed to support "receivers" tend to be comprehensive and have automatic decision rules based on cut scores or other quantitative rules for determining which candidates receive job offers. Selection procedures designed to support "deciders" may have minimum standards on core or basic requirements that determine who the qualified candidates are who will be presented to the deciding manager to make the employment decision. Depending on the tolerance for speed and cost, these processes may also be comprehensive and assess candidates on the full range of important attributes, then reject some of the candidates based on minimum standards, and finally present the remaining candidates and information about their attributes to the deciding manager.

Selection processes designed to support "owners" may take any of several forms. At one end of the spectrum, these may consist of methods for recruiting the candidates sought by the "owner," screening for organization-level minimum requirements such as drug testing and background checks for related convictions and for minimum education or work experience requirements, and then presenting all remaining candidates. Certainly a structured interview process for the "owner's" use would be beneficial. At the other end of the spectrum, the "owner" may be satisfied to approve the specific components of an automatic screening process.

Our experience with large service centers in which many employees occupy the same job is that the hiring managers are usually not inclined to assert an "owner" role in the actual selection process but are satisfied to be "receivers" or "deciders." The design of supervisor and manager jobs in such large centers can result in ratios of service employees to supervisors that might range from twenty-to-one to forty-to-one. Such a large span of control does not allow supervisors and managers sufficient time to be personally involved in all employment decisions.

An important consideration is the manner in which position-specific requirements will be handled. These are requirements that may be important for some positions within a job or job family but unimportant for other positions. For service jobs, these requirements usually involve acquired skills or knowledge, such as typing, foreign language skills or knowledge of specific software, or specific work experiences. Selection processes designed for "receivers" will need to account for these position-specific requirements in the automatic process. However, for "deciders" and "owners," at least some of these position-specific requirements may be left to the hiring manager to evaluate.

Part-Time or Temporary Jobs

A frequent workforce strategy in service organizations is to rely on part-time or temporary employees. On its face, this strategy may not appear to change the attributes required for successful performance or desired contextual behavior. After all, these employees frequently perform the same tasks under the same work conditions as regular, full-time employees. Even if this were true, the utility equation, if you will, changes for the selection process. The use of part-time or temporary employees increases the number of employees necessary to "fill" the prescribed full-time equivalent (FTE) positions. For example, if a service organization uses students to work ten to fifteen hours per week each, the number of employees necessary to fill a specific number of FTEs will be approximately triple the number of regular full-time employees necessary to fill the same number of FTEs. This effect is magnified to the extent that part-time and temporary workers turn over at higher rates than regular full-time employees. For example, a business strategy that uses one-third-time workers who turn over twice as often as full-time workers will require six times as many employees compared to full-time employees. As a result, the cost of the selection process will be six times higher per FTE for positions filled with these part-time workers.

It is instructive to compare this cost impact to the rate of return (utility) for a good-quality selection procedure for entry-level service work. This example will focus only on test-based selection procedures, not other procedures such as drug tests and background checks that might be required by corporate policies regarding workplace safety and security. All of the assumptions described below are based on real costs and representative values in our experience with large call center selection processes. To begin, we make the reasonable assumption that wages for this entry-level service work are $25,000 per year ($12 per hour). Next, we make the rule-of-thumb assumption that the dollar value to the organization of a service worker is two times pay, which is $50,000 per year. The next rule-of-thumb assumption is that the standard deviation of dollar value is one-fifth of the average annual worth, $10,000 per year. Now we consider a modest selection procedure consisting of a test event that combines a cognitive ability test with a personality inventory costing approximately $150 per candidate to schedule, administer, and score, and having a (conservative) validity of approximately .40. Finally, we assume that the organization sets minimum qualification standards such that the top 40 percent pass. The result of these assumptions is that the total cost of testing per new employee is approximately $450. Furthermore, we assume that the turnover rate is 25 percent among full-time employees and 50 percent among part-time employees who work one-third time each. As a result, for each FTE position, 1.25 full-time employees would need to be hired to fill one position for a year (assuming we start with a vacant position) and .25 per year after that. This means that for, say, a four-year period, an average of 2.0 full-time employees would need to be hired per position. In contrast, 4.5 part-time employees would need to be hired to fill one position for a year and 1.5 per year after that, for a total of 9.0 over the same four year period. As a result, for a four-year period, the total cost of selection testing to fill one position and keep it filled with full-time employees is $900 (2 × $450). Over that same four-year period, the total cost of selection testing to fill one position and keep it filled with one-third-time employees is $4,050 (9 × $450).

Given the mean, $50,000, and standard deviation, $10,000, of dollar value, a selection procedure with a validity of .40 and selection ratio of .40 will increase the value per employee hired by approximately $3,900 to $53,900. Over four years, the total dollar benefit is $15,600 (4 × $3,900). In this example, then, for full-time employees, the ratio of benefit to cost over four years is $15,600 to $900, or 17.3 to 1. For positions filled with part-time employees, the ratio is $15,600 to $4,050, or 3.8 to 1. This result shows that the decision to use part-time employees can substantially reduce the utility of selection, although in this example, the utility remains substantial for positions filled with part-time employees.

Without going into as much detail, it is interesting to note the impact of part-time positions on a high-end selection process. Given the same business conditions as above, we make the realistic assumptions that a live telephone simulation was added to the selection process, with the result that validity increased to .50, the overall selection ratio decreased to .20, and the cost of testing per employee hired increased to $1,900. The benefit increases to approximately $9,000 per year per position, or $36,000 over four years. The four-year testing cost for full-time employees is $3,800 and $17,100 for part-time employees. In this case, the benefit-to-cost ratio is 9.5 to 1 for full-time employees and 2.1 to 1 for part-time employees.

The implication of these examples is that the business strategy to use part-time employees can reduce the benefit-to-cost ratio for selection testing substantially, but even for the most elaborate selection processes, the actual dollar benefit is likely to remain substantial.

Salience of Local Employment Competition

In service work such as fast food order taking, telemarketing, and retail clerk work, it is not unusual for service companies to be in active competition for employees with very similar nearby companies. Also, the work and employment conditions can be highly similar precisely because the companies know what one another is offering. In situations where the work, the pay, the working conditions, and the location are all highly similar, differences in the employment processes may have substantial impact on an organization's ability to attract good candidates. Distinctively different selection processes may affect recruiting success.

In our experience with service organizations, three types of selection processes are often viewed by hiring managers as barriers to effective recruiting when other nearby organizations with similar work do not have the same requirements. Drug testing, background checks, and psychological testing are frequently regarded by hiring managers as harming their recruiting interests. Even where managers may understand the benefits of such screens, local competition with nearby similar employers creates pressure to design selection procedures that do not discourage candidates from applying. Discouragement might come from mere inconvenience ("It's easier to apply for jobs over there") to concerns about likely success or privacy. The problem is compounded for plentiful entry-level part-time service jobs that do not offer benefits. It may be difficult for such organizations to convince would-be candidates that the extra effort is worth it.

In any case, the selection designer is well advised to become aware of the selection processes that nearby employment competitors use. It is likely to be difficult to sustain a selection process that is substantially more demanding or perceived as less relevant or less fair than the competitors' selection processes without some countervailing attraction such as schedule flexibility, pay, and promotion opportunities.

References

Austin, J., and Villanova, P. "The Criterion Problem: 1917–1992." *Journal of Applied Psychology*, 1992, 77, 836–874.

Barrick, M. R., and Mount, M. K. "The Big Five Personality Dimensions and Job Performance: A Meta-Analysis." *Personnel Psychology*, 1991, *44*, 1–26.

Barrick, M. R., and Mount, M. K. "Autonomy as a Moderator of the Relationship Between the Big Five Personality Dimensions and Job Performance." *Journal of Applied Psychology*, 1993, *78*, 111–118.

Barge, B. N., and Hough, L. M. "Utility of Interest Assessment for Predicting Job Performance." In L. M. Hough (ed.), *Utility of Temperament, Biodata, and Interest Assessment for Predicting Job Performance: A Review and Integration of the Literature*. Alexandria, Va.: U.S. Army Research Institute for the Behavioral and Social Sciences, 1988.

Bettencourt, L. A., Gwinner, K. P., and Meuter, M. L. "A Comparison of Attitude, Personality, and Knowledge Predictors of Service-Oriented Organizational Citizenship Behaviors." *Journal of Applied Psychology*, 2001, *86*, 29–41.

Borman, W. C., and Motowidlo, S. "Expanding the Criterion Domain to Include Elements of Contextual Performance." In N. Schmitt and W. C. Borman (eds.), *Personnel Selection in Organizations*. San Francisco: Jossey-Bass, 1993.

Brief, A. P., and Motowidlo, S. J. "Prosocial Organizational Behaviors." *Academy of Management Review*, 1986, *11*, 710–725.

Cable, D., and Judge, T. A. "Interviewers' Perceptions of Person-Organization Fit and Organizational Selection Decisions." *Journal of Applied Psychology*, 1997, *82*, 546–561.

Chowanec, G. D. "TQM: Evaluating Service Quality." *Consulting Psychology Journal*, 1993, *45*, 1061–1087.

Costa, P. T., and McCrae, R. R. "Domains and Facets: Hierarchical Personality Assessment Using the Revised NEO Personality Inventory." *Journal of Personality Assessment*, 1995, *64*, 21–50.

Digman, J. M. "Personality Structure: Emergence of the Five-Factor Model." In M. R. Rosenzweig and L. W. Porter (eds.), *Annual Review of Psychology*, vol. 41. Palo Alto, Calif.: Annual Reviews, 1990.

Frei, R. L., and McDaniel, M. A. "Validity of Customer Service Measures in Personnel Selection: A Review of Criterion and Construct Evidence." *Human Performance*, 1998, *11*, 1–27.

Grandey, A., and Brauburger, A. "The Emotion Regulation Behind the Customer Service Smile." In R. K. Lord and R. Kanfer (eds.), *Emotion Regulation at Work*. San Francisco: Jossey-Bass, 2002.

Grandey, A. A., Dickter, D. N., and Sin, H. P. "The Customer Is *Not* Always Right: Customer Aggression and Emotion Regulation of Service Employees." *Journal of Organizational Behavior*, 2004, *25*, 397–418.

Herzberg, F. *Work and the Nature of Man*. Cleveland: World Publishing, 1966.

Hogan, R., and Blake, R. J. "Vocational Interests: Matching Self-Concept with the Environment." In K. R. Murphy (ed.), *Individual Differences and Behavior in Organizations.* San Francisco: Jossey-Bass, 1996.

Hogan, J., Hogan, R., and Busch, C. "How to Measure Service Orientation." *Journal of Applied Psychology,* 1984, *69,* 167–173.

Hogan, J., and Holland, B. "Using Theory to Evaluate Personality and Job-Performance Relations: A Socioanalytic Perspective." *Journal of Applied Psychology,* 2003, *88,* 100–112.

Hough, L. M. "The "Big Five" Personality Variables-Construct Confusion: Description Versus Prediction." *Human Performance,* 1992, *5,* 139–155.

Hough, L. M., and Schneider, R. J. "Personality Traits, Taxonomies, and Applications in Organizations." In K. R. Murphy (ed.), *Individual Differences and Behavior in Organizations.* San Francisco: Jossey-Bass, 1996.

Hunt, S. T. "Generic Work Behaviors: An Investigation into the Dimensions of Entry-Level, Hourly Job Performance." *Personnel Psychology,* 1996, *49,* 51–83.

Hunter, J. E., and Hunter, R. "Validity and Utility of Alternative Predictors of Job Performance." *Psychological Bulletin,* 1984, *96,* 72–98.

McCulloch, M. C., and Silverhart, T. A. "Assessing Person-Organization Fit to Reduce Turnover." Paper presented at the Twenty-Fourth Annual International Public Management Association Assessment Council Conference on Personnel Assessment, New Orleans, La., 2000.

Ones, D. S., Schmidt, F. L., and Viswesvaran, C. "Examination of Construct Validity with Linear Composites and Generalizability Coefficient Corrected Correlations." Paper presented at the annual conference of the Society for Industrial-Organizational Psychology, Nashville, Tenn., Apr. 1994.

Ones, D. S., Viswesvaran, C., and Schmidt, F. "Comprehensive Meta-Analysis of Integrity Test Validities: Findings and Implications for Personnel Selection and Theories of Job Performance." *Journal of Applied Psychology Monograph,* 1993, *78,* 679–703.

O'Reilly, C. A., Chatman, J. A., and Caldwell, D. "People and Organizational Culture: A Profile Comparison Approach to Assessing Person-Organization Fit." *Academy of Management Journal,* 1991, *34,* 487–516.

Organ, D. W., and Ryan, K. "A Meta-Analytic Review of Attitudinal and Dispositional Predictors of Organizational Citizenship Behavior." *Personnel Psychology,* 1995, *48,* 775–802.

Parasuraman, A., Zeithaml, V. A., and Berry, L. L. "A Conceptual Model of Service Quality and Its Implications for Future Research." *Journal of Marketing,* 1985, *49,* 41–50.

Pearlman, K. "Twenty-First Century Measures for Twenty-First Century Work." In A. Lesgold, M. J. Feuer, and A. Black (eds.), *Transitions in Work and Learning: Implications for Assessment*. Washington, D.C.: National Academy Press, 1997.

Pearlman, K., and Barney, M. "Selection for a Changing Workplace." In J. F. Kehoe (ed.), *Managing Selection in Changing Organizations: Human Resource Strategies*. San Francisco: Jossey-Bass, 2000.

Schmidt, F., and Hunter, J. E. "The Validity and Utility of Selection Methods in Personnel Psychology: Practical and Theoretical Implications of Eighty-Five Years of Research Findings." *Psychological Bulletin*, 1998, *124*, 262–274.

Schmit, M. J., and Allscheid, S. P. "Employee Attitudes and Customer Satisfaction: Making Theoretical and Empirical Connections." *Personnel Psychology*, 1995, *48*, 521–536.

Schneider, B. "The People Make the Place." *Personnel Psychology*, 1987, *40*, 435–453.

Schneider, B. "When Individual Differences Aren't." In K. R. Murphy (ed.), *Individual Differences and Behavior in Organizations*. San Francisco: Jossey-Bass, 1996.

Schneider, B., Salvaggio, A. N., and Subirats, M. "Climate Strength: A New Dimension for Climate Research." *Journal of Applied Psychology*, 2002, *87*, 220–229.

Schneider, B., and White, S. S. *Service Quality: Research Perspectives*. Thousand Oaks, Calif.: Sage, 2004.

Smith, C. A., Organ, D. W., and Near, J. P. "Organizational Citizenship Behavior: Its Nature and Antecedents." *Journal of Applied Psychology*, 1983, *68*, 653–663.

Strong, E. K. *Vocational Interests Eighteen Years After College*. Minneapolis: University of Minnesota Press, 1955.

Sujan, H., Sujan, M., and Bettman, J. R. "Knowledge Structure Differences Between More Effective and Less Effective Salespeople." *Journal of Marketing Research*, 1988, *25*, 81–86.

Viswesvaran, C. "Assessment of Individual Job Performance: A Review of the Past Century and a Look Ahead." In N. A. Anderson, D. S. Ones, H. K. Sinangil, and C. Viswesvaran (eds.), *Handbook of Industrial, Work, and Organizational Psychology, Vol. 1: Personnel Psychology*. Thousand Oaks, Calif.: Sage, 2002.

Zeithaml, V. A., Parasuraman, A., and Berry, L. L. *Delivering Quality Service: Balancing Customer Perceptions and Expectations*. New York: Free Press, 1990.

Chapter 6

Staffing and Selection Strategies for Service Quality

Deborah L. Whetzel
Michael A. McDaniel

Have you ever called technical support with a computer-related problem, only to find the representative noncommunicative, generally unhelpful, or even rude? With increased sophistication of goods produced in the United States and abroad, many products are becoming less user friendly, and more customers are turning to service-oriented technical support (for example, one-on-one telephone assistance with an expert) for help. As a result, the notion of quality customer service has gained widespread acceptance as a critical performance feature of many contemporary businesses. This chapter examines the use of a variety of methods for selecting employees with service orientation. We explore the personality characteristics that are associated with good customer service performance and then review methods for predicting the service orientation construct.

Personality Correlates with Customer Service

In the past decade, there has been a resurgence of research on the validity of personality measures for predicting performance. Previously, researchers claimed that individual differences in behavior

were not consistent over time and that behavior was largely determined by situational variables (Mischel, 1968). Two major developments in the field of industrial-organizational psychology have
led to research providing contradictory evidence regarding the use
of personality for predicting job performance: (1) the use of meta-
analysis to cumulate validity results across studies, and (2) the emergence of the Big Five Factor Model as a taxonomy for organizing
personality constructs (Costa and McCrae, 1992; Digman, 1990;
John, 1990). Although there is some disagreement about the content and names of the factors, they are frequently labeled (1) Extraversion, (2) Agreeableness, (3) Conscientiousness, (4) Emotional
Stability, and (5) Openness to Experience (John, 1990). In an
often cited meta-analysis, Barrick and Mount (1991), found that
some of the Big Five factors predicted performance in a number
of occupational settings. For example, Openness to Experience was
a good predictor of training performance. Conscientiousness predicted job performance regardless of occupational category.
Hunthausen, Truxillo, Bauer, and Hammer (2003) found that
when adding an "at-work" frame of reference (that is, instructing
participants to think about how they behave at work when responding to each statement), Extraversion and Openness to Experience scales showed increased concurrent validity in a sample
of customer service managers. Thus, research has shown that personality traits may be a good indicator of customer service. Below,
we discuss four specific traits: service orientation, sales drive, cognitive ability, and vocational interest.

Service Orientation

To the extent that service orientation is a pattern of stable personality characteristics, measurement of this attribute could identify individuals who are predisposed to engage in positive service-oriented
behaviors (Bowen, Siehl, and Schneider, 1989). For example, research on the altruistic personality (Carlo, Eisenberg, Troyer, and
Switzer, 1991) and prosocial behavior in organizations (Brief and
Motowidlo, 1986; Organ, 1988) indicates that stable cross-situational
dispositions may lead to service-oriented behavior (Sanchez, Fraser,
Fernandez, and De La Torre, 1993). To measure these dispositions,
service orientation inventories typically measure sets of personal-

ity traits associated with good performance in customer service jobs. For example, the Service Orientation Index, developed by Hogan and Hogan (1986), contains items that appear to measure emotional stability, agreeableness, and conscientiousness from the Hogan Personality Inventory. The scale's internal consistency (.69) suggests that the index is made up of items from three independent personality scales.

To understand the set of personality characteristics that make up service orientation, most test developers rely on job analysis. Several researchers (Fogli and Whitney, 1991; Hogan and Hogan, 1992; Paajanen, 1991; Saxe and Weitz, 1982) have operationalized service orientation in this way. The authors of the ServiceFirst Inventory (Fogli and Whitney, 1991) identified four constructs that underlie service orientation: active customer relations, polite customer relations, helpful customer relations, and personalized customer relations. Hogan and Hogan (1986) used three factors: virtuous, empathic, and sensitive. As with the Big Five, the factor names differ among service orientation inventories; however, several themes appear to be common among all measures: friendliness, reliability, responsiveness, and courteousness (Frei and McDaniel, 1998). In their meta-analyses of customer service measures, Frei and McDaniel (1998) found that customer service was highly correlated with Big Five measures of Agreeableness (.43), Emotional Stability (.37), and Conscientiousness (.42). These three correlations suggest that service orientation is an expression of a higher-order personality factor labeled "Socialization" (Digman, 1997).

Sales Drive

Intuitively, one would think that customer service employees and salespeople would share similar skills (for example, friendliness, social skills, and responsiveness to customers). There is evidence, however, that personality characteristics associated with good sales performance may not be the same as those associated with good customer service performance. For example, most studies of personality and sales performance find that the traits of extraversion and aggressiveness are good predictors (Deb, 1983; Oda, 1983). Stewart and Carson (1995), however, found a negative correlation between extraversion and performance in customer service occupations. It may be that employees with high sociability or extraversion may give insufficient attention to completing customer interactions in a prompt manner. Although this may please the customer, it may be detrimental to the organization because of increased labor costs. But in an analysis of the relation between service orientation and sales orientation, Frei and McDaniel (1998) reported a moderate correlation of .31 between customer service measures and sales drive.

Cognitive Ability

Research over the past eighty-five years shows that cognitive ability tests are the most valid predictors of performance across all occupations (Schmidt and Hunter, 1998). Hunter and Hunter (1984), however, found that the relation between cognitive ability and sales performance was the lowest among all criteria. Thus, service orientation inventories may be able to add some incremental prediction. Rosse, Miller, and Barnes (1991) administered a service-oriented personality measure and cognitive-perceptual ability tests in a concurrent validation study of medical clerical positions. Their results indicate that service orientation measures can predict job performance beyond cognitive ability tests. This finding is supported by Frei and McDaniel (1998), who found customer service measures to be uncorrelated with cognitive ability tests (−.06).

Vocational Interest

To the extent that a set of stable personality characteristics predicts customer service performance, patterns may emerge regarding other manifestations of personality, such as vocational interest. Holland's Self-Directed Search (1985) is a self-administered vocational counseling tool that operationalizes his RIASEC model of vocational interest. The RIASEC model states that vocational interests can be divided in terms of six primary interest areas: realistic, investigative, artistic, social, enterprising, and conventional. Frei and McDaniel (1998) found a moderate correlation between social vocational interests and customer service (.28) and little to no correlation with the other vocational types. Using a sample of ninety customer service representatives, Fritzsche, Powell, and Hoffman (1999) found that none of the three hypothesized test scores (Conventional, Social, and Enterprising) were significantly correlated with performance, but there was a significant correlation between investigative interest scores and job performance. Given the low number of study participants, this effect may be explained by sampling error.

Validity of Customer Service Measures

Frei and McDaniel (1998) conducted a meta-analysis to determine the criterion-related validity of pencil-and-paper, self-report measures of customer service orientation. The customer service measures included the Service Orientation Scale (Hogan and Hogan, 1992), the Customer Relations Scale (London House, 1992), and the PDI Customer Service Inventory (McLellan and Paajanen, 1994). The criterion-related validity analysis was based on forty-one coefficients with a total sample size of 6,945. The mean corrected validity was .50 for an aggregated supervisor rating of job performance.

Olesen, McDaniel, and Snell (1998) investigated the construct validity of customer service measures. They administered four measures: the Hogan Personality Inventory's Service Orientation Index (Hogan and Hogan, 1992), the PDI Customer-Service Orientation Inventory (Personnel Decisions, 1992), the ServiceFirst measure of service orientation developed by Fogli and Whitney (1991) for CORE CORP and Saville, and Holdsworth's Work Styles Questionnaire—Service (Saville and Holdsworth, 1995), as well as a measure of the Big Five and a measure of cognitive ability. The measures were administered to 356 undergraduate students at a midwestern university. The intercorrelations among the main scales of the customer service inventories ranged from .35 to .52. The customer service measures used in this study were strongly related to three of the Big Five personality dimensions as measured by the NEO Five Factor Inventory and the Hogan Personality Inventory. Specifically the results of their study support the contention that the construct of customer service is a combination of agreeableness, conscientiousness, and emotional stability and thus may be considered an expression of the higher-order personality factor of socialization

(Digman, 1997). They also found that the customer service inventories are largely independent of cognitive ability, supporting the findings of Frei and McDaniel (1998).

The remainder of this chapter provides a brief description of various measures and research results regarding the use of several instruments used to predict the performance of employees in customer service jobs. A new meta-analysis was not conducted because there were insufficient numbers of coefficients to warrant a new analysis.

Review of Customer Service Instruments

This review describes several instruments not included in the Frei and McDaniel (1998) meta-analysis: Development Dimensions International's (DDI) Customer Service Career Battery (CSCB), Unicru's Customer Service Assessment, Employment Technologies' Customer Service Skills Assessment Program (CSSAP), Alignmark's AccuVision Customer Service System, Aon's REPeValuator and Applicant Profile: Service Index and Applicant Profile Snapshot Test Series, and Work Skills First, Inc.'s Judgment at Work Survey for Customer Service. All instruments are administered using the Web.

DDI's measure, the CSCB, consists of three content sets: a situational judgment inventory, a customer service work styles and dispositional inventory, and a behavior-based inventory of past experiences. Unicru's instrument is a computer-administered assessment in which candidates read about situations and select the best alternative. Employment Technologies' measure involves having candidates watch a video that shows a situation and select an answer from four possible video taped responses. Alignmark's Accu-Vision Customer Service System is similar to the measure developed by Employment Technologies Corporation in that it also presents videotaped situations followed by four videotaped response options. Aon's REPeValuator also involves having candidates watch a video and answer questions. The two Applicant Profile tests contain more traditional multiple choice or ranking items that are computer administered. Work Skills First, Inc.'s Judgment at Work Survey is administered over the Web and contains situational items that describe a situation that one might encounter at work in a customer service job. Each situation is followed by several possible actions, and the applicant is asked to evaluate the effectiveness of each action.

This is not a complete list of available instruments. Some considered their data proprietary (for example, eSelex), and others were unable to provide data or information about their selection systems or never responded to the request for information (for example, E-talk and Qwiz).

DDI Customer Service Career Battery

DDI's Customer Service Career Battery (CSCB) has three content sets: Work-Related Judgment, Work Style and Disposition, and Background Experience. The CSCB is a short-form version blending content from three existing inventories: the Situational Judgment Inventory (SJI), the Career Fit Inventory (CFI), and the Applicant Experience Profile (AEP), all of which are designed to predict the performance of applicants for customer service jobs (Sinar, Scott, and Reynolds, 2004). The use of client-specific job analysis and validation information and administering the CSCB on the Web enables the scales administered for each client to be customized. Although the SJI, CFI, and AEP items are typically delivered within the integrated CSCB, we describe them separately below. (For more information about the kinds of reports generated and uses for their tests, go to http://www.ddi.com.)

Customer Service Situational Judgment Inventory

The SJI comprises a series of brief written simulations involving customer service, team membership/leadership, problem solving, continuous improvement, and interpersonal effectiveness. It includes behavioral choice questions that reflect realistic workplace situations. In response to these questions, the respondent must choose the best of four options. Several of the items contain a problem-solving component that involves math or interpreting information from charts and graphs. The remaining items contain situations that are more interpersonal in nature and are designed to reflect face-to-face or telephone-oriented customer interactions. The SJI's test-retest reliability over a one-month time period was .64 ($n = 110$ students). Sinar, Scott, and Reynolds (2003) conducted a meta-analyses to average the validities across studies. Corrected validities ranged from .24 to .33 (n = 654 to 754, number of studies = 6 to 7) with four criterion composites: can-do performance, will-do performance, interpersonal performance, and overall performance.

Customer Service Career Fit Inventory

The CFI collects self-reports of candidates' past behavior, preferences, and motivations as they relate to critical work behaviors. Respondents answer questions using a five-point Likert scale ranging from Strongly Disagree to Strongly Agree. The scales within the CFI are the Team Member scale, the Supervisory Collaboration scale, four behavioral scales (Work Quality, Positive Disposition, Outgoing Disposition, and Adaptability), and one perception scale (Self-Efficacy).

Meta-analytic results of the CFI's internal consistency shows that the reliabilities fell in the range of .65 to .85, with .75 as the average reliability of the seven scales. Using meta-analytic techniques, Sinar, Scott, and Reynolds (2003) found the individual CFI scales to be correlated with the criteria, except for Outgoing Disposition. Corrected scale-level correlations with overall performance ranged from .06 to .25 (n = 524 to 595; number of studies = 5 to 6). Except for the Outgoing Disposition scale and the correlation between interpersonal performance and work quality, none of the confidence intervals included zero. Two additional studies revealed that the CFI also predicted counterproductive work behaviors such as disciplinary actions taken against employees, tardiness, and absenteeism.

Customer Service Applicant Experience Profile

The AEP is a behavior-based selection instrument developed to measure an applicant's past experiences. It contains a series of behavioral statements and several multiple-choice questions related to past work behaviors. For each behavioral statement, applicants indicate if they have performed the described behavior. For each multiple-choice question, applicants choose the response that best describes the applicant's behavior.

The AEP contains five dimension clusters that relate to job performance in customer service environments: ability to learn, interpersonal skills, initiative/innovation, work standards, and customer service experience. Two primary studies have been conducted on the AEP. In the first, corrected validities for the AEP administered verbally ranged from .32 to .37 ($n = 105$ incumbents in call center positions) across the four criteria. In the second study, corrected validities for the pencil-and-paper-administered AEP ranged from .20 to .30 ($n = 164$ incumbents in a customer-oriented operations job family).

Operationally, the CSCB consists of items from the SJI, CFI, and AEP combined into an integrated test, and items from the three content sets are combined into a single score for each candidate. Meta-analytic results for the operational CSCB versions ($n = 1,060$; number of studies = 10) show that the CSCB is a valid predictor of overall performance ($\rho = .47$), can-do performance ($\rho = .38$), will-do performance ($\rho = .41$), and interpersonal ($\rho = .45$). Validity coefficients with absenteeism and punctuality were $\rho = .23$ and .26, respectively. Each of these coefficients was corrected for sampling error, unreliability of the criterion, and range restriction. Differential validity analyses also indicated that regression line slopes and y-intercepts were similar by race and gender, suggesting that the CSCB's prediction of job performance does not differ by applicant subgroup.

Unicru's Customer Service Assessment

Unicru's Customer Service Assessment is a personality-based pre-employment assessment that measures behaviors such as helping and solving people problems, positive behavior (for example, good mood, politeness, empathy), controlling negative behavior (arguing, anger, criticizing), communication, sociability, and working with others (Scarborough, Paajanen, and Ostberg, 2001). The assessment consists of fifty statements of everyday experience, each of which is rated on a four-point scale ranging from 1 = "it is definitely false for you or you strongly disagree" to 4 = "it is definitely true for you or you strongly agree." The customer service assessment is integrated electronically with other parts of a selection system.

The validity of the Customer Service Assessment against a global performance composite score (consisting of management ratings of performance, eligibility for rehire, impact of termination on local operation, and type of termination) was .33 ($n = 213$). (For more information about the kinds of reports generated and uses for the tests, go to http://www.unicru.com.)

Employment Technologies Corporation's Customer Service Skills Assessment Program

The CSSAP is a video-based, computer-scored job simulation designed to assess the competencies essential for success in a customer service position (Employment Technologies, 1990). It measures six primary skill areas critical to providing high-quality customer service: developing positive customer relations, discovering customer needs, responding to customer wants, anticipating customer needs, working together to meet customer needs, and ensuring customer loyalty. Construction of test items and test scenarios was based on individual tasks and critical situations. Thus, test items focused on key behaviors rather than constructs associated with cluster labels.

The test consists of sixteen videotaped scenarios and forty-six test items that appear on the video test. After watching a video, the practice item given in the manual is, "If you were the charge card representative, what would you do next?"

Option A: Tell Tim to send the minimum payment until you can straighten out the bill.

Option B: Ask Tim if other people might have used his charge card.

Option C: Tell Tim he will need to speak to your manager.

Option D: Tell Tim you will check into the matter and will call him back today with an explanation.

The CSSAP reports, including the CareeRx Developmental Report, the List of Participants Report, and the EEO Group Summary Report can be viewed online (http://www.ETC-EASY.com).

The CSSAP criterion-related validity coefficient was estimated to be .40 ($n = 126$ customer service providers at two large automotive companies). In a second sample, the corrected correlation between the CSSAP scores and the performance ratings was .34 ($n = 60$).

The CSSAP also was validated for the job of operator assistance operators whose job consists of assisting customers with a variety of problems, from billing difficulties to the need for emergency services. Successful performance requires a variety of customer service and problem-solving behaviors. The CSSAP test results were correlated with operational quality-of-work ratings yielding a significant correlation of .34 ($n = 65$). When correlated with performance checklist ratings developed for the original validation study, the validity was −.03. The lack of relationship may have resulted because adaptation of the checklist was not entirely successful or because the managers were not as skilled in the use of this new performance measure.

The Call Center Simulation (LaTorre, 2001) is a computer-based, multimedia test that simulates actual call center workstation conditions. Applicants respond to calls from a variety of customers with real-life issues. Some customers are irate, others are confused, and still others are calm. To perform effectively on the assessment, applicants are required to answer customer calls, enter customer information, listen to customer issues, look up relevant information, identify effective responses, and summarize calls. Applicants also are required to demonstrate basic keyboard and navigation skills.

A coefficient alpha measure of internal consistency resulted in an overall test reliability of .83 ($n = 760$). Validities, reported for each of fourteen calls, ranged from .038 to .168. Eleven of the twelve calls had a significant correlation with supervisor ratings of performance. In order to determine the possible range of validity expected from an eight-call test, the developers correlated overall test scores with performance ratings for ten randomly chosen eight-call tests. Results indicated that the uncorrected validity for an eight-call test ranged from .218 to .240. The internal consistency reliability of the final eight-call test was .78. The observed validity of the eight-call test was .24. When corrected for criterion unreliability, the validity was .34, and when corrected for criterion unreliability and range restriction, the validity was .49. Fairness analyses revealed that the test is equally difficult for males and females and for whites, blacks, and Hispanics.

Alignmark's AccuVision Customer Service System

Alignmark's AccuVision Customer Service System (Alignmark, 2001) is a video-based selection test that has been developed to measure customer service skills and abilities. Job analysis information provided the basis for the design and content of the system. For example, varying degrees of customer contact are represented by the different scenarios (for example, employee-to-customer, employee-to-employee videos, and telephone interactions). A set of thirty-four scenarios was developed and reviewed by Subject matter experts (SMEs) for realism. Behavioral response options were rated for effectiveness. The concurrent validation involved using a consortium of three companies representing a mixture of geographical regions and a variety of job titles.

The validity of the test for the total sample was .34 (n = 600). When corrected for criterion unreliability (the correlation between a first and second rating taken six weeks later = .81), the validity was .38. The test-retest reliability was .75 for a sample of thirty-five incumbents. Race and gender differences were found to be negligible when validities were computed separately for the various groups and when the Cleary model was used to test for slope and intercept differences. (For information about the kinds of reports generated and uses for their tests, go to http://www.alignmark.com.)

Aon's REPeValuator and Applicant Profile: ServiceFit Index

Aon's REPeValuator (Aon, 2003b) is designed to simulate a typical call center environment and therefore provides a work sample and a realistic job preview as applicants interact with virtual customers via e-mail or telephone. There are a total of six scenarios (customer chat or voice interactions) involving forty-two items. The items can be completed in approximately sixty minutes. The four competencies measured are Managing Customer Relations (MCR), Providing Accurate Information (PAI), Keyboarding Speed and Accuracy (KSA), and Managing Call Center Time (MCT). An overall score is provided as well as a score for each of the four competency areas.

The reliability of the instrument for each of the four competencies is .37 for MCR, .81 for PAI, .85 for KSA, and .89 for MCT. The reliabilities are all in the very good range for these types of tests except for MCR. This is attributable to the multidimensional nature of the scale. The overall score reliability of the assessment is .85. Concerning subgroup differences, Aon (2003b) found no adverse impact for females and marginal adverse impact for minorities if cut scores are high (d = .60). These studies note that sample sizes available for these analyses are quite small, so results should be interpreted with caution. Concerning validity, the average corrected validity ($n = 134$) for the overall score is .40 against the skill rating composites (ranging from .28 to .51), .47 against the work behavior rating composite (ranging from .38 to .53), and .35 against the three summary (single) ratings (ranging from .25 to .41).

Aon's Applicant Profile: ServiceFit Index (Aon, 2003a) is targeted at predicting turnover and key antecedents of turnover and withdrawal. The test contains ninety items that are designed to measure three core dimensions: Customer Service Orientation (preference for working with a variety of people with whom a person is not familiar), Job Structure Orientation (preference for following prescribed rules and procedures rather than vague or ambiguous direction), and Work Environment Orientation (preference for working quickly and with fast turnaround as opposed to more slowly paced work that does not require the same level of immediate intensity).

These constructs are measured using four item types: paired comparisons (selecting between two things, such as job titles or job activities), rankings (rank order six job activities, work descriptions, or challenges that differ on a core dimension), traditional multiple choice (biodata or personality items), and self-report (criteria) multiple choice (job satisfaction, turnover intentions). Examples of each item type are shown in Exhibit 6.1.

The reliability of the instrument assessed in three studies is .74 ($n = 378$), .76 ($n = 233$), and .74 ($n = 113$). Across all three studies, there were no subgroup differences for females or minorities. The only significant difference on the total score was in favor of female test-takers for a pilot version of the test. Concerning validity against supervisory performance ratings, the results indicate statistical significance for seven of the eight work behaviors, with coefficients ranging from .17 to .42 (average, .31) ($n = 113$). Concerning the prediction of turnover, the number of incumbents who have turned over is still relatively small to date. However, when comparing the top half of performers on the test to the bottom half, the turnover rates are 16.4 percent and 17.4 percent for the top half and 24.6 percent and 25.6 percent for the bottom half. This represents about a 32 to 33 percent decrease in attrition if one simply selected individuals in the top half of test scores. A second study showed that screening out the lowest one-third of the test takers would have reduced turnover (in a call center) by 20 percent and

Exhibit 6.1. Sample Items on Aon's Applicant Profile: ServiceFit Index.

Sample Paired Comparison Items:

I would prefer to have a job as a(n):

   A. School principal

   B. Bus driver

I would prefer a job in which I am . . .

   A. Writing letters

   B. Performing calculations

Please choose which word better describes you in a work context:

   A. Excited

   B. Calm

Sample Ranking Item:

Please rank the list of job activities or descriptions provided based on your work interests and preferences (1 = most important or most desired to 6 = least important or least desired):

____ Communicate with coworkers

____ Document or read information

____ Communicate with persons outside the organization

____ Interact with computers

____ Review documents

____ Resolve conflicts or negotiate with others

Sample Multiple Choice Item:

I am too energetic to stay in one place for any length of time.

   A. Strongly agree

   B. Somewhat agree

   C. Neither agree nor disagree

   D. Somewhat disagree

   E. Strongly disagree

Source: Work Skills First (2005).

screening in only the top third of test takers would have reduced turnover by over 30 percent. A comparison of turnover between the two groups (bottom third to top third) showed that the turnover rate in the bottom third was twice the turnover rate in the top third (Daniel P. Russell, personal communication, Sept. 14, 2004).

Aon's Applicant Profile: Snapshot Test Series is designed for use by businesspeople of nearly any background (health care, manufacturing customer contact, telesales and service, service technician). It consists of an untimed sixty-seven-item test that measures Work Orientation (describes work habits, work preferences, and reliability), Fundamental Skills (measures the ability to understand simple instructions, follow procedures, and reason through basic problems), and Job Judgment (assesses the applicant's ability to apply sound judgment in dealing with everyday job situations). Although there are several versions of the test designed for various industries, all versions have sixty-seven items. Sample questions are shown in Exhibit 6.2.

The validities (corrected for criterion unreliability) of the Snapshot tests against the average performance rating are .36 and .37 with a single-item overall performance rating ($n = 2,126$). There were little or no subgroup differences. Specifically, standardized mean differences for male versus female test performance and minority versus nonminority test performance on the cognitive (Fundamental Skills) items were generally less than .40 standard deviations and far smaller for the other items. (To find out more information about the kinds of reports generated and uses for their tests, information is available on the Aon Web site at http://www.aon.com/talentsolutions.)

Work Skills First, Inc.'s Judgment at Work Survey for Customer Service

The Judgment at Work Survey for Customer Service contains situational stems, each describing a situation that one might encounter at work in a customer service job. Each situation is followed by several possible actions and the applicant is asked to evaluate the effectiveness of each action. An example item is shown in Exhibit 6.3.

Exhibit 6.2. Sample Questions on Aon's
Applicant Profile: Snapshot Test Series.

Sample Work Orientation Question:

Who do you believe is most responsible for ensuring that safe work practices are followed?

   a. Safety experts

   b. Supervisors

   c. Employees

   d. Managers

   e. Trainers

Sample Fundamental Skills Question:

Assigned Area	Monday	Tuesday	Wednesday	Thursday	Friday	Saturday
Area 1	Terry	Pat	Chris	Kelly	Sam	Kelly
Area 2	Sam	Terry	Kelly	Chris	Chris	Terry
Area 3	Kelly	Chris	Terry	Pat	Pat	Sam

Who works neither on Tuesday nor on Wednesday?

   a. Chris

   b. Kelly

   c. Pat

   d. Sam

   e. Terry

Sample Job Judgment Question:

You are busy working. A coworker approaches you and asks for your help for a moment. What would you be MOST likely to do? What would you be LEAST likely to do?

   a. Help the coworker when I am able.

   b. Stop what I am doing and help.

   c. Tell the coworker that I can't help.

   d. Arrange a time when I can help the coworker.

   e. Pretend that I did not hear the request.

Source: Work Skills First (2005).

Exhibit 6.3. Sample Item from the Judgment at Work Survey for Customer Service.

	Extremely Ineffective	Ineffective	Average Effectiveness	Very Effective	Extremely Effective
You are unable to locate a product that a customer insists that you carry.					
You explain to the customer that you do not carry the product.					
You check with a coworker about the availability of the product.					
Tell the customer to check with your manager.					
Suggest that the customer look elsewhere for the product.					
Search more thoroughly for the product.					

Source: Work Skills First (2005).

Situational judgment tests tend to measure multiple constructs because the determinants of behavior in a given situation are typically a function of multiple variables, including general cognitive ability, personality, and job experience. Parallel forms reliability is an appropriate reliability for heterogeneous tests. The parallel forms reliability for the Judgment at Work Survey for Customer Service is .88.

The criterion-related validity evidence rests on two studies. The first is a meta-analysis of the criterion-related validity of a variety of situational judgment measures (McDaniel and others, 2001). The second is a primary validity study using the Judgment at Work Survey for Customer Service. The first study was a meta-analysis of 102 validity coefficients with a total sample size of 10,640 individuals. The mean validity, corrected for measurement error in the criterion, was .34. Almost all criteria used in the study were supervisor performance appraisals. The 90 percent confidence interval for the validity distribution was .16, indicating that situational judgment tests have validity in almost all applications. In the second study, a group of 126 employed adults completed the Judgment at Work Survey for Customer Service. Under anonymous conditions, the study participants also completed a self-report job history and performance appraisal survey that yielded three scales: job performance, attendance, and turnover. The validity coefficients for the Judgment at Work Survey for Customer Service, corrected for unreliability in the criterion measures, were .29 for job performance, .26 for attendance, and .14 for turnover. These validity estimates are likely to be underestimates because no corrections were made for range restriction.

An example score report is shown in Exhibit 6.4. It is intended to be used for all applicants and is e-mailed to the employer. It contains the applicant's score as well as an interpretation of the score and hire or not hire recommendation. (For more information about the Judgment at Work Survey for Customer Service, go to http://www.workskillsfirst.com.)

Summary

This chapter reviewed the personality correlates associated with customer service, including service orientation, sales drive, cognitive ability, and vocational interest. Our review suggested that ser-

Exhibit 6.4. Work Skills First, Inc. Score Report.

Applicant Name: Frank Zappa
Applicant Identification:
Test Administered: Judgment at Work Survey for Customer Service
(Test 110)
Date Administered: Mon Mar 15 11:06:41 2004
SCORE: 4

We offer the following hiring recommendations as reasonable. Applicants with scores of 7, 8, or 9 receive our highest recommendation for hire. Applicants with scores of 4, 5, or 6 receive our next best recommendation for hire. Applicants with scores of 3 and below are not recommended for hire. Very low scores, particularly negative scores, indicate that the applicant responded to the items without reading the questions, read the questions but lacked the reading comprehension skills to understand the questions, or was purposely trying to look bad.

Your company may wish to make its own recommendations for hire based on other information collected on the applicants in the local applicant pool, the performance records of employees who were previously tested, and the adverse impact of the test for your applicants. Technical documentation for the Judgment at Work Survey for Customer Service is available on the Work Skills First, Inc. web site www.workskillsfirst.com.

Source: Work Skills First (2005).

vice orientation was highly correlated with customer service, sales drive was slightly correlated with customer service, cognitive ability was uncorrelated with customer service (suggesting the possibility of incremental prediction of customer service measures over cognitive ability), and social vocational interests were moderately correlated with customer service. We also described the validity and reliability of paper-and-pencil self-report measures of customer service. Meta-analysis findings showed that across forty-one coefficients with a total sample size of 6,945, the validity was .50 for an aggregated supervisory rating of job performance (Frei and McDaniel, 1998). Finally, this chapter provided a description of additional commercially available measures of customer service, including video- and text-based situational judgment tests, self-report inventories, and experience profiles. The research supporting their use showed that there are a variety of ways to predict the construct of customer service.

References

Alignmark. *AccuVision Customer Service System Validation Report.* Maitland, Fla.: Alignmark, 2001.

Aon Consulting. *Applicant Profile: Service Fit Index: Technical Documentation.* Chicago: Aon Consulting, 2003a.

Aon Consulting. *REPeValuator: Technical Documentation.* Chicago: Aon Consulting, 2003b.

Barrick, M. R., and Mount, M. D. "The Big-Five Personality Dimensions and Job Performance: A Meta-Analysis." *Personnel Psychology,* 1991, *44,* 1–26.

Bowen, D. E., Siehl, C., and Schneider, B. "A Framework for Analyzing Customer Service Orientations in Manufacturing." *Academy of Management Review,* 1989, *14,* 75–95.

Brief, A. P., and Motowidlo, S. J. "Prosocial Organizational Behaviors." *Academy of Management Review,* 1986, *11,* 710–725.

Carlo, G., Eisenberg, N., Troyer, D., and Switzer, G "The Altruistic Personality: In What Contexts Is It Apparent?" *Journal of Personality and Social Psychology,* 1991, *61,* 450–458.

Costa, P. T., and McCrae, R. R. "Four Ways Five Factors Are Basic." *Personality and Individual Differences,* 1992, *13,* 653–665.

Deb, M. "Sales Effectiveness and Personality Characteristics." *Psychological Research Journal,* 1983, *7,* 59–67.

Digman, J. M. "Personality Structure: Emergence of the Five Factor Model." *Annual Review of Psychology,* 1990, *47,* 417–440.

Digman, J. M. "Higher-Order Factors of the Big Five." *Journal of Personality and Social Psychology,* 1997, *73,* 1246–1256.

Employment Technologies. *Dealership Employee Selection System: Customer Service Skills Assessment Program Validation Report.* Winter Park, Fla.: Employment Technologies, 1990.

Fogli, L., and Whitney, K. "ServiceFirst: A Test to Select Service-Oriented Personnel." Symposium conducted at the annual meeting of the American Psychological Association, San Francisco, Aug. 1991.

Frei, R. L., and McDaniel, M. A. "Validity of Customer Service Measures in Personnel Selection: A Review of Criterion and Construct Evidence." *Human Performance,* 1998, *11,* 1–27.

Fritzsche, B. A., Powell, A. B., and Hoffman, R. "Person-Environment Congruence as a Predictor of Customer Service Performance." *Journal of Vocational Behavior,* 1999, *54,* 59–70.

Hogan, J., and Hogan, R. *Hogan Personnel Selection Series Manual.* Minneapolis, Minn.: National Computer Systems, 1986.

Hogan, J., and Hogan, R. *Hogan Personality Inventory Manual.* Tulsa, Okla.: Hogan Assessment Systems, 1992.

Holland, J. L. *The Self-Directed Search Professional Manual.* Odessa, Fla.: Psychological Assessment Services, 1985.

Hunter, J. E., and Hunter, R. F. "The Validity and Utility of Alternative Predictors of Job Performance." *Psychological Bulletin,* 1984, *96,* 72–98.

Hunthausen, J. M., Truxillo, D. M., Bauer, T. N., and Hammer, L. B. "A Field Study of Frame-of-Reference Effects on Personality Test Validity." *Journal of Applied Psychology,* 2003, *88,* 545–551.

John, O. P. "The 'Big-Five' Factor Taxonomy: Dimensions of Personality in the Natural Language and in Questionnaires." In L. A. Pervin (ed.), *Hand Book of Personality Theory and Research.* New York: Guilford Press, 1990.

LaTorre, J. *Call Center Simulation: Development and Validation Report.* Winter Park, Fla.: Employment Technologies Corporation, 2001.

London House. *Personnel Selection Inventory Information Guide.* Rosemont, Ill.: London House, 1994.

McDaniel, M. A., and others. "Use of Situational Judgment Tests to Predict Job Performance: A Clarification of the Literature." *Journal of Applied Psychology,* 2001, *86,* 730–740.

McLellan, R. A., and Paajanen, G. *PDI Customer Service Inventory Manual.* Minneapolis, Minn.: Personnel Decisions, 1994.

Mischel, W. *Personality and Assessment.* New York: Wiley, 1968.

Oda, M. "Predicting Sales Performance of Car Salesmen by Personality Traits." *Japanese Journal of Psychology,* 1983, *54,* 73–80.

Olesen, E. P., McDaniel, M. A., and Snell, A. F. "Construct Validity of Customer Service Measures: An Examination of Convergent Validity Evidence." Paper presented at the Thirteenth Annual Convention of the Society for Industrial and Organizational Psychology, Dallas, 1998.

Organ, D. W. "A Restatement of the Satisfaction-Performance Hypothesis." *Journal of Management,* 1988, *14,* 547–557.

Paajanen, G. "Development and Validation of the PDI Customer Service Inventory." Paper presented at the annual meeting of the American Psychological Association, San Francisco, Aug. 1991.

Personnel Decisions. *Draft Technical Manual for the PDI Customer-Service Inventory.* Minneapolis, Minn.: Personnel Decisions, 1992.

Rosse, J. G., Miller, H. E., and Barnes, L. K. "Combining Personality and Cognitive Ability Predictors for Hiring Service Oriented Employees." *Journal of Business and Psychology,* 1991, *5,* 431–445.

Sanchez, J., Fraser, S., Fernandez, D., and De La Torre, P. "Development and Validation of the Customer Service Skills Inventory." Paper presented at the annual meeting of the Society for Industrial and Organizational Psychology, San Francisco, Apr. 1993.

Saville and Holdsworth. *Work Style Questionnaire—Service.* Boston: Saville and Holdsworth, 1995.

Saxe, R., and Weitz, B. "The SOCO Scale Measure of the Customer Orientation of Salespeople." *Journal of Marketing Research,* 1982, *19,* 343–351.

Scarborough, D. J., Paajanen, G. E., and Ostberg, D. E. *Unicru Customer Service Assessment Development and Validation Approach.* Beaverton, Ore.: Unicru, 2001.

Schmidt, F. L., and Hunter, J. E. "The Validity and Utility of Selection Method in Personnel Psychology: Practical and Theoretical Implications of Eighty-Five Years of Research Findings." *Psychological Bulletin,* 1998, *124,* 262–274.

Sinar, E. F., Scott, D. R., and Reynolds, D. H. *Technical Summary Report for DDI's Customer Service Inventories.* Bridgeville, Pa.: Development Dimensions International, 2003.

Sinar, E. F., Scott, D. R., and Reynolds, D. H. *Technical Summary Report for DDI's Customer Service Career Battery.* Bridgeville, Pa.: Development Dimensions International, 2004.

Stewart, G. L., and Carson, K. P. "Personality Dimensions and Domains of Service Performance: A Field Investigation." *Journal of Business and Psychology,* 1995, *9,* 365–378.

PART 3

Organizational Change Management for Service Quality

Chapter 7

Service Encounter Dynamics
Strategies and Tips for Better Customer Service

Diane Catanzaro
Eduardo Salas

In the service organization, the rubber meets the road during the service encounter. While many factors are important in improving service quality, customer perceptions of the quality of service are strongly influenced by the social interactions they experience with employees. These service encounters are transient, emergent events that are challenging for organizations to manage and control but vital to organizational effectiveness, customer satisfaction, and employee job satisfaction. This chapter addresses the important influence of the social dynamics of the service encounter on service quality and presents strategies and tips for improving service encounters.

What Is the Service Encounter?

The interpersonal transaction between a customer and an employee in transmission of a service is known as the *service encounter*. This exchange is characterized by fairly well-defined employee and customer roles. There is a status differential where the service provider is generally expected to defer to the customer (that is, the customer is always right). There is a goal or purpose to the interaction on the part of both parties. During the interaction, both task-related information exchange and nontask social exchange occur, but the primary emphasis is on task-related exchange (Czepiel, Solomon, Surprenant, and Gutman, 1985).

Gutek (1995) suggests that the service encounter is a single interaction between a customer and an employee, as distinct from a service *relationship*, where there is repeated contact between customer and employee and a shared expectation of future interactions. Although service encounters and service relationships differ in a number of ways, the discussion and strategies we suggest in this chapter apply to both.

During the service encounter, both customer and employee are present and participate in the production and transmission of the service, such as when a customer places an order or makes a request and the employee processes the order or fills the request (Shostack, 1977; Berry, 1980). Both customer and employee experience some level of interpersonal communication during this transaction. The service employee is in a boundary-spanning role and represents the organization to the customer (Aldrich and Herker, 1977; Bowen and Schneider, 1985). In fact, the customer may see the employee *as* the organization and form an image of the organization based on the employee's behavior (Lovelock, 1981).

Service organizations can be classified along many dimensions, and the degree to which service encounters are involved in the transmission of services varies (Snyder, Cox, and Jesse, 1982). For example, utility and telecommunications services are provided without the need for human interaction while these services are consumed. Service encounters may occur when initially marketing and selling the service to customers and subsequently regarding billing and technical problems in service delivery. For this type of organization, service encounter dynamics will be salient at times, but transmission of the core service does not occur through a service encounter. At the other end of the continuum are services where the service encounter is inherently part of the primary work process. For example, in physical therapy, restaurant dining, counseling, and nursing home services, the service encounter is an inherent part of the production and consumption of the service, and the experience of the service cannot be divorced from the interpersonal interaction. However, in both types of organizations the service encounter plays an important role.

Why Is the Service Encounter Important?

The service encounter plays an extremely important role in customer evaluations of service quality. Customers' opinions about the quality of service are largely based on their experiences interacting with service employees. The services marketing literature (Shostack, 1977; Lovelock, 1981; Gronroos, 1978) was the first to address how service organizations differ from manufacturing organizations and how services organizations need to (1) focus on the important role of the human interaction between customer and employee during service production and (2) design human resource practices that are aligned with the key goal of effective service encounters (Tansik, 1990). Traditional management and human resource practices, based on a manufacturing organization model where employees and customers do not interact, do not fit the needs of the service organization, where line employees' primary work processes involve communicating with customers (Schneider, 1980).

The service encounter is of such key significance for a number of reasons. Services are relatively intangible (Berry, 1980; Shostack, 1977). In manufacturing organizations, product quality can be measured objectively, but in a service organization, the output is often difficult to measure. Gronroos (1983) noted that perceived service quality comprises two main dimensions: technical quality and functional quality. Technical quality is based on adherence to standards and expectations for accuracy, speed, timeliness, and objective aspects of the service. It is related to the content of the service. The speed with which a cashier scans groceries, the accuracy of a bank teller's end-of-shift balance, and whether a sales clerk greets customers in the first five seconds after they enter the store are examples of technical service quality in the service encounter. Functional quality describes the customer perceptions of the social-psychological process of service delivery and is largely influenced by the social dynamics of the service encounter (Solomon, Surprenant, Czepiel, and Gutman, 1985). The cashier's friendliness, the bank teller's genuinely warm greeting, and the sales clerk's helpful assistance in finding an item are all examples of functional service quality. Although the relative importance of technical and functional service quality depends on the nature of the interaction between employee, customer, and technology, both aspects of service quality are important to the customer (Tansik, 1990).

Customer judgments about both technical and functional service quality are strongly influenced by what transpires during service encounters. Although both aspects of service quality are important, technical aspects are more likely to be emphasized in selection, training, performance appraisal, and other human resource and management practices; functional aspects of the service encounter are often given superficial treatment. When organizational human resource practices do address the functional, process aspects of the service encounter, the strategies (that is, "smile training") can actually be counterproductive. This can occur when the service employee's interpersonal behavior (smiling, greeting, reciting a script) is specified, measured, and controlled in ways that contribute negatively to organizational climate.

Technical quality is more tangible and easily measured than functional quality; therefore, organizational specifications for and evaluations of service quality are likely to focus on technical quality and omit less tangible, functional aspects of the service that are important to customers. In addition, technical aspects of service quality may be difficult for the consumer to evaluate or of sufficient quality or standardization that technical aspects of the service may not differentiate service providers from the customer's perspective (Gronroos, 1983). Because of technology, task-related training, and other factors, any bank teller should be able to process a deposit accurately, any cashier should be able to scan a product and make change, and any nurse should be able to administer an injection. In many industries, organizations are differentiated in the eyes of the consumer more on the basis of interpersonal aspects of service encounter interactions than on technical aspects of service quality, because technical service quality is standardized.

Another reason that the service encounter is important is that the skills, behaviors, attitudes, and emotions of the service employee are apparent to customers during the service encounter (Mills and Moberg, 1982). Employee mood can be transmitted to customers during the service encounter in a process called *emotional contagion* (Hatfield, Cacioppo, and Rapson, 1994). Pugh

(2001) conducted research in thirty-nine branches of a regional bank and found that increased smiling, eye contact, and greetings by tellers were associated with more positive customer mood and better customer judgments about the quality of service. Verbeke (1977) found that salespersons' emotions can infect customers and that display of positive emotion was associated with better customer interactions and higher sales volume. Tsai and Huang (2002) used mystery shopper observers to assess 352 service encounters in 169 retail shoe stores in Taiwan and found that employee greeting, thanking, vocal tone, smiling, and eye contact were correlated with customer judgments of clerk friendliness, customer mood, and length of store visit. Just as employee display of positive emotion is associated with higher customer evaluations of service, employee display of negative emotions is associated with lower customer evaluations of service quality.

Schneider and colleagues' research, also in the banking industry, demonstrated that bank teller perceptions of the internal work environment created by management policies, practices, and human resource orientation correlated with both employee and customer perceptions of service quality (Schneider and Bowen, 1985; Schneider, Parkington, and Buxton, 1980). The human resource practices that are used to manage service employees apparently show to customers in a kind of spillover effect and provide cues that influence customer judgments about quality of service. For example, if management creates a climate where employees do not feel valued or believe that management does not really care about service to customers, employees may develop negative attitudes that customers can detect during the service encounter. If employees feel valued and respected by management and management cares about both employees and giving customers excellent service, the employee is likely to care about giving good service. This may be due to positive mood, organizational commitment, or a desire to represent the company's values positively. Customers are likely to detect this attitude.

Ample and consistent research evidence supports the idea that employee feelings and attitudes about the job and the organizational climate have an impact on customer perceptions of service quality, and this occurs as a result of verbal and nonverbal communication during the service encounter process. With the growth of the service sector comes an increased concern about the importance of quality service, but many organizations use the same human resource strategies developed by business schools and practitioners based on a manufacturing model, where core work processes do not involve interpersonal interactions with customers (Collier, 1990; Shostack 1985).

Because these interpersonal transactions between employees and customers play a major role in customer perceptions of service quality, the organization's human resource and management practices need to be aligned with this objective. It is clear that the service encounter is an important element of service quality, if not the most important. The question is what management can do to improve the quality of service encounters, particularly the elusive interpersonal quality of the service encounter. Significant research conducted in the past twenty-five years, and published in the psychology and marketing literatures, can be instructive for organizational managers striving to improve service quality. The remainder of this chapter focuses on key issues and knowledge gained from this research and suggests specific tips and strategies, based on research and theory, to improve the quality of the service encounter. Because selection of service employees is covered in depth elsewhere in this book, we will not address this topic except to point out that selection of employees who have appropriate skills, attitudes, and service orientation is an important foundation for the strategies that follow.

What Are Important Strategies in Managing and Improving the Service Encounter?

The strategies presented are based on empirical research in the behavioral sciences and are intended to provide guidance to organizational leaders, managers, and human resource practitioners as they strive to improve service quality and create an organizational culture aligned with the service imperative.

Strategy 1: Examine the Impact of How Service Encounter Performance Is Specified and Measured

Although the service encounter is a major influence on customer views of service quality, the behavior of employees during the service encounter is difficult for managers to measure, particularly the functional or process aspects. In addition, the strategies used to measure the service encounter may in fact work at cross-purposes with factors that have a positive influence on service climate, such as employee feelings of autonomy, management support, and organizational commitment.

Measuring service encounter performance is difficult for a number of reasons. The service encounter is a dyadic interaction in which employees and customers each bring their own expectations, behavioral predispositions, attitudes, goals, knowledge, skills, communication styles, and personal demographic characteristics such as gender, age, and race (Klaus, 1985; Solomon, Surprenant, Czepiel, and Gutman, 1985). The emergent nature of the behavior that results as employee and customer influence each other simultaneously defies standardization and occurs rapidly, often without being observed by a manager. The emergent behaviors that are salient to customers may be fleeting microlevel behaviors on the part of the service employee. Tone of voice, eye contact, and facial expression, for example, are readily observable to customers but difficult for a manager to observe and measure systematically enough for performance appraisal and feedback purposes.

Two approaches to measurement of functional service quality are the behavioral approach and the customer evaluation approach. A third, the quantitative approach, is used primarily to measure technical service quality. This last approach looks at objective production outcomes related to the service encounter. Examples of this type of measure are the number of service transactions completed in a time period, accuracy, speed of response, length of transaction, and adherence to script. Collier (1990) presents strategies for measuring and managing technical service quality. Because the functional aspects of service quality such as warmth, consideration, and friendliness are more difficult to measure and often overlooked (Schneider, 1980), this section focuses on the measurement of functional service quality.

Behavioral Approach

The behavioral approach involves measuring specific behaviors, such as smiling, verbalizing a scripted phrase, or asking for specific information. These behavioral specifications can be used as a basis for training, performance appraisal, and reward. This is similar to the product-attribute approach to specifying quality that is used in manufacturing organizations. While this approach is used by organizations and researchers (for example, Komaki, Blood and Holder, 1980; Brown, Malott, Dillon, and Keeps, 1980; Rafaeli, 1989, 1990), it is labor intensive, and the presence of the observing supervisor or rater is likely to influence the behavior of the service employee. This type of observation, measurement, and appraisal of specific observable service encounter behaviors can be useful for research purposes, but it is time-consuming and difficult for managers and supervisors to use consistently. In the research study by Komaki, Blood, and Holder (1980), fast food restaurant managers were asked to objectively record specific behaviors, such as frequency of smiling and talking with customers. They reported that it was difficult to motivate the managers to observe and record these behaviors regularly.

The use of an unobtrusive observer, or "mystery shopper," is one strategy that can be used to assess specific employee behaviors such as smiling, thanking the customer, and eye contact (Komaki, Blood, and Holder, 1980; Rafaeli, 1989, 1990; Tsai and Huang, 2002). This method can be useful for spot checks and research purposes, but may not sample clerk behavior consistently or systematically enough to be useful for normal performance appraisal purposes.

Although the behavioral approach does focus directly on important aspects of employee behavior in the service encounter, there may be negative side effects. Micromanaging service encounter behavior reduces employee perceptions of autonomy and control and requires close supervision and the threat of punishment (or no reward) for failure to comply. A sense of autonomy, choice, and control on the part of employees is associated with feelings of responsibility and is correlated with higher intrinsic motivation and job satisfaction, according to the well-established job characteristics theory (Champoux, 1991; Fried and Ferris, 1987; Hackman and Oldham, 1980) and other research (Spector, 1986). By using the carrot and the stick to require that employees smile, greet customers, and display specific observable behaviors, employee autonomy and felt responsibility is reduced, along with intrinsic motivation and job satisfaction. The focus on extrinsic rewards and punishments (that is, "I am smiling at customers because it is required and there may be consequences if I don't comply," as opposed to "I am smiling at customers because I am in a good mood and care about making customers happy"), can actually reduce intrinsic motivation (Deci, 1972).

Kerr's classic article, "On the Folly of Rewarding A While Hoping for B" (1975), states that basically management gets what it rewards, which is often whatever is most readily measurable. Ideally, service employees would care about giving good service and demonstrate genuine positive emotions, helpfulness, and friendliness to customers. What is actually measured are objective quantifiable behaviors, such as smiling, eye contact, greeting, and timeliness. According to Kerr, focus on the objectively quantifiable as the basis for reward results in goal displacement, where the focus on the rewarded behavior can detract from attention to the real goal of genuine friendliness and helpfulness. This type of "quality control" specification and measurement of interpersonal behaviors can create the type of organizational climate where employees do not care about giving good service and feel little attachment or commitment to the organization.

Another limitation of the behavioral approach to specifying, measuring, and rewarding specific service encounter behaviors is that many of the behaviors that are specified may not actually relate to customer perceptions of service quality. For example, a "service quality" measure of whether a call center employee asks a caller for identifying information before disclosing account information is extremely important, but the presence of this technical service quality may not have a direct impact on customer perceptions of service encounter quality. The absence of this behavior would certainly lead to problems and customer perceptions of poor service quality, but the presence of the behavior is not likely to have a positive impact on customer judgments of service quality. Another example of a "service quality" measure is whether a retail employee greets the customer within five seconds of store entrance. Many customers may perceive this service encounter behavior as scripted, intrusive, or annoying, and it can actually reduce customers' satisfaction with their service experience.

Customer Evaluation Approach

Rather than measure specific employee service encounter behaviors directly, customer perceptions of service quality are closer to the actual phenomena of interest: the views of the customer. Organizations that are interested in improving service quality need to stay close to the customer in terms of gathering relevant information about customer expectations, preferences, and judgments about the quality of service encounter transactions (Parasuraman, Zeithaml, and Berry, 1985; Schneider, Holcombe, and White, 1997). The customer perception approach views service encounter quality not as an objective product attribute but as a judgment or belief held by customers based on impressions largely formed through the interpersonal service encounter interaction. Service encounter quality is in the eye of the beholder. Therefore, customer views of service quality should be assessed and used as a basis for decision making about service quality issues. How, then, can customer views be assessed?

SERVQUAL is a standardized questionnaire that has been used in a wide range of service organizations and for which there is acceptable evidence of reliability and validity (Parasuraman, Zeithaml, and Berry, 1986, 1988, 1991, 1993; Zeithaml, Parasuraman, and Berry, 1990). It assesses customer expectations and perceptions about service encounter behaviors and can be adapted for use in a variety of settings (Catanzaro, 1992; Gotlieb, Grewal, and Brown, 1994; Schneider, Wheeler, and Cox, 1992). In addition, organizational researchers and practitioners often develop their own measures of service encounter quality (Ben-Sira, 1976; Fiebelkorn, 1985; Schneider, White, and Paul, 1998; Susskind, Kacmar, and Borchgrevink, 2003; Tsai and Huang, 2002; Nelson and Nelson, 1995). Questionnaires, interviews, and other methods of collecting data about customer views of service quality should be developed using psychometric theory about test construction and sampling methodology, and the reliability and validity of these measures should be assessed. It is recommended that questionnaires and other methods used to assess customer judgments of service quality include a strong emphasis on actual service encounter behaviors. One limitation of customer questionnaires and interviews is that tying customer views to specific service employees is difficult in many organizational settings because customers are transient and may interact with more than one employee. If this is the case, customer responses will not be useful for performance appraisal or administrative decisions about individual service employees. However, even if customer responses are not tied to individual employees, these responses provide extremely relevant information about group-level service encounter performance in the eyes of the customer.

Regardless of the approaches used, quality data on customer views of service quality, customer complaints, and customer suggestions are key for decision making about how to improve service encounter quality. It is critical to have multiple, systematic methods for collecting data about policies and practices associated with customer dissatisfaction.

Other Strategies for Assessing Service Encounter Effectiveness

Organizations can use feedback cards or formal complaints as mechanisms for gauging customer satisfaction. Voluntary methods such as feedback cards and formal complaints provide some feedback, but their usefulness is limited due to extremely low response rates, especially by satisfied customers. Complaints by customers can be informative, but a very small percentage of dissatisfied customers make a formal or informal complaint, and of these, very few reach decision makers. There is a reluctance among employees to transmit negative information up the chain of command, and in many organizations complaint management is accomplished through a consumer affairs division that is relatively isolated from management decision making (Fornell and Westbrook, 1984). Clearly, a mechanism for encouraging information about customer complaints to be collected and used for decision making is vital; however, what happens in many organizations is the opposite.

Customer complaints may be counted against the employee or the manager; therefore, the employee has an incentive not to record customer complaints or transmit these complaints to management. But without accurate data about customer complaints, decision making regarding service issues is likely to be of poor quality. Organizations can benefit greatly from developing multiple strategies for collecting and recording customer suggestions and complaints. Because these suggestions and complaints are often made during the service encounter, some mechanism to encourage service employees to record and communicate these up the chain of command is critical. If employees perceive that this information may be used against them in any way, then these critical data will not be available for organizational decision making. The impact of this shortcoming can be serious indeed.

One strategy that could both improve complaint management and have a collateral effect on improving service encounters is to involve service employees in systematically recording all customer complaints and suggestions related to policies, practices, or service quality. Employee names should not be used in complaint documentation. There could be a modest incentive for employees based on the number of complaints recorded. This information is sent up the chain of command to provide important data for decision making. The data should not be used to punish employees or managers in any way.

Strategy 2: Ensure Employee Involvement and Participation in Diagnosing and Improving Service Quality

Employees could also be involved in providing information about policies and practices that lead to service encounter difficulties, as well as problem solving to determine solutions to service quality issues. Although this strategy relates to the previous topic of assessing and measuring service quality, it has an additional benefit: by increasing employee involvement and participation in problem identification and solution generation, employees are more likely to experience a sense of ownership of service quality problems, perceive that management considers them important partners in providing services, and think of themselves as empowered to address and solve service quality problems. The powerful influence of participative decision making on employee attitudes is well documented. For example, Goldstein (1978) created participative employee committees to solicit employee suggestions regarding service quality–related problems and solutions in a hospital radiology department, and reported that serious service quality problems were remedied. Spector (1986) summarized the results of eighty-eight research studies and concluded that there is a strong relationship between employee feelings of perceived control, autonomy, and participation in decision making and many behavioral and job satisfaction outcomes. Involving service employees as partners in building a strong service culture helps to create the types of attitudes that make it more likely that employees will care about giving good service to customers.

A number of approaches to employee participation and involvement can be used to tap employee knowledge about service quality and at the same time empower employees as partners in the quest for quality service. Nyquist, Bitner, and Booms (1985) suggest that service employees be interviewed using a critical incidents method (Flanagan, 1954) where they describe specific instances of communication difficulties with customers. Incidents can be classified according to the source (that is, customer expectations were unreasonable, or the firm's or employee's performance failed to meet acceptable standards) and nature (the customer was drunk and disorderly) of the incident. Then employees and management work together to develop strategies to deal with these incidents, which could involve one or more of the four-pronged approaches described in the next section. Schneider, Wheeler, and Cox (1992) used focus group interviews with employees in three financial services organizations and content-analyzed themes relevant to service climate. The resulting knowledge could be used to improve the service climate, an important predictor of employee service encounter behavior (Schneider, 1980). The impact on the service encounter is indirect, through creating a more service-oriented climate, but this approach may actually be more effective in improving service quality than the direct approaches of specifying key behaviors and then rewarding or punishing these behaviors.

Strategy 3: Manage the Conflict Between Customer Expectations and Service Performance

Clear standards for service performance, including goals and objectives, management expectations, and policies and practices aligned with the goal of excellent customer service are a foundation for creating a service culture (Susskind, Kacmar, and Borchgrevink, 2003). Customer dissatisfaction with the service encounter often results from a gap between customer expectations and organizational policies, practices, or ability to meet those expectations (Parasuraman, Zeithaml, and Berry, 1985). The service employee bears the brunt of dissatisfaction created by this gap. A dyadic role perspective, examining behavioral expectations for the employee and customer roles, allows a better understanding of the impact of this gap on the service encounter (Solomon, Surprenant,

Czepiel, and Gutman, 1985). The employee experiences role conflict when two aspects of the service role conflict. The employee role involves implementing organizational policies and practices as well as satisfying the customer. The employee cannot simultaneously follow organizational policies and create a satisfied customer if the policies and practices do not meet or they conflict with customer expectations (Schneider, 1980).

When customers experience dissatisfaction with service policies or practices, they may respond with frustration, anger, or other negative emotions, which can lead to employee frustration and negative emotion. Ryan, Schmit, and Johnson (1996) found a relationship between employee job satisfaction and customer satisfaction, but the results demonstrated that customer dissatisfaction may in fact lead to employee dissatisfaction. Due to the emergent and reciprocal nature of dyadic interactions, it is likely that employee and customer mood and satisfaction transfer between both parties during the service encounter.

This gap between customer expectations and service provided, and the resulting role conflict, can be addressed through a four-pronged approach:

1. Change, improve, or eliminate the policies, procedures, or practices that lead to customer dissatisfaction when feasible.
2. Educate customers prior to the service encounter so their expectations will be more realistic and fit the organization's service delivery system.
3. Train employees how to better handle dissatisfied customers who complain or behave inappropriately.
4. Improve technical service quality to meet or exceed customer expectations for performance.

These four approaches complement each other, and in the next section we offer recommendations for implementing them.

Recommendation 1: Align Organizational Policies, Procedures, or Practices with Customer Service Goals

In some cases, the administrative efficiency or cost benefit of a policy that customers dislike may not compensate for the costs in terms of employee stress, customer goodwill, and loss of repeat business. An example is a store that has a no-refunds policy with only a small sign to alert customers, or a restaurant with a no-substitutions policy. Management establishes a policy that reduces direct costs or is administratively efficient. The service employee is the one who has to deal with the resulting dissatisfaction of irate customers day in and day out. The disliked policy communicates to both customers and employees that customer satisfaction is secondary to management prerogatives. Management communications about the importance of customer service ring hollow to employees, who see the discrepancy between management talk and practice. Of course, in some cases, a policy or practice may be required by law or have a reasonable rationale and is not amenable to change. In this case, one of the other approaches we describe would be appropriate.

Recommendation 2: Provide Customer Education and Communication

A second approach is to educate customers prior to the service encounter about these policies and practices so that their expectations will be more closely aligned with the level of service provided (Parasuraman, Zeithaml, and Berry, 1985). This can happen through various channels such as signage, advertising, promotional literature, and direct communications from service employees. Too often, advertising and promotional literature creates customer expectations that the organization cannot meet. This creates a situation where difficult service encounters are likely to result. For example, an airline whose low-cost strategy involves no meals during flights, or that charges for meals, can incorporate this information in its advertising strategy, have reservation agents provide this information to customers, or clearly provide this information to customers prior to point-of-purchase on its Web site.

Recommendation 3: Provide Employee Training

This recommendation is to train service employees to deal effectively with dissatisfied customers and customer complaints. Some level of role conflict is inevitable, and employees need training specifically designed to help them deal with this aspect of the service role. This training should focus on communication and problem-solving skills to deal with common customer complaints and concerns. Behavior modeling training (Decker and Nathan,

1985; Goldstein and Sorcher, 1974) is the most appropriate method for teaching these specific skills. Information supplied by both customers and service employees should be sought to determine common customer complaints that can be a basis for employee training in dealing with these complaints effectively. Service employees can also be involved in developing the appropriate verbal responses to use as a foundation for the training. This is different from "smile training" in that the focus should be more complex communication and customer-complaint response skills, as opposed to simple behaviors that are already in the employee's behavioral repertoire (smiling, greeting, thanking, suggestive selling). The goal of this training is to help employees develop communication skills that will enable them to manage difficult customer interactions with increased expertise and confidence. These skills could include maintaining control of emotion, acknowledging the customer's complaint, gathering information from the customer about the complaint, explaining the reason for a policy or practice, and offering solutions if appropriate. This training helps empower the employee to handle difficult service encounters more effectively, with resulting benefits to both employee and customer. It also communicates to employees not only that handling difficult customer service encounters is part of the job but also that the organization wants to provide support to help them with what Ashforth and Humphrey (1993) call the emotional labor of the service role.

Recommendation 4: Improve Technical Service Quality Performance

This approach involves improving the capability of the service delivery system to improve the content of service delivery or the ability of the system to meet objective performance standards. If a call center places a customer on hold for twenty minutes, a nurse gives a patient the incorrect medicine, or a restaurant serves undercooked hamburger, clearly the organization is failing to meet technical standards for service quality. Technical aspects of service quality are certainly important in their own right, and in addition will influence the dynamics of current or future service encounters. Since the focus of this chapter is the service encounter, strategies for improving technical service quality (employee training and selection, improved technology, task redesign) will not be addressed here, although the strategies for complaint management and employee involvement in solving service quality problems described earlier would address both functional and technical service quality concerns.

Strategy 4: Assess Organizational Climate for Service

In addition to using this four-pronged approach to managing the service encounter, an understanding of the larger organizational context in which these remedies operate is critical to improving the service encounter. Research by Schneider and his colleagues has shown a clear relationship between employee perceptions of organizational climate and customer perceptions of service quality (Schneider, Parkington, and Buxton, 1979; Schneider, 1980; Schneider and Bowen, 1985). The impact of the service encounter is such that employee attitudes about the job, the organization, and quality of work life correlate with customer perceptions of service quality. Employees cannot be coerced to consistently create good service encounter experiences for customers through external rewards and punishments; service encounters are often not observed, and coercive control strategies detract from the type of organizational climate associated with customer satisfaction. It is far more effective if employee are intrinsically motivated to give good service. Unfortunately, many of the strategies that organizations use to improve technical aspects of service quality can have a negative impact on the employee's intrinsic motivation to provide good service through reducing employee autonomy, increased supervision and monitoring of performance, and focus on external rewards and punishments. Many of these strategies send employees the message that customers are important but the employees are not. In this type of environment, employees may adhere to the "product specifications" for service delivery required by the organization, but if they do not genuinely care about giving good service and creating a positive service encounter, this will be apparent to customers.

For example, a major discount retail organization may require employees to say "thank you for shopping our store" as they hand purchases to customers, but if employees are just reciting words they are required to say a hundred times a day, the phrase will seldom convey warmth or gratitude. If employees feel that the organization does not care about them and that employee quality of work life and job satisfaction are not important to management, then the words could be recited with sarcasm or studied disinterest, yet still adhere to management's technical specifications. Organizations that try to improve service quality by focusing on technical specifications of the service delivery process and treating employees as if they are machines that can be programmed to service delivery specifications may create an organizational climate where it is less likely that employees will be motivated to provide customers with good service.

This trickle-down theory of service has empirical support. Schneider and Bowen (1985) found that employee perceptions of human resource practices such as work facilitation, reward, and supervisory communication consistently correlated with customer perceptions of service climate. Other researchers have noted that employee and customer mood and emotion are "contagious" and have an impact on each other in the service encounter (Pugh, 2001). Unhappy employees can lead to unhappy customers, and vice versa. While the big picture in terms of organizational goals and strategies, technical service quality outcomes, and types of services provided is important, it is also critical for organizations to think small in terms of how various service strategies and goals affect the actual service encounter between employees and customers.

Strategy 5: Think About Service Encounter Behavior as a Type of Organizational Citizenship Behavior

Organizational citizenship behaviors (OCBs) are employee behaviors that go beyond strict role or task requirements in ways that support the organization's goals and objectives (Smith, Organ, and Near, 1983). Motowidlo, Borman, and Schmit (1997) call these behaviors *contextual performance* and propose that these prosocial behaviors are especially important for customer service performance. Although there is a lively debate on whether certain behaviors are truly altruistic or seen by employees as part of the job, there is no question that these behaviors are valuable to organizations. Going the extra mile to complete a task or help a customer or coworker, cooperating with others, volunteering for extra tasks, following rules and procedures, and defending and supporting organizational objectives are all examples of OCBs.

In many ways, OCBs are critical to service encounter performance. A supermarket employee who goes out of the way to help a customer find the miso, a nursing aide who takes the time to listen kindly to an elderly resident's story for the seventeenth time, and an airline employee who offers extra assistance to help a visitor who does not understand English find the correct gate are all examples of OCBs. These specific behaviors are generally not formally required in the position description and are discretionary on the part of the employee. They are often performed without being observed or prompted by a manager or supervisor. While managers may say they expect employees to go the extra mile, whether the employee actually does this is dependent on the employee's mood, altruism, and initiative. These OCBs are in turn influenced by a number of factors related to how employees feel that the organization treats them.

Moorman (1991) found that employee perceptions of interactional justice and employee OCB behaviors as rated by supervisors had a causal relationship. Interactional justice is a type of procedural justice that deals with employee perceptions of fairness regarding how they are treated during interactions with supervisors and other representatives of management. Interactional justice was assessed through questionnaire items that asked whether the supervisor was considerate and kind, whether the supervisor considered the employee's rights, and whether the supervisor dealt with the employee in a truthful manner. Moorman concluded that supervisors can directly influence employee OCB behavior by striving to increase the fairness of their treatment of employees. Although this study was conducted with manufacturing employees, the implications for service employees are clear. If service employees feel they are treated fairly and considerately by supervisors, they are more likely to perform altruistic behaviors on behalf of the organization during interactions with customers.

Bettencourt, Gwinner, and Meuter (2001) conducted research with 325 call center employees in a financial services organization and 144 library employees in customer-contact jobs at five university libraries. They assessed employee-perceived organizational support through items developed by Eisenberger, Huntington, Hutchinson, and Sowa (1986). Examples of items are, "The organization really cares about my well-being," "The organization cares about my opinions," and "The organization shows very little concern for me." In addition, they assessed loyalty OCBs, which concern how the employee represents the organization to outsiders, such as customers. Examples of items are, "Actively promotes the firm's products and services," "Generates favorable goodwill for the company," and "Tells outsiders this is a good place to work" (Van Dyne, Graham, and Dienesch, 1994). Bettencourt, Gwinner, and Meuter found that employee job satisfaction and perceived organizational support were key predictors of loyalty OCBs. Employees who feel the organization genuinely cares about their well-being are more likely to want to represent that organization positively to customers.

There is a well-established connection between positive mood and engaging in prosocial and helping behavior (Rosenhan, Salovery, and Hargis, 1981). George (1991) extended this research to examine the relationship of mood on prosocial customer service behaviors in a sample of 221 salespeople working for a large retailer. Positive mood at work significantly correlated with both customer service behavior as reported by supervisors and sales performance.

What implications does the research on organizational citizenship behavior have for practitioners? In essence, service employees have to be "sold" on the organization so that they want to represent the organization well to customers. If employees genuinely like their jobs, believe they are treated well by management, and have positive feelings for the organization, they are likely to want to create a positive image for the organization in their interactions with customers. If employees do not like their jobs, believe they are treated unfairly by management, and have negative feelings toward the organization, they are not likely to be concerned about representing that organization in a positive manner to customers. Management cannot force an employee to go above and beyond the call of duty, demonstrate authentic concern for customers, or give a genuine smile. Organizations can, however, create working conditions that make employees want to do these things. An organizational environment that fosters employee job satisfaction, perceptions of fair treatment, and feelings that the organization cares about and supports employees creates the conditions in which employees are more likely to care about service quality and treat customers well. Employee feelings regarding these quality of work-life issues translate into service encounter behaviors that impact customers.

Tips for Improving the Service Encounter

The following tips for improving the quality of employee-customer service encounters are based on several decades of research and logical extensions of this knowledge:

• Attempting to micromanage employee service encounter behavior through measuring and rewarding or punishing employees based on compliance with behavioral specifications such as canned greeting, sales, and thanking scripts is counterproductive and actually creates an organizational climate that is less likely to lead to customer satisfaction. This type of strategy reduces employee feelings of autonomy, intrinsic motivation, and genuine emotion. Therefore, *Tip 1: Don't ignore the basics. Create an organizational environment in which employees feel valued, treated fairly, and supported by management.* This type of climate, coupled with standards and expectations for quality service, creates the kind of environment where employees genuinely want to give good service and represent the organization in a positive light.

• Both positive and negative emotions on the part of employees are readily "caught" by customers, and vice versa. Therefore, *Tip 2: Remember that human resource and management practices need to be aligned with the goal of creating an atmosphere where employees feel positive emotions at work.* Management policies and practices that support the goal of quality service, considerate and fair treatment by management and internal service providers, employee involvement in decision making and problem solving, and other strategies that show management concern for both employee and customer welfare are all part of creating a climate where employees feel positively about the organization and their contribution to it. This is particularly true for service jobs that are low in task attributes associated with intrinsic motivation due to low autonomy, little task variety, and low skill challenge, such as call center operator. Because the job is so inflexible and structured, supervisors of these jobs need to exhibit high consideration toward employees.

• Quality data on customer views of service quality are vital for decision making. Organizations need multiple strategies for collecting this data. So, *Tip 3: Get help from your employees. Involve employees in systematically recording customer complaints for a given time period and forwarding this information up the chain of command.* No punishment of employees or managers based on these complaints can follow, or these complaints will not be recorded. This can work only in an organization where there is a high level of trust in management's word that there are no consequences for accurate recording of employee complaints. A modest incentive could also be offered. This approach is a way to collect quality data and also communicates to employees that they are partners with management in working on service quality management.

• *Tip 4: Involve employees in diagnosing service quality problems and subsequently developing solutions to service quality problems.* This approach has several benefits. It generates good information about service quality concerns and weaknesses. Employees, who are close to the customer and bear the brunt of customer dissatisfaction, often have valuable ideas about how to improve service quality. In addition, this process communicates to employees that their input, knowledge, and ideas are valued, creating a sense of ownership and empowerment in resolving service quality issues. These feelings and attitudes will be noticed by customers during the service encounter and can translate into improved customer views of service quality.

• Organizations need a multipronged approach to reducing the gap between customer expectations and perceived service quality. Tips 5, 6, and 7 are three approaches to reducing this gap. *Tip 5: Revise policies and practices that customers dislike when possible.* These policies and procedures may cost more in terms of customer goodwill than the benefits gained through administrative efficiency. *Tip 6: Communicate with customers through a variety of means, including advertising, signage, and interpersonal communications, to provide customers information about policies and procedures in order to create realistic expectations about the service delivery system and the rationale for any policies and procedures disliked by customers.* When a policy or procedure is not amenable to change, clear communication about the policy and its rationale can reduce or prevent customer dissatisfaction. *Tip 7: Train employees to communicate effectively in difficult service encounter scenarios, such as handling a customer complaint.* Behavior modeling training, which involves observation of a model using the behavior, practice, and feedback, is the appropriate method for teaching this type of communication skills. Employees can be involved in developing the key learning points to be used in this training.

• *Tip 8: Create an organizational climate where employees feel attached to the organization and are internally motivated to be helpful to customers.* When employees are satisfied with their jobs, feel well treated by management, and believe that organizational policies and practices support the goals of customer service as well as concern for employee needs, they are more likely to be helpful to customers during service encounters on a voluntary basis, without need for close supervision and monitoring, formal reward and punishment, or service scripts.

Conclusion

The bottom line in trying to improve the service encounter is that it is resistant to overt attempts on the part of management to use the typical management control mechanisms of behavioral specifications, close supervision and monitoring, performance appraisal, and contingent reward. It is more amenable to influence through indirect strategies that focus on creating a climate for service, employee feelings of fair and supportive treatment, and a work environment that causes employees to care about customers. Customers can sense the difference between "positive vibes" and "fake greetings," and only one of these will have a positive influence on customer views of service quality. While many of the principles discussed in this chapter sound a lot like the golden rule, we propose a slightly revised version: "Do unto employees as you would have your employees do unto customers." Consider it organizational karma, but how management treats people counts.

References

Aldrich, H., and Herker, D. "Boundary-Spanning Roles and Organizational Structure." *Academy of Management Review,* 1977, *2,* 217–230.

Ashforth, B. E., and Humphrey, R. H. "Emotional Labor in Service Roles: The Influence of Identity." *Academy of Management Review,* 1993, *18,* 88–115.

Ben-Sira, Z. "The Function of the Professional's Affective Behavior in Client Satisfaction: A Revised Approach to Social Interaction Theory." *Journal of Health and Social Behavior,* 1976, *17*(3), 3–11.

Berry, L. L. "Service Marketing Is Different." *Business,* May-June 1980, pp. 24–29.

Bettencourt, L. A., Gwinner, K. P., and Meuter, M. L. "A Comparison of Attitude, Personality, and Knowledge Predictors of Service-Oriented Citizenship Behaviors." *Journal of Applied Psychology,* 2001, *86,* 29–41.

Bowen, D. E., and Schneider, B. "Boundary-Role-Spanning Employees and the Service Encounter: Some Guidelines for Management and Research." In J. A. Czepiel, M. R. Solomon, and C. F. Surprenant (eds.), *The Service Encounter.* Boston: Houghton Mifflin, 1985.

Brown, M. G., Malott, R. W., Dillon, M. J., and Keeps, E. J. "Improving Customer Service in a Large Department Store Through Use of Training and Feedback." *Journal of Organizational Behavior Management,* 1980, *2,* 251–264.

Catanzaro, D. "The Impact of an Employee Involvement Program on Service Quality in a Nursing Home Organization." *Dissertation Abstracts International,* 1992, *53,* 4403B.

Champoux, J. E. "A Multivariate Test of the Job Characteristics Theory of Work Motivation." *Journal of Organizational Behavior,* 1991, *12,* 431–446.

Collier, D. A. "Measuring and Managing Service Quality." In D. E. Bowen, R. B. Chase, and T. G. Cummings (eds.), *Service Management Effectiveness.* San Francisco: Jossey-Bass, 1990.

Czepiel, J. A., Solomon, M. R., and Surprenant, C. F. (eds.). *The Service Encounter.* Boston: Houghton Mifflin, 1985.

Czepiel, J. A., Solomon, M. R., Surprenant, C. F., and Gutman, E. G. "Service Encounters: An Overview." In J. A. Czepiel, M. R. Solomon, and C. F. Surprenant (eds.), *The Service Encounter.* Boston: Houghton Mifflin, 1985.

Deci, E. L. "The Effects of Contingent and Non-Contingent Rewards and Controls on Intrinsic Motivation." *Organizational Behavior and Human Performance,* 1972, *8,* 217–229.

Decker, P. J., and Nathan, B. R. *Behavior Modeling Training: Principles and Applications.* New York: Praeger, 1985.

Eisenberger, R., Huntington, R., Hutchinson, S., and Sowa, D. "Perceived Organizational Support." *Journal of Applied Psychology,* 1986, *71,* 500–507.

Fiebelkorn, S. L. "Retail Service Encounter Satisfaction: Model and Measurement." In J. A. Czepiel, M. R. Solomon, and C. F. Surprenant (eds.), *The Service Encounter.* Boston: Houghton Mifflin, 1985.

Flanagan, J. C. "The Critical Incident Technique." *Psychological Bulletin,* 1954, *51,* 327–358.

Fornell, C., and Westbrook, R. A. "The Vicious Circle of Consumer Complaints." *Journal of Marketing,* 1984, *48,* 68–77.

Fried, Y., and Ferris, G. R. "The Validity of the Job Characteristics Model: A Review and Meta-Analysis." *Personnel Psychology,* 1987, *40,* 287–322.

George, J. M. "State or Trait: Effects of Positive Mood on Prosocial Behaviors at Work." *Journal of Applied Psychology,* 1991, *76,* 299–307.

Goldstein, A. P., and Sorcher, M. *Changing Supervisory Behavior.* New York: Pergamon Press, 1974.

Goldstein, S. G. "A Structure for Change." *Human Relations,* 1978, *31,* 957–983.

Gotlieb, J. B., Grewal, D., and Brown, S. W. "Consumer Satisfaction and Perceived Quality: Complimentary or Divergent Constructs?" *Journal of Applied Psychology,* 1994, *79,* 875–885.

Gronroos, C. "A Service-Oriented Approach to Marketing of Services." *European Journal of Marketing,* 1978, *12,* 588–601.

Gronroos, C. *Strategic Management and Marketing in the Service Sector.* Cambridge, Mass.: Marketing Science Institute, 1983.

Gutek, B. A. *The Dynamics of Service.* San Francisco: Jossey-Bass, 1995.

Hackman, J. R., and Oldham, G. R. *Work Redesign.* Reading, Mass.: Addison-Wesley, 1980.

Hatfield, E., Cacioppo, J. T., and Rapson, R. L. *Emotional Contagion.* Cambridge: Cambridge University Press, 1994.

Kerr, S. "On the Folly of Rewarding A While Hoping for B." *Academy of Management Journal,* 1975, *18,* 769–783.

Klaus, P. G. "Quality Epiphenomenon: The Conceptual Understanding of Quality in Face-to-Face Service Encounters." In J. A. Czepiel, M. R. Solomon, and C. F. Surprenant (eds.), *The Service Encounter.* Boston: Houghton Mifflin, 1985.

Komaki, J., Blood, M., and Holder, D. "Fostering Friendliness in a Fast Food Franchise." *Journal of Organizational Behavior Management,* 1980, *2,* 151–164.

Lovelock, C. H. "Why Marketing Management Needs to Be Different for Services." In J. H. Donnelly and W. R. George (eds.), *Marketing of Services.* Chicago: American Marketing Association, 1981.

Mills, P. K., and Moberg, D. J. "Perspectives on the Technology of Service Organizations." *Academy of Management Review,* 1982, *7,* 467–478.

Moorman, R. H. "Relationship Between Organizational Justice and Organizational Citizenship Behaviors: Do Fairness Perceptions Influence Employee Citizenship?" *Journal of Applied Psychology,* 1991, *76,* 845–855.

Motowidlo, S. J., Borman, W. C., and Schmit, M. J. "A Theory of Individual Differences in Task and Contextual Performance." *Human Performance,* 1997, *10,* 71–83.

Nelson, S. L., and Nelson, T. R. "RESERV: An Instrument for Measuring Real Estate Brokerage Service Quality." *Journal of Real Estate Research*, 1995, *10*, 99–113.

Nyquist, J. D., Bitner, M. F., and Booms, B. H. "Identifying Communication Difficulties in the Service Encounter: A Critical Incident Approach." In J. A. Czepiel, M. R. Solomon, and C. F. Surprenant (eds.), *The Service Encounter*. Boston: Houghton Mifflin, 1985.

Parasuraman, A., Zeithaml, V. A., and Berry, L. L. "A Conceptual Model of Service Quality and Its Implications for Future Research." *Journal of Marketing*, 1985, *49*(3), 41–50.

Parasuraman, A., Zeithaml, V. A., and Berry, L. L. *SERVQUAL: A Multiple-Item Scale for Measuring Consumer Perceptions of Service Quality*. Cambridge, Mass.: Marketing Science Institute, 1986.

Parasuraman, A., Zeithaml, V. A., and Berry, L. L. "SERVQUAL: A Multiple-Item Scale for Measuring Consumer Perceptions of Service Quality." *Journal of Retailing*, 1988, *64*, 12–40.

Parasuraman, A., Zeithaml, V. A., and Berry, L. L. "Refinement and Reassessment of the SERVQUAL Scale." *Journal of Retailing*, 1991, *67*, 420–450.

Parasuraman, A., Zeithaml, V. A., and Berry, L. L. "The Nature and Determinants of Customer Expectations of Service." *Journal of the Academy of Marketing Science*, 1993, *21*, 1–12.

Pugh, D. "Service with a Smile: Emotional Contagion in the Service Encounter." *Academy of Management Journal*, 2001, *44*, 1018–1027.

Rafaeli, A. "When Clerks Meet Customers: A Test of Variables Related to Emotional Expressions on the Job." *Journal of Applied Psychology*, 1989, *74*, 385–393.

Rafaeli, A. "Busy Stores and Demanding Customers: How Do They Affect the Display of Positive Emotion?" *Academy of Management Journal*, 1990, *33*, 623–639.

Rosenhan, D. L., Salovery, P., and Hargis, K. "The Joys of Helping: Focus of Attention Mediates the Impact of Positive Affect on Altruism." *Journal of Personality and Social Psychology*, 1981, *40*, 899–905.

Ryan, A. M., Schmit, M. J., and Johnson, R. "Attitudes and Effectiveness: Examining Attitudes at an Organizational Level." *Personnel Psychology*, 1996, *49*, 853–882.

Schneider, B. "The Service Organization: Climate Is Crucial." *Organizational Dynamics*, Autumn 1980, pp. 52–65.

Schneider, B., and Bowen, D. E. "Employee and Customer Service Perceptions of Service in Banks: Replication and Extension." *Journal of Applied Psychology*, 1985, *70*, 423–433.

Schneider, B., Holcombe, K. M., and White, S. S. "Lessons Learned About Service Quality: What It Is, How to Manage It, and How to Become a Service Quality Organization." *Consulting Psychology Journal: Practice and Research,* 1997, *49,* 35–50.

Schneider, B., Parkington, J. J., and Buxton, V. M. "Employee and Customer Perceptions of Service in Banks." *Administrative Science Quarterly,* 1980, *25,* 252–267.

Schneider, B., Wheeler, J. K., and Cox, J. F. "A Passion for Service: Using Content Analysis to Explicate Service Climate Themes." *Journal of Applied Psychology,* 1992, *77,* 705–716.

Schneider, B., White, S. S., and Paul, M. C. "Linking Service Climate and Customer Perceptions of Service Equality: Test of a Causal Model." *Journal of Applied Psychology,* 1998, *83,* 150–163.

Shostack, G. L. "Breaking Free from Product Marketing." *Journal of Marketing,* 1977, *41*(4), 73–80.

Shostack, G. L. "Planning the Service Encounter." In J. A. Czepiel, M. R. Solomon, and C. F. Surprenant (eds.), *The Service Encounter.* Boston: Houghton Mifflin, 1985.

Smith, C. A., Organ, D. W., and Near, J. P. "Organizational Citizenship Behavior: Its Nature and Antecedents." *Journal of Applied Psychology,* 1983, *68,* 653–663.

Snyder, C. A., Cox, J. F., and Jesse, R. R., Jr. "A Dependent Demand Approach to Service Organization Planning and Control." *Academy of Management Review,* 1982, *7,* 455–466.

Solomon, M. R., Surprenant, C., Czepiel, J. A., and Gutman, E. G. "A Role Theory Perspective on Dyadic Interactions: The Service Encounter." *Journal of Marketing,* 1985, *49*(10), 99–111.

Spector, P. E. "Perceived Control by Employees: A Meta-Analysis of Studies Concerning Autonomy and Participation at Work." *Human Relations,* 1986, *39,* 1005–1016.

Susskind, A. M., Kacmar, K. M., and Borchgrevink, C. P. "Customer Service Providers' Attitudes Relating to Customer Service and Customer Satisfaction in the Customer-Server Exchange." *Journal of Applied Psychology,* 2003, *88,* 179–187.

Tansik, D. A. "Managing Human Resources Issues for High-Contact Service Personnel." In D. E. Bowen, R. B. Chase, and T. G. Cummings (eds.), *Service Management Effectiveness.* San Francisco: Jossey-Bass, 1990.

Tsai, W., and Huang, Y. "Mechanisms Linking Employee Affective Delivery and Customer Behavioral Intentions." *Journal of Applied Psychology,* 2002, *87,* 1001–1008.

Van Dyne, L., Graham, J. W., and Dienesch, R. M. "Organizational Citizenship Behavior: Construct Redefinition, Measurement, and Validation." *Academy of Management Journal*, 1994, *37*, 765–802.

Verbeke, W., "Individual Differences in Emotional Contagion of Salespersons: Its Effect on Performance and Burnout." *Psychology and Marketing*, 1977, *14*, 617–636.

Zeithaml, V. A., Parasuraman, A., and Berry, L. L. *Service Quality*. New York: McGraw-Hill, 1990.

Chapter 8

"This Call May Be Monitored"

Performance Management for Service Quality

Seymour Adler
Miriam T. Nelson

Imagine designing a performance management system for a job in which virtually every aspect of an employee's performance could be captured. All work-related conversations are digitally recorded. Every computer screen accessed by employees, and the length of time spent on each screen, can be retraced. Every keystroke is recorded. The time employees spend on discrete activities is automatically measured in seconds. Objective measures of productivity for individual employees and for work teams as a whole are electronically logged and available to management in real time.

These are the characteristics of the telephone customer service representative job in large, sophisticated call centers. In contrast with performance management systems that rely extensively on inherently subjective judgments of performance against inherently vague criteria captured retrospectively, performance management in customer service call centers often can be designed in an almost ideal environment.

However, with detailed and precise quantitative service measures so readily available, call center management often cannot resist "metrics mania"—evaluating representatives and their supervisors on a multitude of dimensions. One Fortune 500 technology company evaluates its customer service representatives on thirty-six separate metrics. Supervisors are expected to analyze each of these metrics several times daily and use these analyses to intervene in the deployment, motivation, and behavior of their teams. Not surprisingly, the task of managing performance under these conditions is overwhelming.

In reality, despite the abundance of metrics captured by technology, frontline call center workers, like their counterparts elsewhere, are often forced to guess how well they are performing and where they need to improve. One recent survey of 1,149 frontline call center representatives found that the effectiveness of the performance appraisal process was rated only average (Albrecht and Zemke, 2002). Dissatisfaction is greatest with measures of the core of service quality: the call monitoring ratings that attempt to evaluate how customers are actually treated by representatives on calls.

In this chapter, we describe how call monitoring can be designed and implemented effectively as a key component of performance management to drive customer service quality in the call center. We choose this focus because of the characteristics that make the call center an almost ideal setting to apply the science of performance management. In addition, call center representatives are an increasingly significant part of the workforce providing customer service globally.

Evolving Customer Service Call Center Environment

The customer service call center industry has experienced enormous growth since the first modern call center was created in 1973 as a joint venture of Rockwell Electronic Commerce and Continental Airlines (Durr, 2001). In 2001, there were 55,800 call centers in North America, of which about 90 percent, or 50,200, were located in the United States. Datamonitor, a business intelligence research group, expects the total number of call centers in North America to increase to 58,800 by 2007, representing a compound annual growth rate of 0.89 percent. In 2001, there were 2.9 million call center agent positions in North America. Parallel to this domestic growth is the much discussed trend of booming offshore, or globally sourced, call centers that service the U.S. marketplace from sites in India, Ireland, Israel, the Philippines, and other countries with educated populations of English speakers.

In the early days of call centers, management was challenged simply to ensure that enough staff were in place to answer the telephones. Success was measured by simple quantitative metrics: how quickly calls were answered, the number of calls waiting in queue, abandoned calls, and average talk time. These data, called key performance indicators (KPIs) by call center professionals, were provided by measurement systems attached to the call center's switching technology.

Over the past decade, the service quality construct has become more complex. As a consequence, simple quantitative KPIs captured exclusively through technology, while still important, are insufficient as operational measures of service quality. In order to fully evaluate service quality today, quantitative KPIs need to be complemented by behaviorally based measures that assess the quality of the customer-representative interaction.

This increased complexity is evidenced in a number of ways. First, call centers are often no longer viewed by management primarily as cost centers, a necessary expense for doing business. Rather call centers are expected to contribute to the organization's top and bottom lines. Representatives are commonly expected to respond to inbound service inquiries and smoothly bridge to sell additional products and services. This cross-selling generates new revenue from the customer transaction. Second, innovations in the channels and speed through which service is provided to customers over the past decade have raised the bar on the level of service expected of call center agents. Merely satisfying the customer is no longer acceptable. The service experience is expected to "delight" the customer in order to affect customer loyalty as measured in economic value (for example, spend) over the customer's lifetime. Loyal customers are also more likely to spread positive word-of-mouth, promoting the organization's most effective and cost-efficient customer-acquisition channel (Reichheld, 2003).

A third aspect of this growing complexity is the evolution of the traditional call center into a multichannel contact center. Regardless of the channel through which the customer enters—telephone, Web, chat, e-mail, voice over Internet protocol—customers expect to be provided with consistent service and comparable effectiveness.

Finally, in many cases, the range of products and services provided by an organization to its customers has multiplied, requiring representatives to be versed in many more offerings. For example, at American Express, call center representatives in the card business supported four types of charge cards in 1994. That number had increased by 2004 to over two hundred consumer products supported. In 2005, American Express began issuing cards through partner banks, increasing the range of offerings serviced at these call centers. Correspondingly, representatives have had to become proficient in the newly emergent technology of customer relationship management systems that integrate the often complex multiple business relationships between the organization and the customer. Effective service requires representatives to access this detailed account information, and to retrieve and communicate accurate product information, all the while maintaining positive rapport with the customer.

The evolving complexities of customer service in the contact center environment have resulted in an expansion of the competencies required of frontline representatives. Our competency analysis research indicates that effective contact center representatives are now expected to:

- Treat the customer in a personalized and respectful manner.
- Address customer issues so that they are fixed the first time.
- Balance proactive servicing with efficiency, so as to minimize handle time and cost per call.
- Expose customers to additional services that the customer may value.
- Educate customers on product use, self-service options, and product features of interest.
- Make the service encounter a positive experience that strengthens the link between the customer and the organization, enhancing loyalty and promoting the organization's brand.

In addition, an increasingly critical mission of the contact center, apart from revenue generation and customer service, is to help the enterprise better understand and react to a rapidly changing marketplace. The voice of that marketplace is expressed most clearly and directly during interactions with customers contacting the call center. Beyond the individual-level behaviors that are directed at the customer, agents in effectively managed centers contribute to corporate collective knowledge by learning from customer contacts regarding customer needs to improve business processes. Listening skills and sensitivity to the voice of the customer are critical agent competencies.

In the face of this increased job complexity and associated rising performance expectations, many call centers have simply increased the number of performance measures tracked, using increasingly sophisticated technology. These quantitative KPI measures—call length, volume, wait times, hold times, customer hang-ups, and others—are tracked precisely, are all clearly relevant to overall service quality, and need to be integrated with call monitoring scores within a comprehensive performance management system. Call center managers are generally not as concerned with the precision of measures used to track the behavioral side of service quality and metrics of the way representatives actually treat customers. Although contact center managers frequently tell us that people (typically, their emphasis) are the most important factor in service quality, their efforts to improve quality most often involve investments in technology. The term *performance management* in the contact center world refers more often to the technology systems that measure and report hard metrics of performance—KPIs of talk time, hold time, and number of customers handled (Anton, 1997)—than to processes for measuring and developing skill and enhancing performance familiar to the industrial-organizational (I/O) psychology community. Even the term *call monitoring* is often used by call center professionals to refer to the technology for recording calls rather than to the process of listening to and evaluating behavior on those calls.

Although quality monitoring using observation-based ratings of a representative's performance on customer contacts is widely deployed in call centers—indeed, one study reported that 93 percent of call centers monitor calls (Incoming Call Center Institute, 2002)—little systematic attention has been given to the design and implementation of effective call monitoring procedures as a tool for enhancing service quality. Perhaps that is why the presence or absence of a formal monitoring program in a call center seems to make surprisingly little difference in ratings of customer satisfaction. In one study of over three hundred call centers, those with formal monitoring programs had a 66 percent customer satisfaction rate; those without had a 63 percent satisfaction rate (Service Quality Management Group, 2000).

In this chapter, we share our experiences in designing and deploying call monitoring effectively to drive service quality. Over the past decade, we have studied, designed, and operated call monitoring processes in over fifty organizations across several industry groups and in the public sector. The call center organizations we work with range from seventy-five agents to over three thousand. Our knowledge is based on our experiences with these contact centers, and we share those experiences in this chapter. Although our focus is on performance management in the contact center, we believe that the principles applied to effective contact center performance management, rooted as they are in the fundamentals of psychological theory and research, are relevant to customer service environments more broadly.

Our emphasis is on call monitoring ratings based on direct observation of a service representative's behavior. We emphasize call monitoring in part because it is so widely used in call centers. We also focus on monitoring because its clearly behavioral approach should be of great interest to the I/O psychology community but has been little studied to date. We also address the role of quantitative KPI metrics in service performance management and the interplay between these quantitative metrics and call monitoring ratings. In addition to describing the use of call monitoring to enhance the quality of the service provided to call center customers, we illustrate how monitoring data can be applied to test hypotheses of practical and theoretical interest, for example, concerning the effect of feedback on cognitively driven versus affectively driven behavior.

Process Model

We will refer to a simple process model to guide our work in the design, implementation, and ongoing conduct of monitoring. Exhibit 8.1 depicts the key components of the process model, which we outline here and then apply to structure our discussion of performance management in the balance of this chapter. Briefly stated, the key activities associated with each element are:

Exhibit 8.1. Process Model for Performance Management.

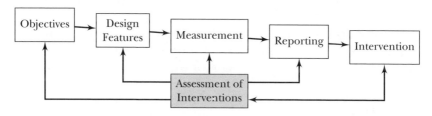

1. Objectives: The objectives of the performance management system are specified and reflect organizational and customer requirements. These objectives, which might include reduced
   customer attrition or lower cost per contact, guide system design.
2. Design features: The key elements of the performance management system are defined. These features include the population to be measured and the performance dimensions on
   which they are measured.
3. Measurement: Quantitative and qualitative evaluations of service performance across multiple dimensions are captured.
   The quality of the measurement methodology is assessed
   against the basic principles of sound scientific measurement.
4. Reporting: Evaluative data are converted into useful information by analyzing the measures collected and teasing out actionable meaning. For monitoring-based evaluations, this
   involves, for example, identifying areas of skill strength and
   areas requiring improvement at the individual and team levels
   or determining, as another example, which agent behaviors are
   most likely to undermine or promote customer loyalty.
5. Intervention: The ultimate purpose of performance management is to improve performance. Activities aimed at improving service quality include feedback, coaching, training, and
   business process redesign. In the intervention stage, strengths
   are leveraged while deficiencies in service performance are
   addressed.
6. Assessment: Monitoring is used to evaluate the effectiveness of
   interventions. The assessment may also result in revising objectives or redesigning the measurement or reporting process. Assessment closes the loop in a continuous effort to improve the

performance management process and ultimately to enhance service quality.

We use this model in the rest of this chapter to structure our description of the development and deployment of an effective performance management system for the call center environment.

Objectives

In order for a performance management (PM) process to drive service quality, it needs to meet the following requisites.

Align with Business Goals

Contact center PM is a means of translating business goals into the KPIs and the expected service behaviors on the individual and unit levels that will be used to define and track customer service. This alignment includes trade-off decisions about staffing levels that balance availability to customers calling in, on the one hand, with labor costs on the other, when setting KPI standards for queue time and handle time. It requires operationalizing broad corporate value statements (for example, "the customer is king") into concrete service delivery metrics (for example, no customers will be kept on hold for more than sixty seconds and every call will end with the representative saying "thank you"), taking into account the costs of customer dissatisfaction. Similarly the use of monitoring data for employee development or for assigning rewards and sanctions will reflect the values of the organization's culture. In addition, the PM system must meet the central criterion applied to every business system: positive return on investment. Its contribution to profitability must exceed the cost of running the system.

Reflect the Customer View

Internal service performance expectations need to be rooted in the needs and experiences of customers. As Schneider and White (2004) point out, in most service encounters, the experience is the service. Performance expectations must reflect customer requirements, and performance management must be directed at improving the customer experience. To meet this objective, designers of PM processes need to capture the customer view both initially and on an ongoing basis. London and Beatty (1993) argue that collecting customer feedback can be a competitive advantage if the feedback is translated into specific processes that focus directly on creating customer value. Initially, this may involve focus groups and customer surveys that define the service behaviors or outcomes expected. Best of all, data on expressed customer experiences, needs, satisfaction, and dissatisfaction can be captured on an ongoing basis during the service call itself, analyzed, and then used to improve the service process.

Define Service Quality

The business objectives and customer experience are the basis for specifying the key tasks, behaviors, and processes required to produce effective customer service. It is imperative that these behaviors and outcomes are well defined, linked to corporate objectives and to the customer experience, and accompanied by specific evaluation standards for each level of performance. An important objective of a customer service PM program is to communicate performance expectations to the frontline organization in specific and achievable terms.

Improve Performance

The PM system must produce information that provides guidance for service improvement on both the individual and unit levels. The system should be designed so that information is clear and accessible to all those who can act on the data to improve service quality. Those with access could include representatives themselves, their management, as well as other departments within the organization (such as product design or marketing). The identification of individual skill deficiencies should trigger training interventions. The identification of knowledge gaps in describing products or service may lead to the development of an online product fact sheet for representatives to use on calls. The frontline call center is a primary point of contact with customers. Data, insights, customer reactions, and customer experience tracked in the contact center are

gold nuggets to be mined for marketplace intelligence and to identify internal processes that need to be changed. When effective information flow is in place, the frontline contact center can truly
serve as a strategic asset.

Design Features

The performance management system in a call center should have
a number of key features, including measures of the quantitative
KPIs, behavioral call monitoring, a defined information flow
process map, databases, clear accountabilities, and training support.
Our focus, as we noted earlier, is on the call monitoring component of the PM system, though we will discuss the relationship between call monitoring and other PM elements.

Service Behavior Model

The model captures the key behavioral dimensions of the representative's customer service performance. Exhibit 8.2 presents an
illustrative model. This is essentially a competency model for the
frontline service position. Often, as in the exhibit, the model is hierarchical, with specific dimensions grouped under more general
competency categories. In building a model, developers should
aim for comprehensiveness. Over time, research may help identify
the specific dimensions that drive customer satisfaction and loyalty,
and developers can gradually refine the model to focus more efficiently only on these critical dimensions.

The methodology for building such a model draws heavily on
the tools of traditional job analysis research. This begins with a review of background documentation, including, if they exist, training manuals, performance appraisal forms, customer survey data,
a customer service vision statement, tapes of model calls, and existing monitoring forms. We like to monitor a sample of calls our-
selves as part of model development. In addition, we interview
incumbents and their supervisors, individually and in focus groups.
Access to a customer focus group also yields telling results. The
model needs to be clear, comprehensive, and easily understood by
managers and representatives.

Exhibit 8.2. Model of Service Behavior.

• Service Orientation
  • Greeted customer
  • Verified customer identity
  • Established rapport
  • Used customer's name
  • Expressed empathy
  • Maintained composure
  • Expressed commitment
  • Offered additional assistance
  • Terminated call appropriately

• Issue Identification
  • Obtained information
  • Listened actively
  • Took responsibility
  • Provided thorough information
  • Summarized actions

• Issue Resolution
  • Took responsibility
  • Provided thorough information
  • Summarized actions

• Communication
  • Projected enthusiastic tone
  • Conveyed confidence
  • Spoke with clarity
  • Used appropriate language

• Call Management
  • Controlled call
  • Used time efficiently
  • Minimized dead air
  • Extended hold courtesies
  • Transferred call appropriately

Rating Scale

Decisions need to be made about the scale that will be used to assign evaluative ratings on each dimension. It is common practice in call centers to use a fairly undifferentiated checklist format, which is essentially a two-point scale, indicating that the representative either did or did not demonstrate the expected behavior. While a checklist reduces the judgmental demands on raters, it simplifies the very real continuum of effectiveness that characterizes most service encounters. Our approach is usually to use either a three- or five-point scale of effectiveness, ranging from Clearly Less Than Adequate to Clearly More Than Adequate. Such a scale makes an explicit differentiation between performance that adequately addresses the customer's presenting problem and performance that delights the customer and turns her into a "raving fan."

The use of a scale that allows for "more than adequate" ratings for some or all competencies presumes that subject matter experts can identify specific, demonstrable service behaviors that reflect that level of skill. In our experience, subject matter experts frequently have difficulty defining such extraordinary behaviors.

Evaluation Guidelines

Evaluation standards should provide five to ten specific expected behaviors for each behavioral dimension to be rated, anchoring each of the points on the rating scale. Exhibit 8.3 provides an illustrative set of guidelines for one service dimension, Terminated the Call Appropriately. In this example, the guidelines provide representative behaviors for the bottom, middle, and top points of a three-point effectiveness scale. The greater the number of behavioral examples, the more detailed the behaviors, and the more representative they are of behaviors that actually occur in that call center, the more useful are the evaluation guidelines. When an agent demonstrates a particular behavior, the task of the assessor is to identify the appropriate dimension reflected in that behavior. Then the assessor needs to match the demonstrated behavior to the examples provided in the guidelines, determine the quality of performance, and assign a rating.

Sampling Strategy

There are essentially two ways of defining the target population for monitoring: the total number of calls handled over a specified period of time by an individual agent, or the total number of calls handled for a specified period by a particular unit. When data are collected on the individual agent level, as few as four or as many as twenty calls may comprise the sample for a particular period, typically a month. With such small samples, sampling error is large, and as a consequence, a month's data on an individual agent need to be interpreted with great caution. Typically only the extremes of highly effective or ineffective performance have any meaning in a given month. Of course, even on the individual level, aggregating data over several months quickly creates a stable estimate of service performance over the population of calls handled. Aggregating

Exhibit 8.3. Sample Evaluation Guidelines for "Terminated Call Appropriately."

- Thanked customer for calling and personalized ending of call, for example, "Thank you for calling [company name], and enjoy your new home."
- Ended the call with a positive statement when customer was irate or upset, for example, "I am truly sorry that you had to call back so many times. I am glad that we were able to answer your question today."

- Thanked the customer by saying: "Thank you for calling [company name]."

___ Did not thank customer for calling

___ Closed with only "Bye, bye"

___ Inappropriate closure (for example, sounded cheerful when the customer is hanging up not completely satisfied)

___ Released customer before customer was finished speaking

___ Hung up on customer, with or without explanation

N/A Call was transferred or customer disconnected prematurely individual-level data across agents for a defined period also provides stable estimates of unit performance.

When monitoring a particular unit as a whole rather than monitoring agents individually, the sample typically has 250 to 500 calls in a given period of time across agents, providing stable estimates of population parameters. While a particular unit may be a defined set of agents, in call centers a "unit" instead may be a particular set of calls. For example, callers to a technical support center may first hear a menu of options and indicate, in response to the menu, that they have a question about a particular product. All such calls are routed to an available agent identified by the "intelligent routing system" as certified in that product. The population of calls to be monitored may be defined by the organization as the total of all inquiry calls about that specific product, even though individual agents may be certified in multiple products.

Assessors

Effective call monitoring requires monitors with strong skills in observing and systematically evaluating service behavior, akin to the skills required to be an effective assessment center assessor. Beyond assessment skills, there may be knowledge requirements unique to the particular business environment. For example, intimate knowledge of procedures, legal requirements, or product specifications may be needed to evaluate accurately whether the agent has satisfactorily responded to a customer's inquiry or has provided incorrect information, which will erode customer loyalty. Call centers typically entrust monitoring to either first-line supervisors or internal dedicated quality assurance specialists.

We have observed that organizations increasingly have outsourced call monitoring to third-party organizations, placing responsibility for monitoring in the hands of outside specialists. Internal assessors are more likely to bring job knowledge to the monitoring task. To the extent that the evaluation of accuracy is critical to evaluating service quality and that evaluating the accuracy of information provided to the customer requires a great deal of technical knowledge, organizations need to rely on internal monitors. However, an internal assessor may be too intimately connected to the representative. For example, knowing that an agent is going through a personal crisis, the evaluator may be forgiving of the agent's brusqueness with customers that day and provide more lenient monitoring ratings. The customer, of course, is unaware of the extenuating circumstances. The customer knows only that the agent was short-tempered or provided a frustratingly terse explanation of a product. Third-party professionals are more likely to bring an objectivity that better captures the customer's perspective. Professional assessors in reputable organizations have specialized skills in behavioral observation and assessment, as well as the discipline and technology to support effective monitoring. These third-party monitoring companies specifically select, train, and manage assessors to monitor effectively as their core mission.

In one large financial services organization, first-line supervisors had conducted all monitoring for years. The organization drew little utility from the call monitoring program. Monitoring scores showed little differentiation across representatives, did not correspond to customer survey data, and did little to drive behavior change. The organization decided to outsource monitoring to a third-party firm. Supervisors received actionable and timely monitoring reports on each representative from the outsourcer, including month-by-month trends and comparisons of the representative's service performance to that of the unit as a whole. On the basis of these reports, and freed from the data-gathering role, supervisors now had the time and tools to provide constructive feedback and coaching to the agents most needing help and then to measure the impact of their coaching through objective, third-party evaluations the following month. Prior to outsourcing, supervisors spent approximately 20 percent of their time monitoring calls. To help fund the cost of third-party monitoring, spans of supervisory control were increased by some 10 percent.

Whether staffed by internal quality assurance staff or outsourced, centralizing monitoring to a single dedicated unit allows more reliable comparisons across units, call centers, and even countries than does entrusting monitoring to frontline supervisors.

Reporting

To maximize the utility of monitoring, the reporting system must provide information in a clear, actionable format. Often this involves the creation of multiple report formats reflecting multiple aggregations of data. For organizations assessing down to the agent level, individual monthly, quarterly, and annual reports are produced on each agent. Additional levels of reporting may include team reports for each supervisor and unit- or center-level reports for more senior management to review. Examples are provided later in this chapter. Within each report, summary scores may be calculated on clusters of dimensions, such as compliance or customer treatment, or for service quality overall. Some call centers publicize call monitoring results widely, going so far as to place posters ranking agents or units on their monitoring scores for the month, just as they do for KPI results.

Technology allows the availability of monitoring reports on a real-time basis. Moreover, sound files with illustrative calls can be attached to the report to facilitate training and coaching.

Measurement

Call monitoring is a form of psychological measurement, translating observations of human behavior into quantitative ratings. The criteria for evaluating the effectiveness of monitoring ratings are the core psychometric criteria used to evaluate all psychological measurement and well known to I/O psychologists.

Representative Sampling

Monitored calls should be representative of the population of calls handled over a designated period of time by the call center. Facets of representativeness include call type (for example, billing inquiries, service complaints), call length, and time of day, week, or month. Representativeness is determined by comparing the frequency distribution of calls handled to the frequency distribution of calls monitored on each of these facets. For example, if 8 percent of the calls received at the center are requests to terminate service, then approximately 8 percent of the calls monitored should also reflect termination requests. If 28 percent of the monitored calls were instead termination requests, the sampling process used to monitor calls is not representative.

Digital recording can be programmed to capture calls on a random basis, yielding a representative sample of calls to evaluate. In call centers where internal first-level supervisors or quality assurance staff are expected to monitor calls live, as they occur, it is virtually impossible to secure representative samples on which to base monitoring evaluations. Most call centers put customer needs first, requiring quality assurance and supervisory staff to jump on the phones and start handling calls when call volumes and wait queues spike.

In one study we conducted at a large credit card company, some 55 percent of the calls monitored by supervisors each month were collected during the last week of the month, as supervisors accelerated their monitoring activity to meet their required quota of ten monitored calls per agent per month. In the same company, 18 percent of monitored calls were collected on Saturdays, when supervisors were undistracted, although only 7 percent of the call flow at that call center occurred on Saturdays.

Reliability

Consistency of measurement requires that a uniform set of rating guidelines be established, raters receive uniform training and on-going calibration on the application of those standards, and inter-rater reliability be continually evaluated. The more specific and behaviorally detailed the rating standards, the more likely it is that monitoring ratings will achieve acceptable levels of reliability.

In one application, a professional staff was fully dedicated to monitoring and used detailed evaluation guidelines. To assess reliability, two hundred calls were independently monitored by two observers; twenty-two different pairs of observers contributed to the sample of dual-monitored calls. Fourteen behavioral dimensions were rated on each monitored call. The intraclass correlation coefficient for this sample was .82, $p < .01$. Some call centers draw on a similar method, called Gage R & R (Rath & Strong, 2002), which was developed to measure a manufacturing process's repeatability and reproducibility. Gage R & R, like the more familiar psychometric reliability statistics (r, chi square, or intraclass correlation coefficient) is applied to monitoring ratings in order to evaluate consistency and ensure calibration between raters.

At the best-practice call centers, some 2 percent of all calls monitored and a minimum of fifty calls per month are dual-rated for each unit being monitored and inter-rater reliabilities calculated. In best-practice monitoring systems, intraclass correlation coefficients of .75 to .85 are typical estimates of the correspondence between ratings of the same set of calls by independent raters. When taped calls are monitored, data to estimate rate-rerate reliabilities can also be collected, although a suitable interval should be allowed between ratings of the same call by the same evaluator to minimize memory effects. Here, rate-rerate correlations of .80 are typical of best-practice centers.

Another useful approach in ensuring reliability is the use of statistical process control (SPC), a method of monitoring, controlling, and, ideally, improving a process through statistical analysis. Its four basic steps are measuring the process, eliminating variances in the process to make it consistent, monitoring the process, and improving the process to its best target value.

In one third-party monitoring organization, all monitoring ratings are captured online. Calls to be monitored are randomly distributed to assessors. Consequently, if assessors showed perfect inter-rater reliability, variations in mean monitoring ratings across assessors should exclusively reflect sampling error. Statistical process control automatically flags assessors whose mean monitoring ratings overall or on any given behavioral dimension are outside the parameters of chance fluctuation (for example, more than two standard errors from the grand mean across all assessors). SPC can also flag an assessor whose ratings one week are different beyond chance levels from his own ratings over a prior period (for example, the previous twenty weeks).

These data not only allow reliability assessment; they need to drive reliability improvement. This typically involves reinforcement of initial assessor training in the monitoring process and standards. Often, merely providing assessors with ongoing SPC results stimulates realignment with standards. Discrepancies across assessors in ratings should be addressed by conducting regular calibration sessions, where several assessors listen to and discuss their evaluations of a call. Lack of consistency in rating a particular behavioral dimension can also stimulate clarification and redefinition of that dimension. Best-practice call centers run calibration sessions for monitors as often as once a week.

Validity

Monitoring processes are designed to assess the quality of service delivered. The validity of inferences about the level of service quality drawn from monitoring data can be evaluated using models familiar to I/O psychologists from other contexts. The service behavior model should be rooted in the empirical job analysis methods typically used by I/O psychologists that capture the critical dimensions of service performance and the tasks or behaviors associated with effective and ineffective performance on each of these dimensions.

The validity of monitoring ratings can be estimated through both content- and criterion-oriented strategies. Subject matter expert ratings should be collected to evaluate the relevance of each behavioral dimension to service quality. These experts are typically call center supervisors and quality assurance specialists. However, the subject matter expert panel may also include trainers, marketers, and customer satisfaction researchers. The validation process follows the same content validation procedures employed to validate a set of behavioral guidelines to be used in evaluating candidate skills in an assessment center or on a behavioral interview. Subject matter experts review each element in the service behavior model and rate the behavior's relevance to customer satisfaction. They also scale the level of effectiveness reflected by that behavior. Do subject matter experts agree, for example, that the use of incorrect grammar two or three times on a call reflects inadequate oral communications skills? Procedures for analyzing consensus ratings, such as Lawshe's content validity ratio (1975), can be used to estimate the job relatedness of the service behavior model. Similar consensus ratings can be used to evaluate the validity of how the evaluation guidelines are scaled. Essentially the content validation approach evaluates the extent to which the service behavior model captures the content of the customer experience.

Criterion-oriented strategies involve correlating call monitoring ratings with customer evaluations of the treatment they received on the calls monitored. Several years ago, we worked with a large financial services firm that had a team of professional external assessors monitor 10,500 customer calls over a three-month period. First-line supervisors from inside the organization also rated some 10,500 calls over the same period. Satisfaction surveys were sent to all 21,000 customers within a week of their call. With a 20 percent response rate, about 2,000 data points were available to evaluate the validity of each method of monitoring. The correlation between monitoring ratings and customer evaluations was .04

for supervisor ratings and .42 for the professional assessors. The ratings provided by external raters were valid in that they predicted customer satisfaction; those supplied by first-level supervisors were not. As a consequence of this study, the company removed monitoring responsibility from its first-line supervisors and ever since has had third-party professional assessors conduct monitoring on an ongoing basis.

In validating monitoring ratings of such sales-related dimensions as influencing, listening, and problem-solving skills, monitoring scores can be correlated with hard sales measures. Relatedly, we found in a study at a credit card collections center that monitoring scores on several dimensions were significantly correlated with dollars collected from customers for a population of over two hundred collection agents over a three-month period across over one thousand monitored calls. The multiple correlation for the predictive behaviors with dollars collected was .32.

Over time, criterion validation of call monitoring scores against external service and sales criteria can help refine models of effective service and sales behavior.

Discriminability

On virtually every customer service call, some behaviors are performed effectively and some ineffectively. There are also opportunities to go beyond the customer's stated request—behaviors that exceed the customer's expectations. Monitoring results must reflect these distinctions. A set of clearly distinguishable dimensions can help identify areas of strength and weakness on each call. A scale also helps to identify behaviors that exceed expectations and should be encouraged and rewarded.

Organizations commonly use a two-point scale in their monitoring programs in the hope that ratings are clear and undisputable; rating disputes are a bane of monitoring programs. Although a two-point scale simplifies the rating process, variance in ratings may be low, and the usefulness of the data for coaching purposes will be limited.

We have often been asked by clients to assess or audit their existing call monitoring systems and develop recommendations for improvement. In one such assignment, at a Fortune 500 bank, we found what our academic colleagues refer to as "grade inflation": over 90 percent of representatives scored 90 or above on the 100-point rating scale used to summarize overall service performance. Moreover, those rated high on one quality dimension were almost invariably rated high in all dimensions, a strong halo effect. Such undifferentiated ratings had little value in identifying top performers to reward and encourage. More critically, the relatively flat profiles yielded by the monitoring process made it difficult to coach agents to develop skill deficiencies and leverage strengths.

Statistical process control can be used not only to track the drift in central tendency that we described earlier but also to track possible drift in the distributional characteristics of monitoring scores. Assessors who show consistently low intra-individual discrimination—that is, halo—can be provided feedback and coaching. Dimensions that are consistently rated adequate across agents and assessors may need to be examined. Typically in such cases, the evaluation guidelines provide too few examples for inadequate or more-than-adequate skills. Examples that are too vague leave assessors little choice other than to use the midpoint as a default in the absence of a useful set of standards for the extremes. Improved guidelines are likely to reduce such central tendency errors.

Reporting

Reporting involves summarizing and analyzing monitoring ratings in order to guide interventions aimed at enhancing service performance. Reports can reflect rather simple summaries of individual-level performance, comparisons across individuals and units, correlations between behavioral measures of service quality and objective KPIs, insights into the customer experience collected by monitors, and links between service behavior, on the one hand, and direct measures of the customer experience, on the other. Effective service organizations do not invest in monitoring per se; their intent is not merely to measure service behavior. Organizations invest in building and operating a monitoring process in order to extract information that has a business value from the monitoring data. It is critical that timely, actionable, and clear reports are generated.

Monitoring Reports

In their most basic form, monitoring reports provide an evaluation of performance at the target level (for example, a single agent) and, on an aggregated basis, at levels above the target (for example, the service team). The basic report presents or summarizes the specific ratings assigned on each target dimension and on some composite index or indexes.

An effective PM process might include reporting at several levels of aggregation. The most fundamental level is the call-specific report provided to the representative or her supervisor (or both) at the time the call was monitored. This report might have the actual recorded call electronically attached. The PM process would also include an agent-level performance summary report at the conclusion of a month, aggregating her monitoring results over the five, ten, or twenty calls representatively monitored in the course of the entire month. This report would identify, on a dimensional and behavioral level, the agent's strengths and developmental opportunities. Here again, one or two recorded calls can be attached to the monthly report as an example of the agent's own particularly outstanding service that month or as an example of weak performance that needs to be addressed through concentrated development. In addition, normative scores, based on the entire population of agents monitored, can be presented on reports in order to provide relative, as well as absolute, performance feedback.

Exhibit 8.4 is an example of a monthly summary report produced by Aon Consulting for a particular agent. In this example, the frequency distribution in the center section of the report indicates how consistent the agent was on each of the individual behaviors over the course of the month. The stars in the right column provide a symbolic representation of the agent's performance profile on a five-point scale. For each behavior, the number of stars is computed by first averaging the individual scores for each behavior across all calls monitored during the month, and then categorizing the resultant continuous composite score into one of the five performance categories symbolized by one to five stars on the report.

An effective reporting process also produces aggregated team- and center-level reports, averaging ratings across all monitored

Exhibit 8.4. Sample Individual Monitoring Report.

	CONFIDENTIAL
COMPANY Y MONITORING	Individual-Level Report

Representative:	Pat Thompson	Monitoring Period:	04/01/04–04/30/04

This Report presents Aon's monitoring of a random sample of calls conducted by you with callers. The competencies included in this Report were identified as critical drivers of customer satisfaction. Aon's assessors use the standards to evaluate customer service behavior.

The following page provides a view of your skill profile. Each of the five Competency Scores represents your average level of performance on the behaviors comprising the Competency. Beneath each Competency Score is a listing of the behaviors comprising the Competency. For each behavior, two pieces of information are provided: a breakdown of the ratings across the calls monitored (in the middle columns), and the average level of performance on the behavior (represented by the number of stars in the right-hand column). The Summary Rating provides a view of your skill profile overall, based on your average level of performance across all monitored behaviors.

This report is intended to provide a profile of the customer contact skills demonstrated by you. Notice the behaviors that were found to be particularly strong, as well as those behaviors that provide opportunities for further development. Use this profile to develop a plan to improve those areas needing development.

COMPANY Y MONITORING		Individual-Level Report
Representative:	Number of Monitors:	Monitoring Period:
Pat Thompson	10	04/01/04 – 04/30/04

	SCALE	
Competency Ratings:	20–100	
Behavioral Ratings:	*****	Exceeds Expectations
	****	
	***	Meets Expectations
	**	
	*	Needs Development

Exhibit 8.4. Sample Individual Monitoring Report, Cont'd.

				CONFIDENTIAL
COMPANY Y MONITORING		Individual-Level Report		
Representative:	Pat Thompson	Monitoring Period:	04/01/04–04/30/04	
I. Service Orientation	+	√	–	59
1. Greeted customer	3	5	2	***
2. Verified customer	3	6	1	****
3. Established rapport	3	6	1	****
4. Used customer's name	2	7	1	***
5. Expressed empathy	1	5	4	**
6. Maintained composure	2	6	2	***
7. Expressed commitment	1	5	4	**
8. Offered additional assistance	1	8	1	***
9. Terminated call appropriately	1	6	3	**
II. Communication	+	√	–	62
1. Animated tone	2	7	1	***
2. Conveyed confidence	2	7	1	***
3. Spoke with clarity	3	9	1	***
4. Used appropriate language	2	7	1	***
III. Issue Identification	+	√	–	66
1. Asked probing questions	4	4	2	****
2. Listened actively	3	3	4	***
IV. Issue Resolution	+	√	–	72
1. Took ownership	3	6	1	***
2. Addressed customer's issues	8	2	0	*****
3. Summarized actions	2	6	2	***
V. Call Management	+	√	–	72
1. Controlled call	1	8	1	***
2. Used time efficiently	1	4	5	**
3. Extended hold courtesies	1	4	5	**
4. Extended transfer courtesies	0	3	7	*
5. Minimized "dead air"	1	6	3	***

calls within the team or center. These reports tend to mirror the format of individual agent–level reports but contain aggregate ratings data.

Trends over Time

At the agent, team, and center levels, monitoring reports can provide important indexes of change over time. Report formats can be programmed to produce summary data for each of the past three to four months on each dimension measured. Overall composite scores can be tracked over time as well. This information is important in recognizing and rewarding performance improvement.

We have been using monitoring trend data to identify service behaviors that are more or less amenable to change over time. In one of our studies with a Fortune 100 financial services organization, over three hundred customer service representatives were monitored and provided with monitoring-based feedback and coaching over the course of one year. Their service behaviors for the first quarter of the monitored year were compared with performance during the fourth quarter. We classified service behaviors into three categories: interpersonal behaviors (building rapport, expressing empathy), simple cognitive behaviors (courtesies related to putting a caller on hold or transferring a call), and complex cognitive behaviors (addressing the customers' issues, assuming ownership of the caller's problem). We found that simple cognitive behaviors and interpersonal behaviors improved significantly over the year, but performance on complex cognitive behaviors did not. We suspect that complex cognitive behaviors may be more resistant to feedback and coaching because of the greater level of learning that is required. Looking at such trends within a range of service contexts may suggest, more generally, which service behaviors should be the focus of routine coaching interventions, which behaviors might require more extensive training for incumbents, or, for behaviors that are particularly difficult to change, which require more rigorous preemployment assessment.

Linking KPI and Monitoring Results

A comprehensive picture of service performance at the agent, team, and center levels requires linking the reports emerging from quantitative technology-based KPI measurement to the reporting that is generated from the monitoring process.

There is a widespread assumption in call centers that effective customer service quality, as measured by monitoring how customers are treated, comes at the expense of call center productivity as measured by the quantitative KPIs. Productivity is an overarching goal within the call center environment. Requiring an action as simple as saying to each customer, "Thank you so much for your call, and have a pleasant day," will result in increased talk time of three or four seconds a call, which, when multiplied by hundreds of thousands of calls, can have a significant impact on the business. Similarly, a procedural change—for example, asking the customer for his mother's maiden name or to verify her home address—increases call handling time by as many as twenty to thirty seconds and changes the entire operational and financial dynamic of managing that call center.

The issue of the trade-off between the quality and quantity of performance has been addressed in the I/O literature. Until recently, the studies examining the relationship between quality and productivity have used one-dimensional measures of quality and productivity (Audia, Kristof-Brown, Brown, and Locke, 1996; Gilliland and Landis, 1992). In the call center context, however, it is possible to examine multidimensional aspects of performance quantity (talk time, hold time, after-call work) and multidimensional aspects of performance quality (communications, problem-solving, and interpersonal skills). In our own studies linking monitoring and KPI measures, interesting relationships have emerged. For example, of the service quality dimensions, communication skills are most strongly and positively related to productivity. In our research, representatives who communicate more effectively with customers—particularly by using more grammatical speech, avoiding unfamiliar terminology, and speaking more concisely—handle calls more efficiently and quickly (forty seconds less talk time, on average, in one of our studies, compared to those with poor communications skills). Conversely, representatives who more effectively and thoroughly solve customer problems have longer average talk time, hold time, and time spent on after-call work. Presumably, though, the additional time spent on resolving the customer's problems yields greater customer satisfaction and less frequent, costly customer callbacks. While it is commonly believed that the expected telephone courtesies, such as those needed to build rapport with customers, take more time on calls, we have consistently found that these behaviors are largely unrelated to productivity measures. By linking multidimensional service quality and KPI measures into a comprehensive report of service performance, management can make more informed choices about the behaviors expected of representatives when they are on calls with customers in order to maximize overall utility.

Cross-Unit Comparisons

A primary macro-PM objective in large call center organizations is to make direct comparisons in service quality across units and sites to ensure consistent service quality. This issue has become particularly important as organizations have provided service in parallel through both internal call centers and outsourced call centers. From the customer's perspective and the organization's, it should be immaterial whether a representative in Phoenix, in Jacksonville, or in Bangalore is serving the customer. The service experience that is integral to the company's branding should be identical. The primary advantage of using a centralized monitoring group to conduct this monitoring—whether that centralized unit is internal to the organization or provided by a third-party monitoring firm—is the objectivity and consistency with which the same service standards are applied across all units. Reports to senior leadership should provide sound comparisons across locations.

To illustrate the value of cross-unit comparisons, we describe a case study in which third-party monitoring of service performance in a large U.S.-based credit processing organization is providing us with an opportunity to compare the skills of agents across U.S. and Indian call centers. Agents from these call centers serve the same American customer base.

In this case study, call monitoring is designed to assess three broad dimensions: service orientation (courtesy and professionalism toward customers), communication (clarity of speech and grammar), and call management (using time efficiently on the telephone).

On a summary score level, agents from both countries are not significantly different in their overall service effectiveness. However, analysis of specific performance dimensions reveals a number of significant differences between the two groups:

- Representatives from the India call center outperformed U.S.-based representatives in service orientation by 21 percent. India-based agents were especially skilled in using the customer's name to personalize the call, offering additional assistance, and closing the call with appropriate courtesies.
- U.S.-based agents were rated 14 percent higher in overall communication skills than were India-based representatives. Most notably, agents operating from the U.S. call centers sounded more confident, spoke more clearly, and used language that was more appropriate for the call.
- Representatives from the U.S. call centers were rated about 10 percent higher in overall call management. They were particularly more adept than Indian agents at controlling the call, using time efficiently, and extending transfer courtesies.

The data emerging from this case study illustrate the value of creating cross-unit reports off a consistent, standardized, centralized monitoring process.

Identifying Opportunities to Improve Business Processes

More in-depth analysis of call monitoring ratings in conjunction with other data captured by call monitors can yield important insights into the organization's business processes. External observers, we have found, are more accurate and detailed than agents themselves in classifying call type into primary and secondary descriptive categories (for example, billing inquiry or complaint or request for product information). Call type can then be associated in the monitoring database with call monitoring ratings. Average monitoring scores can be calculated by call type to identify which call types are most and least likely to be handled effectively and be satisfying to the customer. Agent monitoring scores can then be matched to assign the strongest agents to handle the "gates" through which the toughest calls flow.

As we noted above, an effective service organization will capture key information on the voice of the customer from each interaction. While the burden of capturing customer experiences, inquiries, and concerns falls primarily on the agents themselves, monitors can play an important complementary role. While observing calls, and not burdened by having to respond to the customer, the assessor can systematically code customer attitudes and experiences and link these directly to the monitoring ratings. Representative behaviors that lead to customer dissatisfaction—failure to provide first-call resolution, lengthy holds, and dial transfers to other departments—can be systematically tracked, analyzed, and acted on. Individual analyses and cross-tabulations of customer and representative behavior can be used to produce reports that identify better ways to explain services to the public, address frequently asked questions, understand issues that create customer confusion or anger, and uncover cues for offering additional services—in sum, provide more effective business processes. Call monitoring is often used in this way when call centers adopt Six Sigma methodology to enhance service quality. Six Sigma methods use defined metrics to assess baseline quality and then measure improvements in quality as business processes are changed (Rath & Strong, 2002). Call monitoring thus becomes core to such quality initiatives in the call center environment.

Exhibit 8.5 provides an illustrative report prepared for a financial services firm. The report tracks sources of customer dissatisfaction. At this organization, third-party call assessors code incidents of expressed dissatisfaction while listening to recorded calls. As indicated in the bottom row of the table, customers openly expressed dissatisfaction on slightly over 10 percent of all monitored calls. The assessors categorized the expressed reason for dissatisfaction and this report summarizes the sources of dissatisfaction across the organization's customer service, sales, and collections teams. With careful analysis, the tracking categories can be refined over time and can be further supported and enriched with qualitative "verbatims" captured by the evaluators.

In our case study comparing Indian and U.S. call centers, we also looked at differences in business processes across sites. Business process measures tracked include the percentage of calls dial transferred out by agents and the number of repeat calls—those in which the customer indicated that he or she was calling back about an issue that had not been resolved on a prior call.

Exhibit 8.5. Causes of Dissatisfaction by Group.

Source of Dissatisfaction	Total Number of Calls	Total Percentage of Calls	Percentage of Calls: Customer Service	Percentage of Calls: Sales	Percentage of Calls: Collections
Other[a]	78	33.8	35.0	26.5	40.0
Customer data error	36	15.6	14.7	20.4	12.0
Repetitiveness of error	29	12.5	12.1	12.3	16.0
Time frames	29	12.5	14.6	10.2	4.0
Integrity of process/information	23	10.0	9.6	12.2	8.0
Disagreed with policy/procedure	15	6.5	7.0	4.1	8.0
Previously provided incorrect/conflicting information	11	4.8	3.8	8.2	4.0
Customer interaction	7	3.0	1.9	4.1	8.0
Product/features	3	1.3	1.3	2.0	–
Total calls with dissatisfaction	231	10.3	10.6	13.3	6.3

[a]The most typical other sources of dissatisfaction include the customer not being informed of increasing insurance rates; the customer not being informed that his or her escrow account was depleted, insufficient itemization of billing statements; and letters being sent to the customer in error. These specific sources of dissatisfaction will be tracked as separate dissatisfaction categories in the future.

We found a number of significant differences in several of the business process measures. Four percent more calls were transferred by U.S.-based representatives than by India-based representatives. However, agents from the call center in India received almost twice as many repeat calls as did their U.S.-based counterparts. This suggests that representatives within the U.S. call centers are more effective at resolving a customer's issue themselves, or at directing a call to where it can be successfully resolved, on the first call. The measure of first call resolution is arguably the most important KPI for call centers, with impacts on customer satisfaction and cost per call.

Other business process measures reveal that calls routed to the India-based call center were placed on hold twice as often as were calls sent to the U.S. centers (32.1 percent versus 13.7 percent), but for much shorter periods of time (an average of forty-nine seconds versus an average of ninety seconds of wait time in the U.S. centers). In addition, the customer verbally expressed dissatisfaction on the call in 6.3 percent of calls handled within the India-based center, compared to only 3.4 percent of calls handled within the U.S. centers.

Linking Monitoring and Customer Surveys

We already mentioned that monitoring scores could be linked to customer surveys in order to provide criterion-oriented validation data with which to evaluate the effectiveness of the monitoring process. On an ongoing basis, customer survey data can be linked to aggregate monitoring data to present a richer, more holistic view of service quality from multiple perspectives.

In our U.S.-India case study, for example, customers who have contact with the company's agents are surveyed through a follow-up telephone call from a third-party organization. The telephone survey assesses the customer's overall satisfaction with the call as well as satisfaction with specific dimensions of the agent's performance.

On a regular basis, a consolidated report combining both monitoring and telephone survey results on the same service quality dimensions is prepared and presented to management. In a recent quarterly report, overall monitoring ratings across the U.S.- and India-based agents were comparable, but customer survey results for the two countries were not. Representatives within the U.S. call centers on average scored significantly higher on the survey in overall customer satisfaction. India-based agents were rated substantially lower on nine of ten specific dimensions of performance. The largest difference in survey scores was, as on monitoring scores, on the dimension of communicating clearly, where representatives in the U.S. call centers were rated about 15 percent higher than their India-based counterparts. In contrast with monitoring results, U.S.-based agents were perceived to be slightly more courteous than were India-based agents. Despite these differences, customers whose calls were handled by the Indian call center were just as likely to recommend the company to others as were those whose call was handled by one of the U.S. centers.

Linking call monitoring and customer survey results for these populations reveals interesting insight into the differences between how representatives within the U.S.-based and India-based centers handle calls and in how customers perceive their service. The stronger monitoring scores on service orientation behaviors of India-based agents seem to reflect a greater adherence to trained service behaviors, although these behaviors are often executed by rote. The less developed communication and call management skills of India-based representatives, combined with their more frequent failure to resolve problems immediately, lead U.S.-based customers to be generally less satisfied with their experiences with these agents as compared to their experiences dealing with agents at American call centers. This generally negative view seems to color customer perceptions of the agent's service orientation, even though objective, professional third-party monitors rate Indian agents as more effective in demonstrating service orientation behaviors.

For managers evaluating offshore call centers, these more holistic results that link monitoring and customer surveys present a more complex and realistic evaluation of service quality. In our case study, it may well be that the low call management skills of India-based representatives stem from the fact that the call center industry in India is relatively new. Our research has found that there tends initially to be a trade-off between service orientation skills and call management skills among new agents, but that this trade-off diminishes as representatives become more experienced and receive more training. As we continue collecting and reporting on both monitoring scores and customer survey results, we may well see changes in the overall patterns we find in the future.

Interventions

The ultimate goal of monitoring is to provide management with information to drive customer satisfaction and loyalty. The value of the monitoring data comes from the impact that interventions stemming from monitoring have on the organization and the customer.

According to a 2002 study by the Incoming Call Center Institute and AC Nielsen (D'Ausilio and Anton, 2003), organizations monitor for the following reasons:

- Measure agent performance: 77 percent
- Identify additional agent training needs: 72 percent
- Evaluate level of customer satisfaction: 54 percent
- Identify customer needs and expectations: 49 percent
- Let agents "listen and learn": 36 percent
- Educate other departments about customers: 12 percent

While other chapters in this book focus in depth on interventions intended to drive service quality generally, we will highlight more specifically several of the common interventions that flow from the monitoring system in the call center environment.

Individual-Level Coaching and Feedback

One important use of monitoring data is to support skill development. In this light, monitoring evaluations should be communicated to representatives in accordance with the principles of effective feedback. Feedback should be timely and should focus on specific, changeable behaviors. Recording technology enables representatives, alongside their supervisor or some other coach, to listen to calls while reviewing the monitoring ratings. This direct, unmediated self-observation may be the most powerful intervention of all.

While sophisticated call centers certainly do not lack the data points necessary for coaching and feedback, the challenge for the frontline supervisor is often how to carve out the time necessary for these activities, particularly in the light of the wide spans of control (often over twenty) typical in those environments. One of the benefits of an effective call monitoring process is that it allows the frontline supervisor to "triage" her team members, determine the few who most require coaching, and concentrate on those specific competencies needed by each agent in the high-priority group.

Training Needs Analysis

Aggregate profiles across both qualitative monitoring dimensions and KPIs yield detailed information on the strengths and developmental needs of the agent population as a whole, or specifically identified subgroups such as those with less than six months' tenure or those at a particular site. We have found that beyond the monitoring scores themselves, it is good practice to run focus group sessions periodically with assessors to identify the specific procedures or areas of product knowledge on which they need training or performance support tools. New technologies can automatically deliver customized electronic training in the form of one- to ten-minute learning objects directly to a specific agent's desktop and headset based on two factors: that agent's specific developmental needs uncovered through monitoring and the agent's availability for those few minutes based on current and projected call flows.

Reward and Recognition

Most monitoring programs develop a composite performance score that is included in the representative's performance appraisal. Often the organization links compensation to the composite score. Organizations use such links to compensation in order to communicate and reinforce the organization's business strategies and culture. By rewarding representatives in part for their demonstrated skill in handling customers, management nurtures a customer-focused service culture that will result in improved business performance.

The quality metrics generated by the monitoring process are typically balanced with productivity metrics, such as average talk time, calls handled per hour, or sales closed—in linking pay to performance. In addition to annual compensation, many call centers also immediately flag and recognize or reward a monitored call on which the agent demonstrated outstanding service. Such recognition is not only motivating, but also helps position monitoring as a tool for development rather than as a threat.

Driving Customer Satisfaction

Improving the customer experience is the ultimate goal of any quality process. Call monitoring is arguably the best tool for measuring the level of service provided to the customer. Over time, customer treatment levels are tracked by the organization, and patterns of service effectiveness can be identified across call types, teams, and centers on both global and detailed behavioral levels. Customer-driven organizations recognize that monitoring results are a leading indicator of customer satisfaction. Improvements in the way agents treat customers will result, other factors controlled, in improvements in the level of customer satisfaction and loyalty (Johnson and Gustafsson, 2000). One major credit card company used regression analysis to determine that a five-point increase in overall call monitoring score predicted a two-point increase in customer survey score three months later. A two-point increase in customer survey score was further determined to predict a very financially meaningful 0.2 percent decline in customer attrition. When management sees a decline in monitoring scores, customer-focused organizations can act promptly to change agent behavior rather than wait for the subsequent decline in customer survey results.

Halting Egregiously Negative Behavior

While we have focused on the collection and aggregation of monitoring data over time, there is an aspect of call monitoring that is very incident specific: addressing the occurrence of behaviors such as sexual harassment, verbal abuse, aggressive threats, and gross rudeness. Procedures need to be established and codified as part of the PM process so that when monitors observe agents acting in such ways to customers, the behavior is carefully documented (if possible, recorded) and communicated immediately to a designated contact in the call center. We have termed these reports "hot-line" communications, and they are intended to initiate two types of intervention: disciplining, often resulting in terminating, the agent and repairing the damage to the organization's relationship with the customer. These incidents are relatively rare in our experience, with a hot-line communication initiated approximately once every ten thousand calls monitored. Nonetheless, with larger call centers handling many times that volume monthly, egregious agent behavior can be an almost daily event.

Assessment

The monitoring process itself can be used to assess the effectiveness of quality improvement initiatives:

• Monitoring scores can indicate to supervisors and trainers whether their coaching is having the intended impact on agent or team behavior or on performance on a particular target dimension. This assessment is, of course, less likely to be biased if based on monitoring ratings provided by third-party assessors who are blind to the sources and targets of intervention.

• The rate of improvement in service performance of newly hired agents can be used to assess the quality of the training initially provided to these new agents. With sufficient numbers of agents, monitoring scores and the rate of improvement in those scores can be used to evaluate the effectiveness of trainers and of training curricula.

• Monitoring scores can be used to assess the validity of agent selection procedures. A few years ago, we developed selection procedures for a large credit card company and used monitoring data, collected for six months after hire, as a primary criterion. Resulting validities ranged from the low .40s to the low .50s. Of course, customer treatment as measured by monitoring should not be the only criterion used for assessing the validity and utility of an agent selection process, but in a service-oriented culture, it is essential. Similarly, team-monitoring scores are a legitimate, if insufficiently comprehensive, criterion for assessing the validity of call center supervisor selection procedures.

• Crucially, call monitoring should be used to assess and enhance the quality of the PM process itself. As we noted earlier, reliability, accuracy in predicting customer satisfaction, and discriminability of monitoring scores serve to identify areas where the PM process needs to be redesigned. To maintain effectiveness, it is common to redefine objectives in the light of emerging business needs, redesign critical reports to extract information more relevant to decision makers, change the call sampling plan to focus on specific agents or call populations that reflect important customer or product segments, and revise evaluation guidelines in synch with changing customer or organizational expectations.

Conclusion

Although this chapter focuses narrowly on our experience designing and implementing PM processes in the call center context, we believe that this experience provides a great number of more general lessons for the use of PM as a tool for driving service excellence. We see three key lessons:

- Broad service quality objectives must be translated into specific, actionable, controllable behavioral expectations that are communicated to service providers, on which service providers are trained, and against which the performance of those providers is appraised and rewarded or sanctioned. Service culture needs to be rooted in concrete service behaviors.
- Performance management procedures need to be viewed systemically. Business goals and constraints must guide PM design and execution at all times, which means that as these goals and constraints change, PM processes and content must change. PM has an effect on, and is affected by, other human resource and business systems in the service organization. As we illustrated in this chapter, PM produces information with implications for training and development, selection, reward and compensation, staffing, technology, product and service design, and operations.
- In line with a message embedded in other chapters in this book, a key lesson of our call center experience is that I/O psychology has much to offer customer-focused organizations. The potential for realizing that contribution in order to enhance service quality is great. Few organizations attend, for example, to the psychometric criteria that we as a profession routinely use to design

and assess sound performance measures. In our experience, few service organizations have implemented PM processes that fully reflect our field's state-of-the-art knowledge base.

Finally, for the reasons we gave at the beginning of this chapter, we view the call center environment as a wonderful setting for productive, theory-driven research. We described studies that we have done over the past five years on differential skill development over time, quality-quantity performance trade-offs, the link between agent behavior and customer experiences, and cross-national performance differences. Much more can be done, drawing on models that already exist within I/O psychology. Issues such as the interplay between the expressed emotions of customers and agents; the impact of respites (breaks, weekends, vacations) on performance; how internal factors such as supervisory style and skill, climate, and culture affect customer treatment; how the relative influence of ability and personality variables changes over time and criterion type; and countless others, can be rigorously studied under fairly controlled conditions within a real-life field setting. We have found the call centers to be an environment where sample sizes are large, customers and agents are usually randomly matched, and service quality can be rigorously measured. For scientist-practitioners looking for field research sites, it almost never gets better than that.

References

Albrecht, K., and Zemke, R. *Service America in the New Economy.* New York: McGraw-Hill, 2002.

Anton, J. *Call Center Management by the Numbers.* West Lafayette, Ind.: Purdue University Press, 1997.

Audia, G., Kristof-Brown, A., Brown, K. G., and Locke, E. A. "Relationship of Goals and Microlevel Work Processes to Performance on a Multipath Manual Task." *Journal of Applied Psychology,* 1996, *81*, 483–497.

D'Ausilio, R., and Anton, J. *Customer Service and the Human Experience.* Santa Maria, Calif.: Anton Press, 2003.

Durr, W. *Navigating the Customer Contact Center in the Twenty-First Century: A Technology and Management Guide.* Duluth, Minn.: Advanstar Communications, 2001.

Gilliland, S. W., and Landis, R. S. "Quality and Quantity Goals in a Complex Decision Task: Strategies and Outcomes." *Journal of Applied Psychology,* 1992, *77*, 672–681.

Incoming Call Center Institute. *Report on Customer Relationship Management.* Farmington Hills, Mich.: Thomson-Gale, 2002.

Johnson, M. D., and Gustafsson, A. *Improving Customer Satisfaction, Loyalty, and Profit: An Integrated Measurement and Management System.* San Francisco: Jossey-Bass, 2000.

Lawshe, C. H. "A Quantitative Approach to Content Validity." *Personnel Psychology,* 1975, *28,* 563–575.

London, M., and Beatty, R. W. "360-Degree Feedback as a Competitive Advantage." *Human Resource Management,* 1993, *32,* 353–372.

Rath & Strong. *Rath & Strong's Six Sigma Pocket Guide.* Lexington, Mass.: Rath & Strong, 2002.

Reichheld, F. F. "The One Number You Need to Grow." *Harvard Business Review,* Dec. 2003, pp. 46–54.

Schneider, B., and White, S. S. *Service Quality: Research Perspectives.* Thousand Oaks, Calif.: Sage, 2004.

Chapter 9

What We Need to Know to Develop Strategies and Tactics to Improve Service Delivery

Lawrence Fogli

Over the past two decades, *customer service* delivery has become a catchphrase for businesses, as well as an inescapable part of modern life. Not a day goes by without multiple opportunities to engage in service transactions at grocery stores, banks, restaurants, and a host of other businesses. The service sector has become the largest part of the U.S. economy (Collier, 1983), claiming 90 percent of the nonagricultural jobs added to the U.S. workforce between 1950 and 1980 (Heskett, 1986). This explosive growth of the U.S. service sector, coupled with every company's need to compete for market share, has resulted in a large number of books being published that address the issue of customer service, such as the following: Albrecht and Zemke (1985); Bell and Zemke (1992); Berry (1985); Bowen, Chase, Cummings, and Associates (1990); Connellan and Zemke (1993); Czepiel, Solomon, and Surprenant (1985); Desatnick (1987); Gerson (1993); Finch (1994); Goodman (2000); Heskett, Sasser, and Schlesinger (1997); Hochschild (1983); Lovelock (2001); Martin (1989, 1993); Rust and Oliver (1994); Schneider and White (2004); Whiteley (1991); and Zemke and Schaaf (1989).

The goal of this chapter is to integrate the knowledge of the previous chapters and other customer service literature, before describing organizational strategies and tactics to improve customer service delivery. To do so, the following topics are summarized:

- What are services?
- Understanding customer behavior and service delivery
- The importance of service encounters
- The employee: The key to effective service encounters
- The relationship between employee attitudes, customer attitudes, and service delivery
- Strategies and tactics for improving service delivery
- Service delivery in an era of unprecedented change

What Are Services?

Defining service has been a difficult preoccupation for many of the customer service delivery writers and researchers, with different authors offering different variations. For example, in his book *Services Marketing*, Lovelock (2001) offers two definitions—one behavioral and the other economic:

Behavioral: "A service is an act or performance offered by one party to another. Although the process may be tied to a physical product, the performance is essentially intangible and does not normally result in ownership of any of the factors of production" (p. 3).

Economic: "Services are economic activities that create value and provide benefits for customers at specific times and places as a result of bringing about a desired change in—or on behalf of—the recipient of the service" (p. 3).

However, a number of authors, in an effort to define service, focus more on differentiating services from goods, with a common thread being that products are physical objects, whereas services are actions or performances.

In addition to the definitions above, Lovelock described distinctive characteristics that differentiate services from goods. First and foremost, customers do not obtain ownership of services, as service products are intangible performances. Another characteristic of a service product is the greater level of involvement of customers in the production process, with other people possibly forming part of that product. There is a greater degree of variability in operational inputs and outputs, and delivery systems may involve both electronic and physical channels. Furthermore, the time factor is relatively more important, and there are no inventories following the production of a service. Finally, many services prove difficult for customers to evaluate.

Similarly, Kendall concludes in Chapter One that services differ from products because they are intangible, simultaneous, and involve customer participation. Most authors agree that services are intangible (they cannot be touched, held, or stored). One approach to distinguish between goods and services is to consider how the good or service is evaluated or classified on a scale of bipolar opposites (tangible to intangible):

- Pure tangible good (such as candy or paper clips)
- Tangible good with accompanying service (for example, cars or computers)
- Hybrid combining roughly equal parts of goods and services (for example, a fast food chain)
- Major service with accompanying minor goods and services (for example, air travel)
- Pure service (such as consulting or policing)

Schneider and White (2004) make a distinction between the "how" and "what" components of service delivery. The "what" is the product, for example, a meal served in a restaurant, and the "how" (the process of reservations, seating, serving, and attention received) is the service delivery. Although the "what" of the product is critically important to customers' judgments of service quality, the focus of this chapter is on the "how" or process delivery of service.

In addition to defining services and contrasting them with products, Lovelock classified services based on both the nature of the services act (tangible/intangible) and who or what is the direct recipient of the service process (people/possession). He thus developed four categories of services:

1. *People* processing involves *tangible* actions to people's bodies. Examples of people-processing services are passenger transportation, hairdressing, and dental work. Customers need to be physically present throughout service delivery to receive the desired benefits of such services.

2. *Possession* processing includes *tangible* actions to goods and other physical possessions belonging to the customer. Examples of possession processing are air freight, lawn mowing, and cleaning services. In these instances, the object requiring processing must be present, but the customer need not be.

3. Mental stimulus processing refers to *intangible* actions directed at *people*'s minds. Services in the mental stimulus–processing category include entertainment, spectator sports events, theater performances, and education. In such instances, customers must be present mentally but can be located either at the same location where the service is being created, such as a lecture hall or sports stadium, or in a remote location connected by broadcast signals or telecommuting linkages.

4. Information processing describes *intangible* actions directed at assets in a customer's *possession*. Examples of information-processing services are insurance, banking, and consulting. In this category, little direct involvement with the customer may be needed once the request for service has been initiated, and even that can be undertaken remotely by mail, phone or internet.

Understanding Customer Behavior and Service Delivery

According to Lovelock (2001), when customers decide to buy a service, they often experience a complex purchase process involving three separate stages—the prepurchase stage, the service encounter stage, and the postpurchase stage. These stages are detailed in Exhibit 9.1.

These three stages of the purchasing process for services (prepurchase, service encounter, and postpurchase) and their components have several important implications for our understanding of customer service needs, expectations, satisfaction, and loyalty.

Customer needs have expanded beyond mere physical or basic needs, such as food and shelter, to a vast variety of perceived social

Exhibit 9.1. The Purchase Process: Customer Activities in Selecting, Using, and Evaluating Service.

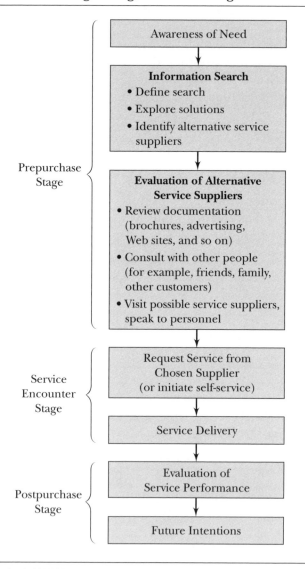

Source: Lovelock (2001).

and egocentric needs as the result of industrial expansion and globalized economies. Needs become needs in part due to greater disposable incomes for products and services that are produced and marketed to develop a demand for products and services that fulfill ego and social needs—for example, vacations, entertainment, health and fitness, and anti-aging products and services. This demand for products and services is directly related to the demographics of different geographical populations and values of cultures; for example, in North America, consumers want memorable experiences (Lovelock, 2001). Needs change fast, and organizations must adapt their service offerings to meet changing and evolving needs.

Customer expectations about service delivery vary from person to person, product to product, service to service, culture to culture, business to business, industry to industry, and country to country. The dynamics of the relationships among customer needs, expectations, and consequences of service delivery are illustrated in Exhibit 9.2.

As customer needs vary by person, product, service, culture, business, industry, and country, so do customer expectations. What leads to those expectations? According to Lovelock (2001), expectations

Exhibit 9.2. Factors That Influence Service Expectations.

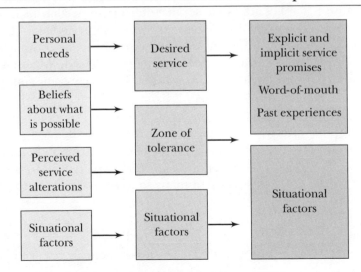

Source: Lovelock (2001).

develop based on people's prior experiences with the organization or individual providing the service, as well as with that service provider's competition and providers of similar services. If a customer has no such experience, then expectations may develop based on what the customer has heard about the service provider through marketing, word-of-mouth, or the media. These past experiences and reputations contribute to the development over time of norms for what to expect, which may vary considerably both within and among different service industries. To use Lovelock's example (2001), "Americans don't expect to be greeted by a doorman and a valet at a Motel 6, but they certainly do at a Ritz-Carlton hotel, where service levels are known to be much higher" (p. 114).

Exhibit 9.2 illustrates the factors that determine expectations, including desired service (what should be delivered) and the zone of tolerance, which encompasses adequate service (minimal service required) and predicted service (what would be delivered based on previous experiences). Kendall states in Chapter One that customers do not have to receive the absolute best quality of service to be satisfied: a "zone of tolerance" exists and is the gap between desired service and adequate service that a customer will accept. Some customers will trade off certain advantages (price, time) for smaller concessions of quality.

Failure to meet adequate service delivery expectations results in customer dissatisfaction. When customers experience long wait times, late deliveries, rude or incompetent service, or complicated procedures (for example, automated telephone systems), they respond with dissatisfaction in various ways. They may complain, pursue legal action, stop purchasing from the service provider, tell others about their experiences, or do nothing. For example, circulating the Internet is the letter in Exhibit 9.3, allegedly written by a ninety-six-year-old woman to her bank; Chronwatch.com, "a media watchdog and conservative news site, with a focus on the *San Francisco Chronicle*," is one of many sources where this letter can be found.

Complaint resolution and service recovery is critical when expectations are not adequately met. According to Lovelock (2001), customers whose complaints have been satisfactorily resolved have

Exhibit 9.3. Complaint Letter to Bank.

Dear Sir:

I am writing to thank you for bouncing my check with which I endeavored to pay my plumber last month.

By my calculations, three nanoseconds must have elapsed between his presenting the check and the arrival in my account of the funds needed to honor it. I refer, of course, to the automatic monthly deposit of my entire salary, an arrangement which, I admit, has been in place for only eight years.

You are to be commended for seizing that brief window of opportunity, and also for debiting my account $30 by way of penalty for the inconvenience caused to your bank. My thankfulness springs from the manner in which this incident has caused me to rethink my errant financial ways.

I noticed that whereas I personally attend to your telephone calls and letters, when I try to contact you, I am confronted by the impersonal, overcharging, pre-recorded, faceless entity which your bank has become.

From now on, I, like you, choose only to deal with a flesh-and-blood person. My mortgage and loan repayments will therefore and hereafter no longer be automatic, but will arrive at your bank, by check, addressed personally and confidentially to an employee at your bank whom you must nominate.

Be aware that it is an offense under the Postal Act for any other person to open such an envelope. Please find attached an Application Contact Status which I require your chosen employee to complete. I am sorry it runs to eight pages, but in order that I know as much about him or her as your bank knows about me, there is no alternative. Please note that all copies of his or her medical history must be countersigned by a Notary Public, and the mandatory details of his/her financial situation (income, debts, assets and liabilities) must be accompanied by documented proof.

In due course, I will issue your employee with a PIN number which he/she must quote in dealings with me. I regret that it cannot be shorter than 28 digits but, again, I have modeled it on the number of button presses required of me to access my account balance on your phone bank service. As they say, imitation is the sincerest form of flattery.

Exhibit 9.3. Complaint Letter to Bank, Cont'd.

Let me level the playing field even further. When you call me, press buttons as follows:

1. To make an appointment to see me.
2. To query a missing payment.
3. To transfer the call to my living room in case I am there.
4. To transfer the call to my bedroom in case I am sleeping.
5. To transfer the call to my toilet in case I am attending to nature.
6. To transfer the call to my mobile phone if I am not at home.
7. To leave a message on my computer, a password to access my computer is required. Password will be communicated to you at a later date to the Authorized Contact.
8. To return to the main menu and to listen to options 1 through 7.
9. To make a general complaint or inquiry.

The contact will then be put on hold, pending the attention of my automated answering service. While this may, on occasion, involve a lengthy wait, uplifting music will play for the duration of the call.

Regrettably, but again following your example, I must also levy an establishment fee to cover the setting up of this new arrangement.

May I wish you a happy, if ever so slightly less prosperous New Year?

Your Humble Client,
Rosemary Reeves Martin

Source: Essary, http://www.chronwatch.com/content/contentDisplay.asp?aid=7428

a repurchase rate of 69 to 80 percent, whereas the rate fell to 17 to 32 percent when the complaint had not been settled to the customer's satisfaction.

How do customers judge service delivery quality? The answer to this question has been the focus of researchers in marketing and psychology for over two decades. Because service delivery is intangible and multifaceted, it is harder for a customer to evaluate than is good. The seminal and landmark research on the dimensions on which customers make service quality judgments was done by Parasuraman, Zeithaml, and Berry (1985, 1988, 1994). These researchers developed a survey instrument called SERVQUAL based on focus group feedback. From the original dimensions of service delivery quality (Tangibles, Reliability, Responsiveness, Competence, Courtesy, Credibility, Security, Access, Communication, and Understanding the Customers), they refined SERVQUAL to the following factors:

1. Reliability (dependable, accurate performance)
2. Tangibles (physical elements)
3. Responsiveness (promptness and helpfulness)
4. Assurance (competence, courtesy, credibility, and security)
5. Empathy (access, communication, and understanding the customer)

Schneider and White (2004) thoroughly reviewed the latest research on service quality dimensions and concluded that SERVQUAL is not universally applicable to all situations without modifications. In particular, the five factors may be too broad for some services and too specific for others. Nevertheless, Schneider and White (2004) clearly described how SERVQUAL can be successfully used in most organizations:

> Our sense is that, for many purposes, the SERVQUAL measure and its underlying dimensions can usefully serve as a base for the development of service quality surveys in many settings and in many industries. But notice the focus on the words "base for": We are of the opinion that it is more important to capture the service quality issues for a particular organization or industry than it is to slavishly rely on the published version of SERVQUAL—and this is in agreement with the way Parasuraman, Zeithaml, and Berry (1988) proposed the measure be used. Of particular importance in this regard is the relative sparseness of items having to do with Tangibles in SERVQUAL.

For researchers and consultants working to understand service situations or improve service delivery, the dimensions of SERVQUAL provide an initial way to obtain a general understanding of how customers judge the quality of service delivery. Four of five SERVQUAL dimensions are intangible (Reliability, Responsiveness, Assurance, and Empathy), and Schneider and White (2004) recommend that as tangibles increase in saliency to the customer, more specifics be identified to determine service quality.

The Importance of Service Encounters

The focal point of any customer service interaction is the employee. Berry, Zeithaml, and Parasuraman (1985, p. 48) note that "customer-contact personnel provide the link between the company and customer. To the customer, they are the company." Indeed, many customers equate organizational service quality with the individual employee who serves them (Schneider and Bowen, 1985; Shostack, 1977). Thus, because a single poor service interaction can adversely affect a customer's view of an entire company, some organizations with weak customer relations strategies have allowed employees with poor customer orientations to tarnish the organization's image (Kurman, 1987).

Heskett, Sasser, and Schlesinger (1997) described four types of service encounters: (1) face-to-face encounters with services *visible* to the customer, (2) face-to-face encounters with services *invisible* to the customer, (3) human to machine, and (4) machine to human. In this book we have focused on better understanding face-to-face encounters with services *visible* to the customer and human-to-machine encounters.

Catanzaro and Salas made some conclusions in Chapter Seven with regard to face-to-face encounters. A service encounter is the interpersonal transaction between a customer and an employee during the transmission of a service; both roles are well defined, but the employee is expected to defer to the customer during the transaction. The employee may be the only representative of the entire organization whom the customer interacts with and may form an opinion about the company based solely on that one transaction. Different organizations in different industries require service encounters at varying stages of providing service—some mostly at the initial phase of marketing and selling and when handling problems and others at every stage. Service encounters are so important because customers' opinions of the organization can be largely based on these interactions; services are intangible and the quality of service interactions can be difficult to measure; and customers can tell the difference between genuine functional service quality (and employees can often transfer their positive emotions and behaviors to customers) and employees who are being controlled and ordered to provide friendly, courteous service.

Heskett, Sasser, and Schlesinger (1997) also identified the conditions that lead to successful service encounters, which are set out in Exhibit 9.4.

Lovelock (2001) described two factors when classifying service encounters: (1) degree of contact (high-low) and (2) type of contact (human or equipment). High contact with services personnel include hairstyling, dental services, branch banking with a teller, and nursing home care, while high contact with equipment can be Internet- or telecommunication-based communication—online purchasing of products or services (airline tickets, hotel reservations, retail products), for example, and automated telephone ordering or appointments (medical appointments, credit card purchases).

With the growing trend toward using equipment or technology to deliver service, many service encounters are shifting to human-to-machine contact. However, although there are significant customer segments (based on demographics—for example, baby boomers and their parents) demanding high human contact from services that include their banking and investment needs,

Exhibit 9.4. Conditions That Lead to Successful Service Encounters.

Face-to-Face Encounters (with service visible to customer)	Human-to-Machine
• Careful customer segmentation and selection	• Easy-to-understand procedures
• Frontline server selection emphasizing human skills	• Easy-to-access technology
• Easy access for customers	• Verification of service performance
• Pleasant, comfortable surroundings	• Fast response
• Good support technology	• Access to humans, if necessary
• Well-trained employees	• Information and transaction security
• Customer and employee loyalty	• Fail-safe mechanisms and procedures
• Timely, dependable service	
• Employees whose appearance and behavior engender trust	

Source: Heskett, Sasser, and Schlesinger (1997).

Lemon concludes in Chapter Four that service has become more depersonalized due to information technology and the streamlining or elimination of the traditional person-to-person encounter. Customer service encounters have been "engineered out" of organizations.

The Employee: The Key to Effective Service Encounters

The employee or the frontline service provider is critical in the eyes of the customer for effective face-to-face service encounter delivery. Heskett, Sasser, and Schlesinger (1997) described the service relationship triangle of (1) the service organization, (2) the frontline service provider, and (3) the customer. They elaborated on the importance of the frontline service provider as the key to the service encounter and further emphasized the importance of service employees by describing the critical employee performance requirements in the cycle of capability (see Exhibit 9.5). Effective service encounter performance is directly related to hiring, training, leading, and motivating the right employees.

In Chapter Five, Kehoe and Dickter provide comprehensive insight into service jobs, service competencies, and strategies for selecting service providers. In almost all service jobs, extensive job knowledge is crucial. When job knowledge changes frequently and is easy to acquire (such as customer service positions), employers rely more heavily on training than selection. The opposite is true for positions where job knowledge requires considerable education and experience: employers will devote more resources to selection than training.

The research on service performance indicates that service-oriented jobs are complex and vary depending on employees, organizations, managers, situations, work environments, and other factors. Industrial-organizational psychologists have had difficulty researching and classifying dimensions of service performance; in contrast, extensive research has been conducted about the difference between task performance (formal activities required to perform the job) and contextual performance (going beyond job description and contributing to the organization's success and effectiveness). Distinguishing between what employees can do and what they will do is distinguishing between what they are capable of and required

Exhibit 9.5. Cycle of Capability.

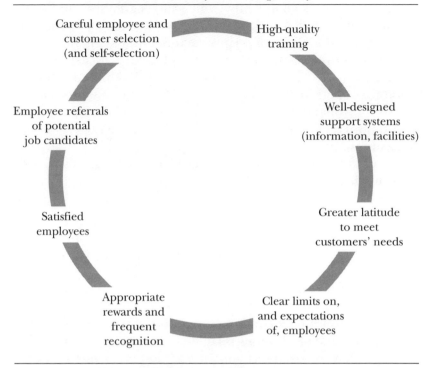

Source: Heskett, Sasser, and Schlesinger (1997).

to do and what they are motivated to do to in order to help the service transaction.

According to Kehoe and Dickter, organizations often value selection strategies that help to improve outcomes for its service providers, which in turn have a positive impact on the customer, the supervisor, and the organization. When looking to find employees for service-oriented jobs, organizations can design selection strategies that focus on employee attributes that relate to job performance, such as life experience, aptitudes and abilities, acquired skills and knowledge, personality, and values, interests, and attitudes. These generally apply to performance and behavior in all work situations, but they often relate specifically to service work. A selection strategy should also consider the major features of service work that are significant in determining the importance of experience, abilities, acquired skills and knowledge, personality, and values and interests: (1) work complexity (which varies greatly from, for example, valet attendants to nurses), (2) work structure (policy and procedures, guidelines or scripts, factors influencing the service provider in the course of their interactions), (3) customer engagement (higher levels of customer interaction increases the importance of personality attributes and values and interests relating to interpersonal behavior), and (4) customer influence (the extent to which employees' behavior can influence the customer's desired response).

In Chapter Six, Whetzel and McDaniel provide an excellent review of selection techniques and instruments being used to identify service-oriented employees during the hiring process, such as the following:

Development Dimensions International's Customer Service Career Battery, which provides three inventories that predict the performance of applicants for customer service jobs: one is a series of brief written simulations where respondents pick one of four options; the second is a self-report of past behavior, preferences, and motivations related to work behaviors; the third is a behavior-based instrument that measures an applicant's past experiences.

Unicru's Customer Service Assessment, a personality-based pre-employment assessment that measures behaviors with fifty statements of everyday experience and uses a four-point scale of agreement.

Employment Technologies Corporation's Customer Service Skills Assessment Program, a video-based computer-scored job simulation that assesses competencies for customer service and measures six skill areas related to helping customers: developing good customer relations, discovering customer needs, responding to customer wants, anticipating customer needs, working together to meet those needs, and ensuring customer loyalty.

The Call Center Simulation, a computer-based test that simulates actual call center workstation conditions, testing applicants to respond to calls from customers with real issues (some are irate, others confused, some are calm, and so forth).

Whetzel and McDaniel also concluded that most test developers rely on job analysis to understand the personality characteristics linked with a service orientation; several tests have used various names for the same attributes: friendliness, reliability, responsiveness, and courteousness. In the development of ServiceFirst, I identified the eleven customer service competencies in Exhibit 9.6 by integrating job analysis, literature, and focus group research (Fogli, 1991, 1995).

Customer service employees and salespeople do not share the same personality characteristics, and both approach their transactions with customers differently and to different ends; salespeople demonstrate extraversion and aggressiveness, while customer service personnel perform poorly when showing those same traits. Whetzel and McDaniel also discussed that for almost a century, cognitive ability tests have proven to be the most valid predictors of performance across all occupations.

The Relationship Between Employee Attitudes, Customer Attitudes, and Service Delivery

In *The Service Profit Chain,* Heskett, Sasser, and Schlesinger (1997) provide specific evidence from company studies to show the relationship between customer and employee satisfaction for several well-known companies (MCI, XEROX, Merry Maids). We know that customer and employee satisfaction go hand in hand. However, the cause and effect is not clear. Some organizations have a motto, "employees first, customers second" because of their belief that you can have satisfied customers only when you have satisfied employees. It should be noted that the studies reported by Heskett and others involve services that are face-to-face (with services visible to the customer—office machine servicing, cleaning services, restaurant employees, branch bank employees, and so on).

In Chapter Three, Brooks, Wiley, and Hause offer a new and different approach to understanding employee and customer attitudes related to organizational performance. According to the service-profit chain concept, when customers are satisfied, they are loyal, and their loyalty drives profit and revenue growth in service; also, customers will perceive the value of service as being higher when they are served by satisfied, loyal, productive employees. However, while organizations have traditionally cared about keeping customers

Exhibit 9.6. ServiceFirst Job Analysis.

ServiceFirst: Customer Service Competencies

1. Empathy

The ability to think and feel as the customer does in order to better identify and fulfill customer needs and better handle customer complaints.

- Listens to and understands customer problems; does not become defensive in complaint situations.
- Is able to respond to both the content and feeling of a customer's message. (Example: "As I see it, Mr. Jones, it makes you angry to receive products that are not up to your standards. It makes me angry too. Tell me more about it.")
- Is able to see situations from the perspectives of both customer and management.
- Expresses sympathy and concern for customer problems.

2. Behavior Flexibility

The ability to modify or alter one's expressive behavior to fit different situations.

- Alters behavior to better show the customer feelings of concern, wanting to help, etc.
- Gauges how to behave by observing the behavior of the customer.
- Acts differently at different times, with behavior appropriate to the situation at hand.

3. Activity Level/Energy

The ability to maintain a high energy level throughout the day and to perform numerous activities without tiring.

- Performs tasks quickly and productively.
- Works with liveliness and vitality.
- Can work on more than one thing at a time.

Exhibit 9.6. ServiceFirst Job Analysis, Cont'd.

4. Assertiveness/Dominance

The tendency to take the initiative and exercise leadership in customer-oriented situations.	• Is self-confident in dealing with customers. • Actively offers assistance to customers rather than waiting for them to ask for help. • Takes the lead when working on group projects.

5. Sociability

The inclination to seek out and enjoy social interaction that fosters a friendly working/shopping environment.	• Is friendly to customers. • Enjoys talking with customers. • Participates in group activities. • Works well with others.

6. Personalized

The ability to make shopping a more familiar and personal experience for customers.	• Gets to know customers' names. • Addresses customers by name when known. • Takes an interest in customers' specific requests/needs.

7. Politeness

The ability to be courteous to customers at all times, using consideration and correct manners in dealing with others.	• Appropriately uses phrases such as please, thank you, excuse me. • Smiles at customers. • Is courteous to customers even when they are rude.

8. Helpfulness

The readiness to offer assistance to customers and serve them willingly.	• Shows customers where things are rather than telling them. • Offers extra assistance to customers as needed. • Goes out of his or her way to satisfy customer needs or desires.

Exhibit 9.6. ServiceFirst Job Analysis, Cont'd.

---

9. People Orientation

The tendency to enjoy being with people rather than being alone; to be active rather than passive; and to be extroverted rather then introverted.	• Prefers working in a group to working alone. • Likes people. • Enjoys helping customers.

---

10. Discretion/Judgment

The capacity to distinguish between alternatives and make reasonable decisions.	• Can tell the difference between appropriate and inappropriate job behaviors. • Chooses appropriate job behaviors.

---

11. Customer/Management/Self-Orientation

The extent to which the employee places his or her own, the customer's, or management's interests as top priority.	• Customer Orientation: Places the customer's interest above all others. • Management Orientation: Places management's interests above all others. • Self-Orientation: Places his or her own interests above all others.

Source: Fogli (1991).

happy, research has shown that happy customers do not often translate into loyal customers. In Chapter Three, Brooks, Wiley, and Hause discuss linkage research, which collects data from employees about their work environment, and the connections between customer satisfaction and loyalty and the performance of the business and its financial success. They conclude that a high-performance work environment promotes a more positive customer experience. There are two problems with the employee-customer-performance linkage: human resources focuses too much on employee satisfaction as the start of this chain, when they should focus initially on employee perceptions of leadership, and many organizations do not fully understand these models and have trouble executing them or do not see the link between performance areas (employee opinions and customer loyalty) and the financial bottom line. Observations from the authors' case study, which included an employee survey, a customer survey, and business results, are as follows: (1) to relate customer opinions to financial results, there must be a time lag (taking into consideration repurchase cycles of products and other factors), (2) overall customer satisfaction is not the most influential customer opinion, and (3) the employee opinion of climate-for-service is more relevant than employee satisfaction.

The "father of service climate research" is Benjamin Schneider, who has written and co-written several books and articles about the subject. In 2004, he provided a comprehensive definition of *service climate:*

> We define service climate as the shared employee perceptions of the policies, practices, and procedures and the behaviors that get rewarded, supported, and expected with regard to customer service and customer service quality. Basically, a service climate represents the degree to which the internal functioning of an organization is experienced as one focused on service quality. As noted earlier, it is a pattern across policies, procedures, and rewarded behaviors to which employees attach the meaning, "Service Quality is important here." So, when employees perceive that they are rewarded for delivering quality service and when employees perceive that management devotes time, energy, and resources to service quality and when employees receive the training they require to effectively deal with diverse customers, then a positive service climate is more likely to be the theme or meaning attached to these experiences [Schneider and White, p. 100].

Furthermore, Schneider provides data supporting his model that climate correlates with customer perceptions of service quality. The drivers of service climate are organizational work facilitation (leadership to support service delivery) and internal service (the level of service provided to internal departments inside the organization). Service climate correlates with customer perceptions of service quality.

Strategies and Tactics for Improving Service Delivery

This section describes strategies and tactics to improve service delivery at two levels: (1) the service encounter and (2) total service delivery (TSD).

Service Encounters

Catanzaro and Salas identified in Chapter Seven important strategies in managing and improving service encounters, the first of which is to examine the impact of how service encounter performance is specified and measured. The behavioral approach measures specific employee behaviors (smiling, using a script, probing customers for information) and uses this to train, appraise, and reward employees. This approach uses the company's labor resources poorly, influences how the employee really acts, and is hard to use for anything other than short-term research (for example, putting supervisors in charge of watching all transactions). Micromanaging employees takes away from the feelings of autonomy, control, and responsibility that correlate with employee motivation and job satisfaction. The customer evaluation approach gathers information from customers about their views of their expectations, preference, and experiences of service encounter transaction. Questionnaires like SERVQUAL and others assess customer expectations and perceptions of service encounter behaviors and have been used in many industries with evidence of reliability and validity.

Another strategy is to reduce and manage conflict between customer expectations and service performance. Customer dissatisfaction occurs when there is a gap between customer expectations and organizational policies, practices, or the ability to meet those expectations; the employee bears the brunt of this. There is a conflict of roles for the service employee, who has to both adhere to the company's policies and serve customers to their satisfaction. Four methods can be used to close this gap: (1) improve company policy to increase customer satisfaction, (2) educate customers so their expectations are more realistic, (3) train employees to better deal with dissatisfied customers, and (4) improve service quality to meet or exceed customer expectations.

Catanzaro and Salas also discuss how to improve the organizational climate for service, as research shows a correlation between employee perceptions of organizational climate and customer perceptions of service quality. Many companies have policies that imply that the customers are far more important than employees, which results in employees' not genuinely caring about service quality. Employee and customer emotions can be contagious—

both good and bad. Employees will be significantly more effective at giving good service if they are intrinsically motivated. Service encounter behavior may be thought of as a type of organizational citizenship behavior (OCB), which are employee behaviors that support the organization's goals and objectives by going the extra mile to help a customer or coworker, volunteering for more work to help others, obeying rules, and other behaviors that ask employees to step out of their job description to help others. OCBs can have an impact on service quality because they require employees to use their discretion to help customers without supervision or direction.

Following is a summary of key strategies for improving the service encounter:

- Organizations should create an environment where employees feel valued, treated fairly, and supported by management, which creates employees who want to give good service to customers and positively represent the organization.
- Human resources and management need practices in place that create an atmosphere where employees feel positive and pass those feelings on to customers, which can be involving employees in decision making and problem solving.
- Employees have more customer contact than managers, and their opinions can be valuable for improving service quality, which results in empowering employees who will provide good service.
- Organizations can use the four-prong approach mentioned above to close the gap between customer expectations and their perceived quality of service.

In Chapter Eight, Adler and Nelson discuss the ways in which call center customer service has become complex in today's marketplace. Call centers, which respond to customer complaints and inquiries and are also responsible for selling additional products and services, have increased in importance in management's eyes; they now affect the top and bottom lines of a company. Customers expect more from call center agents, and their loyalty is earned when those expectations are met or exceeded. Loyal customers who spread positive word of mouth create the most effective and cost-efficient method of acquiring new customers. Call center representatives are now expected to interact with customers in several ways—telephone, Web, chat, e-mail, and other voice services. They have to be well informed about the multitude of products and services companies now offer; to be effective, they must know about more products and services and maintain a positive conversation with customers.

Adler and Nelson describe a performance management process that shows dramatic and significant improvement in call center service delivery encounters. For a performance management process to improve service quality, it must meet the following requisites:

- Align with business goals to turn corporate initiatives into service delivery metrics that the representatives can convey to customers, to reward employees for following these initiatives, and prove profitable for the business.
- Reflect customers' views of their needs and expectations both initially and on an ongoing basis so performance management can be used to improve customers' experiences. Focus groups and surveys can be used in the beginning, and customers can be asked during calls to continue tracking those data.
- Service quality must be clearly defined so that employee behavior and company processes can be tailored to produce effective customer service.
- Help the company improve service at both individual and group levels.

Total Service Delivery

Heskett, Sasser, and Schlesinger (1997) prescribe key organizational drivers and capabilities that lead to improved service delivery and profitability. (See Exhibit 9.7 for the design that outlines basic relationships behind the service-profit chain.) The implications of the service-profit chain for management are landmark and critical to changing leadership for service delivery. Service-profit chain thinking is causal, and company leaders are given a prescription on how to improve service delivery. The causal links in the service-profit chain are:

Exhibit 9.7. Service-Profit Chain.

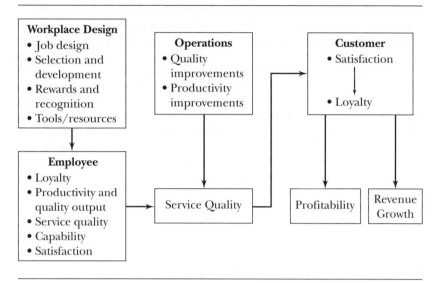

Source: Heskett, Sasser, and Schlesinger (1997).

- Customer loyalty drives profitability and growth.
- Customer satisfaction drives customer loyalty.
- Value drives customer satisfaction.
- Employee productivity drives value.
- Employee loyalty drives productivity.
- Employee satisfaction drives loyalty.
- Internal quality drives employee satisfaction.
- Top management leadership underlies the chain's success.

The change process I call Sales and Service Excellence evolved from more than a decade of consultation to improve Total Service Delivery (TSD) in the retail sector (Fogli, 2004). It starts with a sales and service strategy and a plan to improve sales and service delivery. Total Service Delivery is the result of improved employee hiring, training, motivation, communication, performance measurement, rewards, specific service delivery initiatives, and job changes. The ultimate objectives are to improve customer satisfaction, retain existing customers and develop customer loyalty,

attract new customers, increase revenues and profits, develop a reputation as a service leader, differentiate the market, obtain a competitive advantage, and achieve long-term growth. A sales and
service culture is developed by focusing on the key levers of
change: human resource practices, communication flow, strategy,
structure, and business and information processes as shown in Exhibit 9.8.

Experience has shown that the following must be a part of the
strategic plan to create a change in sales and service delivery. The

**Exhibit 9.8. Sales and Service Excellence:
Integrated Delivery System.**

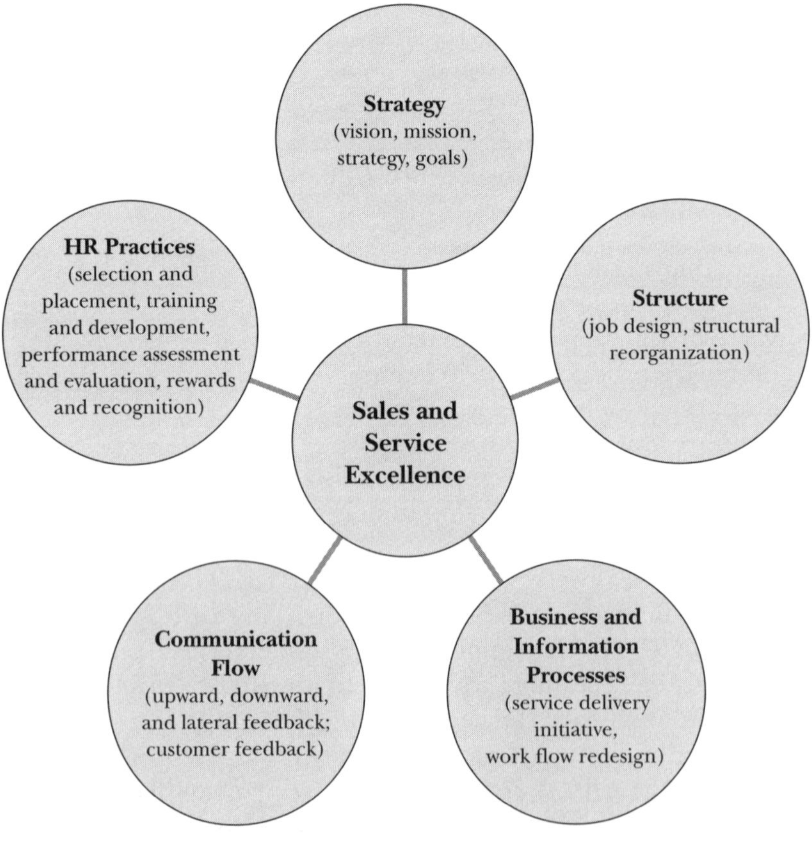

Strategy
(vision, mission,
strategy, goals)

HR Practices
(selection and
placement, training
and development,
performance assessment
and evaluation, rewards
and recognition)

**Sales and
Service
Excellence**

Structure
(job design, structural
reorganization)

**Communication
Flow**
(upward, downward,
and lateral feedback;
customer feedback)

**Business and
Information
Processes**
(service delivery
initiative,
work flow redesign)

Source: Fogli (2004).

implementation plan for the Sales and Service Excellence System is designed to ensure that the following are present:

1. Include service as a strategic objective in the vision, mission, or strategy: set at the top, communicated companywide, and translated into goals, objectives, and action.
2. Train and encourage top management to champion, sponsor, lead, and support service initiatives by "walking the talk."
3. Create a coalition of people committed to Sales and Service Excellence: a Sales and Service Excellence steering committee with an urgent commitment to action.
4. Keep it simple: pick a few high-impact, added-value actions, and implement them well.
5. Allow for early wins ("quick fixes").
6. Measure performance, and hold managers and employees accountable (manager role, shopper surveys, 360-degree evaluations).
7. Strive for a broad-based culture change in the long-run—a Sales and Service Excellence culture.
8. Set and communicate standards for service and sales (for example, staffing standards).
9. Provide training and support for needed changes.
10. Motivate and inspire employees to champion and deliver superior service.
11. Hire employees who have the right skills and personal qualities.
12. Remember the golden rule: "employees first, customers second."

Exhibit 9.9 illustrates the three phases of Sales and Service Excellence change: the current state, the transition state, and the desired state. This is a familiar change model of unfreezing old practices (deciding what you will do differently), testing new practices (pilot testing new procedures), and refreezing effective practices (reinforcing what works).

When customers go to a retailer, their expectations for service fall into five categories:

- Reliability (employees perform the promised service dependably and accurately—most important)
- Assurance (employees are knowledgeable and courteous, and convey trust and confidence)

Exhibit 9.9. Three Phases of Sales and Service Excellence Change.

Current State	→	Transition State	→	Desired State
• Establish need and sense of urgency • Form steering committee • Create and shape vision, mission, strategy, and goals • Evaluate structure, work processes, communication flow, HR practices • Identify areas for change and design initiatives • Communicate vision, mission, strategy, and goals and change initiatives • Mobilize commitment • Establish milestones		• Improve employment hiring • Implement training and motivation program for managers • Implement service values • Implement service initiatives • Implement mystery shopper program • Implement 360-degree feedback • Make structure changes • Make workflow changes • Empower others to act • Create short-term wins • Monitor and communicate progress • Consolidate and leverage improvements		• Key systems and processes aligned with strategy • Service or sales culture emerging • Top management walks the talk and champions change • Goal is sustaining and leveraging changes • Institutionalize new approaches • Communicate best practices and heroic acts • Raise the bar and set new standards • Enforce accountabilities

Source: Fogli (2004).

- Tangibles (good appearance of physical facilities, product quality and variety, equipment, personnel, and communication materials)
- Empathy (employees provide caring, individualized attention)
- Responsiveness (employees are willing to help customers and provide prompt service)

Sales and Service Excellence is designed to implement initiatives for total service delivery. They are the centerpiece of Sales and Service Excellence. They are specific actions that change service levels within a store. Four types of initiatives are implemented in stores:

- Tangible initiatives (specific store procedures that are delivered to create a consistent look and feel of exceptional service)

- GUEST or behavioral and performance initiatives (specific actions that staff will carry out in interacting with customers to ensure an exceptional service experience)
- Measurement initiatives (store service levels that will be measured through mystery shops, with results given to stores on a weekly basis)
- Senior management support initiatives (the district manager and the retail leadership group will work with stores to reinforce exceptional service; successful stores will receive service recognition rewards).

To further illustrate total service delivery initiatives, Exhibit 9.10 presents a listing from ABC Food & Drug and XYZ Coffee.

The Sales and Service Excellence System is a systematic change process of education, training, motivation, feedback, and accountability. To meet these diverse expectations, retail store managers need to

- Understand customer expectations and how to meet them.
- Learn customer service strategies and tactics.
- Develop service management skills.
- Be motivated and empowered to do what it takes to satisfy the customer.

Exhibit 9.10. Total Service Delivery Initiatives.

Tangible initiatives	Specific store procedures that are carried out to create a consistent look and feel of exceptional service.
G.U.E.S.T. / Behavioral and Performance Initiatives	Specific actions that staff will carry out in interacting with customers to ensure an exceptional service experience.
Measurement Initiatives	Store service levels will be measured through mystery shoppers. Stores will receive their results weekly.
Senior Management Support Initiatives	The district manager and the retail leadership group will work with stores to reinforce exceptional service. Successful stores will receive service recognition rewards.

Source: Fogli (2004).

- Receive feedback on their performance.
- Be held accountable for their performance.
- Understand how Sales and Service Excellence fits in with the bigger picture—the vision, mission, values, and goals of the organization.

Store managers receive feedback from two perspectives. Feedback from the customer's point of view is provided through "mystery shopper" evaluations and customer feedback (external assessment), and multirater feedback is provided on how managers are running the store from the perspective of employees and management (internal assessment). Together, these assessments give managers what they need to know about how they are facilitating employee performance and customer satisfaction, as managers are accountable for creating change in their stores. Exhibit 9.11 illustrates same-store sales increases after two years of implementing total service delivery in ABC Food & Drug. Same-store sales increased 8.6 percent after two years, compared to the industry average same-store sales increase of 1.7 percent. Exhibit 9.12 shows an improvement in mystery shopper ratings of 60 to 90 percent on GUEST service delivery.

Exhibit 9.11. ABC Food & Drug Sales Increase.

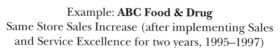

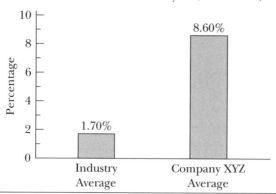

Source: Fogli (2004).

At XYZ Coffee, Sales and Service Excellence was designed to evaluate effectiveness based on the results of the mystery shoppers. Mystery shoppers were trained to shop stores and evaluate tangible and intangible service delivery in the following seven store areas: entryway, sales floor, bar service, bean or tea service, drink pickup service, restroom service, and condiment area. There were twenty intangible items included, fifteen of which were GUEST items:

Greet: Were you greeted?

Understand: Did the employee understand your order?

Engage and suggest: Were you offered anything else?

Serve: Were you provided with timely and accurate service?

Thank: Were you thanked?

The study of effectiveness was designed in four phases:

Phase 1: Preimplementation.

Phase 2: Implement Sales and Service Excellence pilot.

Phase 3: Make changes to pilot, and evaluate.

Phase 4: Make further changes to pilot, and evaluate.

Exhibit 9.12. ABC Food & Drug GUEST Service Delivery.

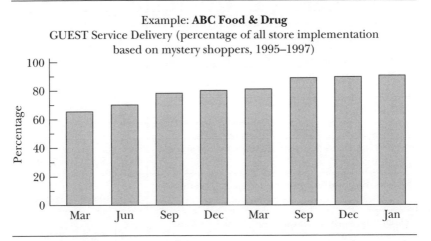

Example: **ABC Food & Drug**
GUEST Service Delivery (percentage of all store implementation based on mystery shoppers, 1995–1997)

Source: Fogli (2004).

Results of the study are shown in Exhibits 9.13, 9.14, and 9.15. Exhibit 9.13 shows items with the greatest improvement across the study in service delivery in the coffee shops (for example, wearing a name badge or apron, thanking customers for their orders, helping customers with a sense of urgency, recommending an additional product, calling customers by name, and thanking customers at the end of the transaction).

Exhibit 9.14 shows changes from the beginning of the study to the end. Both GUEST (intangible items) and tangible delivery improved from the start. GUEST delivery went from 66.5 to 89.7 percent effectiveness, and tangible delivery improved from 67.6 to 93 percent. All customer service areas in the store showed improvement (see Exhibit 9.15), except for the restrooms. Bar service improved the most from just under 50 percent to almost 92 percent.

Exhibit 9.13. Pre- and Post-Comparisons: Greatest Improvement.

Improvement of more than 40 percent and Post-Pilot 2 results greater than 70 percent.

Item	Pre-Pilot	Post-Pilot 2	Percentage increase
32. Was the counter cashier wearing a name badge and apron?	0.0	95.5	95.5%
41. Was the barista wearing a name badge and apron?	0.0	92.1	92.1
18. Was the bar counter cashier wearing a name badge and apron?	4.2	95.4	91.2
16. Were you thanked for your order by the bar cashier?	4.0	92.0	88.0
10. Were all employees actively engaged in helping customers with an appropriate sense of urgency?	21.4	92.3	70.9
34. Did the counter cashier suggest at least one additional product recommendation?	25.0	94.6	69.6
39. Did the barista call out your drink by using your name?	50.0	93.7	43.7
40. Did the barista thank you for your order?	33.3	75.6	42.3

Source: Fogli (2004).

**Exhibit 9.14. GUEST and Tangible Service
Delivery: Pre- and Post-Comparisons.**

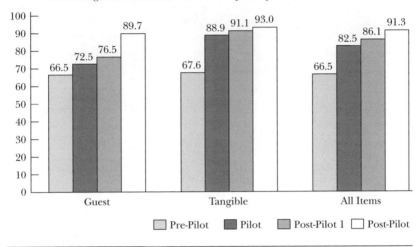

The average across **Guest** items went up 23.2 points (increase of 35%).
The average across **Tangible** items went up 25.4 points (increase of 38%).
The average score across **All** items went up 24.8 points (increase of 37%).

Source: Fogli (2004).

Sales and Service Excellence is designed from the experiences and knowledge of subject matter experts—for example, retail managers, industrial-organizational psychologists, and, in small part, previous research. Sales and Service Excellence implementation is a form of actionable research. The key reasons for success are buy-in from senior management, clear linkage to business results, broader culture change, feedback and measurement, accountability, support for development, and simplicity and focus.

Service Delivery in an Era of Unprecedented Change

Over the past twenty years, organizations have gone through unprecedented change both within and between organizations. Customers, jobs, and employees have been affected by the massive reshaping of the workplace. The following are the drivers of organizational change (Fogli, 2004):

Exhibit 9.15. Pre- and Post-Comparisons
for Customer Service Areas.

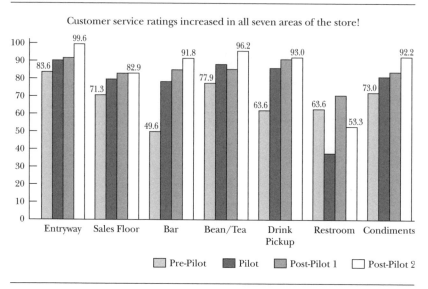

Customer service ratings increased in all seven areas of the store!

Legend: Pre-Pilot | Pilot | Post-Pilot 1 | Post-Pilot 2

Source: Fogli (2004).

- *Changing demographics.* The aging of the U.S. population (baby boomers), ethnic diversity (increases in Hispanic and Asian populations), and women comprising over 45 percent of the workforce; multiple generations (baby boomers, Generation X, and Generation Y) with different needs and expectations.
- *Advances in technology.* Cyberspace, Internet, voice, and wireless communication and information sharing.
- *Increased competition and globalization.* Multinational companies; outsourcing and offshoring of jobs; and producer, supplier, and distributor partnerships and alliances.
- *Increased customer expectations.* Customers want more for less, they want it faster, and they want it customized to their needs.
- *Increased shareholder pressure.* The drive for increasing stock prices on Wall Street has resulted in unexpected mergers and acquisitions.

The drive to develop high-performance organizations and economically successful organizations has resulted in merged, acquired, downsized, and reorganized corporations. Many of the "new" corporations have changed their vision, mission, strategies, and tactics in the delivery of their products and services. To do so efficiently, internal processes have been reengineered, reshaped, and reinvented (Lawler, Mohrman, and Ledford, 1998). Several of these organizational changes have implications for service delivery. Company structures have been shaped around the customer, for example, in health care, fast food, and retail banking. Total Quality Management systems and Six Sigma have been implemented to improve product quality and reduce cost in manufacturing. Competencies, best practices, and benchmark behaviors for service delivery are now a part of human resource management; for example, "Focus on the Customer," "Reliability," and "Responsiveness" are customer service delivery competencies.

Customers today can be described as more demanding, which in part is due to the variety of choices available and the competition that drives new products to the marketplace. In general, consumers expect more for less, greater variety, customization, and faster delivery. They are less brand loyal and more willing to switch brands than in the past.

Organizations have had a role in "creating" this consumer by both creating new products and services to meet anticipated customer needs and expectations and by responding to the customer purchasing and satisfaction results. Over ten thousand new products are introduced to the marketplace each month in the United States. Ten years ago, the average product life cycle was about two years; today it is six months. In retail, new businesses are emerging from old categories of merchandise. Specialty retailers like PetSmart and Bed, Bath and Beyond represent new store formats from old categories in supermarkets and general merchandise retailers. Inventories are better managed using time-based completion and just-in-time delivery systems. Strategic partnerships between retailers and suppliers (for example, Wal-Mart) in category management have made pricing competitive. Private labels have emerged to be both price and quality competitive to entice switching behavior and erode customer loyalty.

Robert Vance in Chapter Two clearly points out the use of technology by organizations to become more efficient in customer delivery. Post-2000 changes to the workforce included companies' investing in technology to increase worker productivity, outsourcing becoming more and more popular as hiring new American workers became less popular (reducing costs of benefits and wages to companies and weakening American labor unions), manufacturing jobs being created in other countries with cheaper labor and products, stock prices rising, and executives being compensated more for instituting these changes. Companies across many industries can use technology to improve and implement programs to help customer service, even companies where employees do not deal with customers extensively (manufacturing). The Internet and customer relationship management software have made those initiatives possible and easier to implement. Technology is cheaper than labor, and companies are offering great incentives to customers who can use it, from buying airline tickets online to shopping at online stores without storefronts. Another advantage is that companies can reach customers twenty-four hours a day, seven days a week by utilizing various technologies.

Lovelock (2001) cited five factors that drive increased demand for services and more competition to deliver services:

- Government policies (for example, regulations, privatization, consumer protection laws)
- Social changes (for example, rising consumer expectations, immigration)
- Business trends (such as strategic alliances, franchising)
- Advances in technology (convergence of computers and telecommunications, wireless networking, and so forth)
- Internationalization (international mergers and alliances, offshoring of production)

The U.S. Bureau of Labor Statistics (2003) projects that by the year 2010, 20.5 million jobs will be added to the U.S. economy, and the majority of these will be in retail and professional services. The significant customer segments for 2010 will be baby boomers, who will turn fifty to sixty-four, and women, who will comprise 45 percent of the labor force, and, according to Tom Peters (2001), make the majority of the purchase decisions about products and services. Asians and Hispanics will be the fastest-growing members of the labor market with more and different needs for services and products.

Exhibit 9.16. Old and New Models.

Old Model	New Model
Service with a smile	Service with empowerment
Customer is always right	Focus on the right customers
Customer satisfaction at all costs	Build the brand-service-profit chain
Complaint department	Seek and reward feedback
We don't care, and we don't have to	We care because it's good business

Source: Lemon (2006).

In Chapter Four, Lemon described externalities by corporations that are both positive (lower prices, more efficient delivery of products, increased selection and choices, increased access to more product information) and negative (loss of privacy, identity theft, loss of customer trust and loyalty, and depersonalization of service) for the customer. Service delivery will become more complex as more products are introduced, technology delivery systems develop, and market segments expand worldwide. Companies are expanding across the globe and finding that customer satisfaction can be driven by different factors in different countries—lower cost is more important in Latin America, quality in Southern Europe, and so on. To meet the challenges, Lemon suggests that we may need new models of service delivery, as shown in Exhibit 9.16.

References

Albrecht, K., and Zemke, R. *Service America! Doing Business in the New Economy.* Homewood, Ill.: Dow-Jones-Irwin, 1985.

Bell, C., and Zemke, R. *Managing Knock Your Socks Off Service.* New York: AMACOM, 1992.

Berry, L. L., Zeithaml, V. A., and Parasuraman, A. "Quality Counts in Services, Too." *Business Horizons,* Mar. 8, 1985, pp. 9–20.

Bowen, D., Chase, R., Cummings, T., and Associates. *Service Management Effectiveness: Balancing Strategy, Organization, and Human Resources, Operations, and Marketing.* San Francisco: Jossey-Bass, 1990.

Collier, D. "The Service Sector Revolution: The Automation of Services." *Long Range Planning,* 1983, *16*(6), 10–20.

Connellan, T., and Zemke, R. *Sustaining Knock Your Socks Off Service.* New York: AMACOM, 1993.

Czepiel, J. A., Solomon, M. R., and Surprenant, C. F. *The Service Encounter.* San Francisco: New Lexington Press, 1985.

Desatnick, R. L. *Managing to Keep the Customer.* San Francisco: Jossey-Bass, 1987.

Essary, M. "A Woman's Message to Her Bank," 2004 [http://www .chronwatch.com/content/contentDisplay.asp?aid=7428]

Finch, L. *Twenty Ways to Improve Customer Service.* Menlo Park, Calif.: Crisp, 1994.

Fogli, L. "ServiceFirst: A Test to Select Service Oriented Personnel." Paper presented at the annual meeting of the American Psychological Association, San Francisco, 1991.

Fogli, L. "Construct Validity of ServiceFirst from CORE Corporation: Theory and Measurement of Customer-Service Orientation." Paper presented at the Tenth Annual Conference of the Society for Industrial and Organizational Psychologists, Orlando, Fla., 1995.

Fogli, L. "Sales and Service Excellence: Exceptional GUEST Service." Paper presented at the Dearborn Conference, Washington, D.C., May 2004.

Gerson, R. *Measuring Customer Satisfaction.* Menlo Park, Calif.: Crisp, 1993.

Goodman, G. *Monitoring, Measuring, and Managing Customer Service.* San Francisco: Jossey-Bass, 2000.

Heskett, J. *Managing in the Service Economy.* Boston: Harvard Business School Press, 1986.

Heskett, J., Sasser, W. E., and Schlesinger, L. *The Service Profit Chain: How Leading Companies Link Profit and Growth to Loyalty, Satisfaction, and Value.* New York: Free Press, 1997.

Hochschild, A. R. *The Managed Heart.* Berkeley: University of California Press, 1983.

Kurman, M. "Customer Relations: The Personnel Angle." *Personnel,* Sept. 1987, pp. 38–40.

Lawler, E. E., III, Mohrman, S. A., and Ledford, G. E., Jr. *Strategies for High-Performance Organizations: Employee Involvement, TQM, and Reengineering Programs in Fortune 1000 Corporations.* San Francisco: Jossey-Bass, 1998.

Lovelock, C. *Services Marketing: People, Technology, Strategy.* (4th ed.) Upper Saddle River, N.J.: Prentice Hall, 2001.

Martin, W. *Managing Quality Customer Service: A Practical Guide for Establishing a Service Operation.* Menlo Park, Calif.: Crisp, 1989.

Martin, W. *Quality Customer Service: A Positive Guide to Superior Service.* (3rd ed.) Menlo Park, Calif.: Crisp, 1993.

Parasuraman, A., Zeithaml, V., and Berry, L. "A Conceptual Model of Service Quality and Its Implications for Future Research." *Journal of Marketing,* 1985, *49,* 41–50.

Parasuraman, A., Zeithaml, V. A., and Berry, L. "SERVQUAL: A Multiple-Item Scale for Measuring Consumer Perceptions of Service Quality." *Journal of Retailing,* 1988, *64,* 17–39.

Parasuraman, A., Zeithaml, V. A., and Berry, L. "Alternative Scales for Measuring Service Quality: A Comparative Assessment Based on Psychometric and Diagnostic Criteria." *Journal of Retailing,* 1994, *70,* 201–230.

Peters, T. "Rollercoaster Days: Learning to Rock and Roll." Presentation for Raymond James Financial Services, Las Vegas, 2001 [http://www.tompeters.com/slides/content.php?year=2001].

Rust, R., and Oliver, R. *Service Quality: New Directions in Theory and Practice.* Thousand Oaks, Calif.: Sage, 1994.

Schneider, B. "HRM—A Service Perspective: Towards a Customer-Focused HRM." *International Journal of Service Industry Management,* 1994, *5,* 64–76.

Schneider, B., and Bowen, D. E. "Employee and Customer Perceptions of Service in Banks: Replication and Extension." *Journal of Applied Psychology,* 1985, *70,* 423–433.

Schneider, B., and Bowen, D. E. *Winning the Service Game.* Boston: Harvard Business School Press, 1995.

Schneider, B., and White, S. *Service Quality: Research Perspectives.* Thousand Oaks, Calif.: Sage, 2004.

Shostack, G. L. "Service Positioning Through Structural Change." *Journal of Marketing,* 1977, *51,* 34–43.

U.S. Bureau of Labor Statistics. "BLS Releases 2000–2010 Employment Projections," Dec. 2003 [http://www.bls.gov/news.release/ecopro.nr0.htm]

Whiteley, R. *The Customer Driven Company.* Reading, Mass.: Addison-Wesley, 1991.

Zemke, R., and Schaaf, D. *The Service Edge: 101 Companies That Profit from Customer Care.* New York: Plume, 1989.

Name Index

Subject Index